The 2019 From Reason to Revolution con_____ces of the ordinary British soldier in the era 1721-1815, from enlistment, through service at home, to life on campaign and the experience of battle. This book presents the proceedings of that conference in full, along with an introduction by series editor Andrew Bamford.

This was an era in which the social position of the soldier began to change, as did the relationship between the Army and society at large. Soldiers saw service against Jacobite rebels in Scotland and anti-Catholic rioters in London. Campaign service overseas stretched from garrison duties in the growing empire to pitched battles in Flanders and the Iberian Peninsula. Lack of indigenous manpower led to the enlistment of foreigners in large numbers into the British Army itself by the end of the period, whereas in earlier days the shortfall had been made up by hiring mercenaries. As the idea of a social contract became embedded, it was necessary to make provision for pensions for maimed or superannuated soldiers, as well as the more obvious need for medical care for the sick and wounded. The chapters contained in this volume all address aspects of these topics, drawing upon focussed case studies from across the long eighteenth century.

Andrew Bamford is editor of the From Reason to Revolution series and has written extensively on the wars of the eighteenth century and Napoleonic era.

Life in the Red Coat
The British Soldier 1721-1815

Proceedings of the 2019 From Reason to Revolution Conference

Edited by Andrew Bamford

Helion & Company

Helion & Company Limited
Unit 8 Amherst Business Centre
Budbrooke Road
Warwick
CV34 5WE
England
Tel. 01926 499619
Email: info@helion.co.uk
Website: www.helion.co.uk
Twitter: @helionbooks
blog.helion.co.uk/

Published by Helion & Company 2020
Typeset by Mach 3 Solutions Ltd (www.mach3solutions.co.uk)
Cover designed by Paul Hewitt, Battlefield Design (www.battlefield-design.co.uk)

Text © Individual Contributors 2020
Cover: 1st Regiment of Foot Guards c.1790, by Reginald Augustus Wymer
(Anne S.K. Brown Collection).

Every reasonable effort has been made to trace copyright holders and to obtain their permission for the use of copyright material. The author and publisher apologise for any errors or omissions in this work, and would be grateful if notified of any corrections that should be incorporated in future reprints or editions of this book.

ISBN 978-1-913118-94-5

British Library Cataloguing-in-Publication Data.

A catalogue record for this book is available from the British Library.

All rights reserved. No part of this publication may be reproduced, stored in a retrieval system, or transmitted, in any form, or by any means, electronic, mechanical, photocopying, recording or otherwise, without the express written consent of Helion & Company Limited.

For details of other military history titles published by Helion & Company Limited, contact the above address, or visit our website: http://www.helion.co.uk

We always welcome receiving book proposals from prospective authors.

Helion and Company gratefully acknowledges the support of the Society for Army Historical Research (https://www.sahr.org.uk/) and the British Commission for Military History (http://www.bcmh.org.uk/) in sponsoring the conference from which these papers are drawn.

Contents

Contributor Biographies viii
Introduction: The British Soldier 1721-1815
    Andrew Bamford x

1   The Life of a Soldier Before and After Service as Revealed by the Out-Pensioner Records of the Royal Hospital, Chelsea
    Andrew Cormack 17

2   The Rank and File of the British Army at Culloden
    Jonathan Oates 31

3   A Serious Inconvenience? Foreign Prisoners of War and Deserters in Wellington's Peninsular Army 1808-1814
    Robert Griffith 54

4   John Wesley's War: Methodism off and on the Battlefield, 1739-1789
    Alexander Burns 82

5   The Role of the Army in Suppressing the Gordon Riots, 2–9 June 1780
    Brendan Morrissey 102

6   'No British Ship Sighted': The British Garrison on Minorca and the Siege of St Philip's Castle, 1756
    Robert Tildesley 131

7   'Another Tarnish for British Valour': Responses to Success and Failure in Wellington's Peninsular Army
    Zack White 153

8   'Stand fast and defend yourself to the last!': the Experience of Battle in the French Revolutionary and Napoleonic Wars
    Carole Divall 172

General Index 190
Index of Regiments and Corps 193

Contributor Biographies

Alexander Burns is a PhD Candidate working with Dr Katherine Aaslestad at West Virginia University. His dissertation, 'The Entire Army Says Hello: Common Soldiers in Britain and Prussia, 1739-1789', examines the local and religious identities of soldiers in the North Atlantic world in the second half of the eighteenth century. In addition to writing his dissertation, Alex is the editor of a forthcoming Festschrift for well-known eighteenth-century military historian Christopher Duffy.

Dr Andrew Cormack FSA, FRHistS worked in military museums throughout his career. His edition of *The Journal of Corporal William Todd, 1745-1762* was published by the Army Records Society in 2001. He has contributed many articles on eighteenth-century subjects to the *Journal of the Society for Army Historical Research* and became its editor in July 2008. His PhD (2017) was a study of the Out-pension of the Royal Hospital, Chelsea, which he published as *'These Meritorious Objects of the Royal Bounty'; The Chelsea Out-Pensioners in the Early Eighteenth Century* in the same year.

Carole Divall FINS has a long-standing interest in the period of the Revolutionary and Napoleonic Wars as a time of great social, political, and cultural change. Her particular interest is the organisation and campaigns of the British Army in this period, with particular focus on the human perspective. She has published six books; most recently a study of Sir Ralph Abercromby and the Revolutionary Wars, and *The British Army in Egypt 1801* published by Helion. She was a member of the Waterloo200 education committee, and edited the Waterloo200 website.

Robert Griffith's passion has always been history, especially the Napoleonic period. He grew up reading C.S Forester, Dudley Pope, Bernard Cornwell and George MacDonald Fraser. His first book, *Riflemen: A History of the 5th Battalion 60th (Royal American) Regiment*, was published by Helion in 2018. His research into the 5/60th sparked a deep interest in the foreign corps and light infantry of the British Army during the period, and also in the Peninsular War. His second title for Helion, *At the Point of the Bayonet*, which covers the battles Arroyomolinos and Almaraz, will be published towards the end of 2020.

Brendan Morrissey was born in London, and attended Wimbledon College in the 1970s, during which time he visited events at the British Museum and National Maritime Museum, to commemorate the Bicentennial of the American War of Independence. He also famously scored '0' in a history essay on that conflict by writing entirely about the military operations and not mentioning the politics once. After reading law and briefly training as a solicitor he entered the world of public relations, initially with British Aerospace Military Aircraft, then later with agencies and as a freelancer. He has written a number of books on the American War of Independence, and been a guest lecturer at the National Army Museum, where he also organised an annual 'Revolution!' weekend involving re-enactors and guest speakers from the UK, the US, Germany and France. More recently, he has advised leading manufacturers of wargames figures on their American War of Independence ranges. He lives on the Surrey/Hants/Sussex border with his long-suffering (and infinitely more talented) wife and whichever of his two sons are visiting for the weekend because they need their laundry done.

Robert Tildesley is currently completing his DPhil in History at Wolfson College Oxford. His primary research focus is on the development of military logistics during the Early Modern Period, particularly how it relates to the strength and power projection of the fiscal-military state. His thesis looks at the development of logistical networks in Iberia during the War of the Spanish Succession.

Dr Jonathan Oates has been interested in the Jacobite campaigns since he was 11 years old, especially its military aspects. In this he was encouraged by his late father; watching the few relevant films, reading the popular books, visiting the battlefields in Scotland and later record offices together. In 1990 his undergraduate dissertation at Reading University considered responses in Newcastle upon Tyne to the Jacobite insurrection of 1715. Eleven years later there was a doctoral thesis at the same institution concerning the responses in the north-eastern counties of England to the 1715 and 1745 Jacobite rebellions. His recent Jacobite titles from Helion include *The Crucible of the Fifteen: Sheriffmuir* (2017), *Killiecrankie and the Jacobite Campaign of 1689-1691* (2018), and *King George's Hangman: Henry Hawley and the Battle of Falkirk 1746* (2019). He is currently working on a study the prisoners of the '15.

Zack White is a Doctoral Researcher, and holder of the Archival Scholarship at the University of Southampton, specialising in crime and punishment in the British Army during the early 19th century. He has previously written on public interest in the developments of the Peninsular War, and the relationship between the Duke of Wellington and his troops during the same conflict. He was founder and inaugural Editor-in-Chief of the research journal *Romance, Revolution & Reform*, and runs the online hub and discussion forum www.thenapoleonicwars.net. He is Postgraduate liaison for the British Commission for Military History, and runs the Commission's 'Next-Gen Network', and the conference paper sharing site www.historygoeson.com. He is also the presenter of the Napoleonic era podcast 'The Napoleonicist', co-presenter of the military history review podcast 'Khaki Malarkey' and is co-leader of the 'Bones of Burgos' Project.

Introduction: The British Soldier 1721-1815

Andrew Bamford

The goal of the 2019 From Reason to Revolution conference, the papers of which form the basis of this book, was to explore the experiences of the British soldier in the long eighteenth century. As well as wanting to cover the full chronological extent of the 1721-1815 period that the series deals with, it was also the intention to cover the full extent of experiences potentially inherent in a military career. Thus, speakers looked at enlistment and training; peacetime duties including domestic policing; active service overseas; the experience of combat both in siege warfare and on the battlefield. The conceit of the conference, replicated in the structure of this book, was to follow the soldier from enlistment to battle. Inevitably, this has not entirely worked out, such that we have a taste of mid-eighteenth century battle as early as Chapter 2, and, indeed, the fact that the best source for data on men's pre-enlistment background and subsequent careers is the records kept by the Royal Hospital, Chelsea, means that the opening chapter also looks at life after the Army for those individuals fortunate enough to survive their service and qualify for an Out Pension. By and large, however, we have kept to our theme and jumped back and forth through the era to accommodate it: that being so, it seems useful to employ this Introduction as a means to provide an overview of the British Army during the period with which we are concerned, and so place the chapters in their wider historical and historiographical context.

1721 found Britain once again at peace following the conclusion of the War of the Quadruple Alliance, which, uniquely for the period, had seen her allied with France. The bulk of British fighting against the Spanish foe had been in the maritime sphere, although the attack on Vigo had seen the employment of a sizeable land force. At home, the Jacobite threat had been revived with Spanish aid, only for the '19 Rising to be crushed at Glenshiel. That this had required the assistance of allied Dutch forces was an indication of the relatively small size to which the military establishment had shrunk after the conclusion of the War of the Spanish Succession, from which there would be no great expansion for the best part of two decades. The brief Anglo-Spanish War of 1727-1729 saw only a limited requirement for land forces, with the disastrous expedition to Porto Bello falling primarily on the Royal Navy's shoulders whilst Gibraltar was successfully held through the dispatch of only three regiments of foot to reinforce the four weak battalions that were already there.[1] It was not until the renewal of war with Spain in 1739, prefiguring involvement in a growing global conflict that would last the best part of a decade, that significant expansion took place, but the initial focus on colonial operations meant that the priority remained with the Royal Navy and with the raising of Marine and colonial regiments to support its operations in the Americas and West Indies.

The first two decades of our period may therefore be characterised as an era in which the main problems were what John Houlding has called the 'Frictions of Peace'; that is to say, all the petty concerns that distracted and dispersed those troops available at home, very often to the detriment of their military effectiveness.[2] Detachments might well be doing useful service keeping the peace, assisting the Excise, or building roads through Scottish glens, but their deployment in penny packets in this way gave them little by way of training for war. Economy, too, kept many regiments in the same stations for years on end and although a rotation system was introduced that ended the situation where regiments could be left for decades in the same colonial garrison – the 38th Foot in the Caribbean for 49 years being the worst such case – there were several cavalry regiments that spent upwards of a half-century on the Irish Establishment, barely above cadre strength, seemingly leaving their officers little to do but play at local politics.[3]

When Britain became involved with the European war in earnest from 1742, a more substantial expansion of the Army took place, but even the old-established regiments that formed the initial deployment to Flanders and then marched into Germany for the Dettingen campaign of the following year showed a certain rustiness that also extended upwards to many of their commanders. Just as victory in 1743 was down more to luck than judgement, however, conversely the defeats at Fontenoy (1745), Rocoux (1746), and Lafeldt (1747) saw the British regiments fight far more effectively, with the causes of allied failure to be found elsewhere. The British contingent at Rocoux, however, was little more than a token to her allies due to the recall of the bulk of British troops to meet the threat of the last of the Jacobite Risings. The inability of home-based troops to carry out effective training was highlighted by the poor performance of those engaged at Prestonpans on 21 September 1745, but even veterans of Flanders allowed themselves to be unnerved and bested at Falkirk the following January. The Duke of Cumberland's final victory at Culloden, discussed in more detail in Chapter 2 of this work, was essentially an exercise in the deployment of overwhelming force, albeit not without some sharp fighting for those regiments that found themselves directly opposing the Highland charge.

---

[1] For a recent treatment of the War of the Quadruple Alliance, see Jonathan D. Oates, *The Last Spanish Armada: Britain And The War Of The Quadruple Alliance, 1718-1720* (Warwick: Helion, 2020); the 1727-1729 conflict would merit a modern study.

[2] J.A. Houlding, *Fit for Service: The Training of the British Army 1715-1795* (Oxford: Clarendon, 1981), pp.1-98.

[3] See, for example, 9th/12th Royal Lancers Regimental Museum, Derby, 912L:2088/43: 'Letterbook of Col. W. Bury [sic] and Col. W. Pitt 1767-1772', containing the correspondence of two successive commanding officers of the 12th Dragoons (in Ireland continually 1718-1793), which is taken up almost entirely with letters pertaining to civil and ecclesiastical patronage.

The '45 Rising had led to the raising of a number of new units to oppose the Jacobites, several of which were briefly taken into the line, but all but one of these was disbanded once the threat was past.[4] The sole survivor lasted only until the end of the European war, which also occasioned substantial reductions across the rest of the army, and peacetime retrenchment seems to have taken its toll more widely, as the case of the Minorca garrison, discussed in Chapter 6 of this work, makes plain. The fall of Minorca was only one of a number of disasters to mark the early years of the Seven Years War, with embarrassing setbacks in North America and much effort diverted into a series of raids on the French coast which achieved relatively little and culminated in a defeat at St Cast where the British forces were attacked while re-embarking and suffered heavy losses. Lessons learnt in these operations were, however, learnt in sufficient time to be applied on the other side of the Atlantic in the capture of Louisbourg in 1758 and of Quebec the year after, and although the final reduction of New France owed something to the application of the proverbial sledgehammer to crack a nut, the nut was a particularly tough one and its cracking required the British Army to perfect new skills and doctrines.[5]

Back in Europe, British regiments serving as part of an allied force in western Germany from 1758 onwards did so with increasing effectiveness, the infantry covering itself in glory at Minden in 1759 and the cavalry gaining equal renown at Emsdorf and Warburg the following year. The division of forces between such different theatres, however, led to the emergence of opposing 'European' and 'American' schools of tactics that continued to divide opinion for much of the rest of the century. Recent scholarship of the American Revolutionary War has nevertheless demonstrated that this, the British Army's next major commitment, saw it employ a far more sophisticated tactical repertoire than the idea of two opposing schools would suggest, in which conventional 'European' linear firepower and 'American' open order tactics had their place, along with a willingness to charge home with cold steel which has been identified elsewhere as a recurrent theme in British unit-level infantry tactics back into the 17th century.[6]

The American struggle for independence can be seen as symptomatic of a shift in the politics of the eighteenth century, the movement from reason to revolution that gave this book series its name, and it was not just those Britons who had relocated to the colonies who challenged the status quo that the British Army was obliged to defend. Whereas riots in earlier years were direct responses to immediate and

---

4   See Andrew Bamford (ed.), *Rebellious Scots to Crush: The Military Response to the Jacobite '45* (Warwick: Helion, 2020); in particular Andrew Cormack's chapter 'The Noblemen's Regiments', pp.76-100.
5   On this war in general, and the adaptations necessary to fight it, see *Redcoats: The British Soldier and War in the Americas, 1755-1763* (Cambridge: Cambridge University Press, 2006); on amphibious operations, see also Hugh Boscawen, *The Capture of Louisbourg 1758* (Norman: University of Oklahoma Press, 2011), in particular pp.152-194.
6   On the American War, see Matthew H. Spring, *With Zeal and Bayonets Only: The British Army on Campaign in North America, 1755-1783* (Norman: University of Oklahoma Press, 2008); on the longer-term evolution of British infantry tactics through into the mid-eighteenth century, see David Blackmore, *Destructive and Formidable: British Infantry Firepower 1642-1765* (Barnsley: Frontline, 2014).

often localised concerns – hunger and unemployment – the threats in the latter part of the era were more overtly politicised, in a manner that would continue on into the 19th century with Reform and Chartism. Chapter 5 of this work explores the military response to the Gordon Riots of 1780, the largest non-battlefield deployment of British troops against British subjects during the era with which we are concerned, but the threat soon switched from reactionary anti-Catholic bigotry to political radicalism and the threat of political suborning of the armed forces was a genuine concern in the 1790s and onwards into the new century.[7] Nor, indeed, was it one entirely lacking in justification, for the 5th Dragoons was disbanded in the aftermath of the Irish Rebellion of 1798, its ranks having been infiltrated with those whose sympathies were with the United Irishmen. Insofar as other troops became disaffected, however, the concerns were over service and conditions, with the prospect of drafting men off for service in the West Indies leading to unrest in more than one unit, and precipitating the disbanding of some of the high-numbered regiments of the line briefly added to the establishment at the outset of the French Revolutionary War.[8] There was, however, nothing in the Army to match the Spithead and Nore mutinies that briefly paralysed the Royal Navy.

In many respects, the opening years of the long war against Revolutionary and Napoleonic France that lasted, with only two brief interruptions, from 1793 to 1815 saw a combination of all the errors that had marked Britain's entry into the previous major conflicts of the era. The peacetime army had been run down, and the few regiments that were available to go to Flanders at the outbreak of the war were weak in numbers. Mass expansion saw the raising of new regiments rather than building on the existing structure, and many of the good troops that were available were frittered away on peripheral operations or condemned to the fevers of the West Indies. The main front in the Low Countries was never the absolute priority that it ought to have been, although it is questionable whether or not the internally-divided First Coalition could have ever been successful even if Britain had thrown her full weight behind it. One point of note that did develop from these campaigns, however, was that an increasing number of foreign troops were taken directly into British pay, rather than serving as auxiliaries either through terms of an alliance like the Dutch and Hessian troops brought over to combat the Jacobites or simply as a result of a financial arrangement as was the case during the American War. To be sure, the army that the Duke of York led in Flanders in 1793-1794 contained large numbers of Hessian and Hanoverian troops in the old fashion,[9] but also a number of regiments of French émigrés in British pay. As the war went on, and more of Europe fell

---

7   The shifting challenges are discussed in Clive Emsley, 'The Military and Popular Disorder in England 1790-1801', *Journal of the Society for Army Historical Research*, Vol.61, No.245 (Spring 1983), pp.10-21 and No.246 (Summer 1982), pp.96-112.
8   For a case-study, see T.H. McGuffie, 'The Short Life and Sudden Death of an English Regiment of Foot: An Account of the Raising, Recruiting, Mutiny and Disbandment of the 113th regiment of Foot or "Royal Birmingham Volunteers" (April, 1794, to September, 1795)', *Journal of the Society for Army Historical Research*, Vol.33, No.133 (Spring 1955), pp.16-25, and No.134 (Summer 1955), pp.48-56.
9   For a detailed examination of which, see Paul Demet, *'We Are Accustomed to do our Duty': German Auxiliaries with the British Army 1793-1795* (Warwick: Helion, 2018).

under French dominion, so did the number of these forces grow until by 1814 they represented a significant portion of the total available manpower, as is detailed in Chapter 3 of this work.

For over a decade after the last British troops were pulled out of North Germany in 1795, the primary focus became one of defending the British Isles against invasion. With the expansion of Militia, Fencibles, and Volunteers, as well as the regular British Army, society was exposed to a military presence on a far greater level than had been seen in previous conflicts. Nevertheless, overseas expeditions were mounted to North Holland in 1799 and then to the Mediterranean the following year, and the long process of learning what not to do paid off with Abercromby's successful campaign to evict the French from Egypt in 1801.[10] Out of these campaigns emerged many of the commanders who would serve with distinction in the Peninsular War and at Waterloo; in parallel with them, the Duke of York redeemed his failings as a field commander by overseeing a comprehensive reform of the Army's internal organisation.[11]

With hindsight, it is easy to see the British Army's campaigns in the Peninsula as a string of successes leading slowly but surely to the final victorious crossing of the Pyrenees and advance into Southern France. In reality, as Chapter 7 of this work explores, success seemed by no means as certain at the time, and managing morale and discipline, as well as public opinion back home, was of paramount importance. Both 1808 and 1812 saw major retreats that were accompanied by major collapses in discipline, whilst the conduct of British troops in the aftermath of the sieges of Ciudad Rodrigo, Badajoz, and San Sebastian continues to arouse controversy and debate. Nevertheless, the victories were well-deserved and the manner in which they were achieved sufficiently versatile to discredit the idea that Wellington was merely a defensive general. One only has to compare the long strategic game played out over 1810 and 1811 to defeat the French offensive against Lisbon, the coup d'oeil and decisive resolve that won Salamanca in 1812 after a long campaign of manoeuvre, or the coordination of multiple corps in the battles of 1813 and 1814 to see a talent that even a French observer conceded had not been seen in British service since Marlborough's day.[12]

Focus on Wellington and his Peninsular victories, however, detracts from the fact that Britain was fighting a global war and that the British Army had to juggle multiple commitments. As late as 1809 there was still no firm commitment to the Peninsula, with the main effort in that year being the expedition against Antwerp that bogged down in the fever-swamps of Walcheren. The Mediterranean remained an active secondary theatre throughout the war, French and Dutch colonial possessions

---

10   These campaigns, and Abercromby's role in preparing the British Army for them, are detailed in Carole Divall, *General Sir Ralph Abercromby and the French Revolutionary Wars 1792-1801* (Barnsley: Pen and Sword, 2019).

11   For a summary of which, see Richard Glover, *Peninsular Preparation: The Reform of the British Army 1795-1809* (Cambridge: Cambridge University Press, 1963); a full study focusing on York as reformer and administrator still remains to be written.

12   *Général de Division* Maximilien Foy, quoted in Rory Muir, *Salamanca 1812* (New Haven: Yale University Press, 2001), p.208. Muir's account stands as a model for Peninsular battle-studies.

returned under the Peace of Amiens needed capturing for a second time and garrisoning thereafter, and Britain's own empire needed to be defended. Opportunism on the part of the United States opened up a new front in Canada from 1812, and the need to show a commitment to the Sixth Coalition's main effort in Northern Europe saw a rag-tag force sent to Germany and the Low Countries in 1813-1814. From the latter, reinforced from home and by troops brought back from America, was formed the 'infamous' army that fought at Quatre Bras and Waterloo in 1815, and advanced to Paris thereafter.[13]

Such, then, is the briefest of overviews of the campaigns of the British Army in the period 1721-1815, but what of the men in the ranks? How can we understand their experiences of service at such a chronological remove? Memoirs are, for the early part of the period, extremely rare and even if we supplement accounts from the ranks with those of officers there is nothing approaching what might be considered a representative sample. William Todd of the 30th and 12th Regiments of Foot and James Wood of the Royal Artillery do provide two noteworthy accounts of service in the ranks during the Austrian Succession and Seven Years War era, whilst the letters of Richard Davenport provide a useful perspective on the same approximate timeframe from a junior officer, but other accounts owe more to previous published sources than to personal recollection.[14] The collected accounts of soldiers who were, or became, Methodists provide a useful insight and are discussed in Chapter 4 of this work, although they do of course represent a self-selecting sample. Undoubtedly there is more material out there that would benefit from the same annotated treatment that Todd's memoirs were given, and Ilya Berkovich's impressive study of the motivation of ordinary soldiers in the eighteenth century identifies a number of archival holdings and long-out-of-print volumes that will hopefully be seized upon by future scholars and made available to a wider audience.[15]

Necessarily though, with so few personal accounts it becomes necessary to turn to other records to obtain more details of the men in the ranks, with one such example being the use of pension records as in Chapters 1 and 2 of this work; readers desirous of further detail on the administration of the Chelsea Out-Pension, and the records deriving from it, are directed to Andrew Cormack's detailed study.[16] Careful reading

---

13 The issues of overstretch, and the effect it had on the British Army's systems of manpower organisation, are discussed in Andrew Bamford, *Sickness Suffering and the Sword* (Norman: University of Oklahoma Press, 2013).
14 Andrew Cormack and Alan Jones (eds), *The Journal of Corporal William Todd 1745-1762* (Stroud: Sutton for the Army Records Society, 2001); Rex Whitworth (ed), *Gunner at Large: the Diary of James Wood RA 1746-1765* (London: Leo Cooper, 1988); C.W. Frearson (ed.) *"To Mr Davenport" being Letters of Major Richard Davenport (1719-1760) to his brother during service in the 4th Troop of Horse Guards and 10th Dragoons, 1742-1760* (Aldershot: Gale and Polden for the Society of Army Historical Research, 1968).
15 Ilya Berkovich, *Motivation in War: the Experience of Common Soldiers in Old-Regime Europe* (Cambridge: Cambridge University Press, 2017). Note, for example, the 'Memoirs of an Invalid' in the Centre of Kentish Studies, the account of 'Jonas' published as *A Soldier's Journal* in 1770, or the account of William Pell in the Grenadier Guards Archive, extracts from which are to be found quoted in Chapter 5 of this work.
16 Andrew Cormack, *'These Meritorious Objects of the Royal Bounty' The Chelsea Out-Pensioners in the Early Eighteenth Century* (London: Published by the Author, 2017).

of the personal accounts left by officers can also reveal a great deal about the men under their command, and their relations with them. Returning to official records, much can also be gleaned from the records of courts martial, although, albeit in a very different way to their Methodist comrades, the men ending up facing military discipline might also be considered a self-selecting sample! Still, much can be gleaned from them and from the records of enlistments and reports on regimental inspections, which grow steadily more detailed as the period goes on. By the time we reach the Napoleonic era, therefore, it becomes increasingly possible to produce a coherent and representative regimental history even for a unit lacking in rank and file memoirs, as indeed has been done by several of the contributors to this volume: Carole Divall on the 30th, Robert Griffith on the 5/60th, and the present editor on the 12th Light Dragoons.[17]

Considering the sheer volume of accounts that are now in print from men who served under Wellington, albeit many of the later ones suffering through the author having relied on Napier's history of the conflict to refresh a failing memory, it may perhaps come as a surprise to realise that such gaps exist in the eyewitness coverage. Nevertheless, it remains the case that there are Peninsular and Waterloo regiments where we lack even much by way of a written record from the commissioned ranks, let alone those who served under them. Equally, it is tempting to question (with tongue firmly in cheek) how the Light Division ever managed to find time to fight the French, when so many of its members were apparently engaged in note-taking for a future literary career. Thus, we are left with something of an imbalance in perceptions of the experience of the common soldier in this final period of our study, and care needs to be taken – as in Chapter 8 of this work, which uses these accounts to investigate the experience of battle – to ensure that one's coverage encompasses the army as a whole and not just its self-identified and ever-popular elites.

It should be clear, therefore, that there are numerous ways to gain a greater insight into the experience of the common soldier during the long eighteenth century. Naturally, this collection of chapters cannot begin to explore them all, but it is hoped that it will facilitate and inspire continued study of 'that article there' – the British redcoat – on whose shoulders even the greatest of captains recognised lay the real difference between victory and defeat.[18]

---

17 Carole Divall, *Redcoats Against Napoleon: The 30th Regiment During the Revolutionary and Napoleonic Wars* (Barnsley: Pen and Sword, 2009) and *Inside the Regiment: The Officers and Men of the 30th Regiment During the Revolutionary and Napoleonic Wars* (Barnsley: Pen and Sword, 2011); Robert Griffith, *Riflemen: The History of the 5th Battalion, 60th (Royal American) Regiment 1797-1818* (Warwick: Helion, 2019); Andrew Bamford, *Gallantry and Discipline: The 12th Light Dragoons at War with Wellington* (Barnsley: Frontline, 2014).
18 Wellington in conversation with Thomas Creevy prior to Waterloo, quoted in Richard Holmes, *Redcoat: The British Soldier in the Age of Horse and Musket* (London: Harper Collins, 2001), p.12.

1

The Life of a Soldier Before and After Service as Revealed by the Out-Pensioner Records of the Royal Hospital, Chelsea

Andrew Cormack

This chapter is founded largely on a database of 25,000 Chelsea Out-Pensioners who appeared before the Royal Hospital's Commissioners between 1715 and 1755 that was compiled in the course of writing my PhD and subsequent book *These Meritorious Objects of the Royal Bounty – The Chelsea Out-Pensioners in the early Eighteenth Century*. It will explore the socio-economic backgrounds and the ages of the men at the time of their enlistment and will examine the conditions of service that they signed up to when becoming soldiers. Of course, most of them were actually unable to sign their own names and in consequence very few of them left any account as to why they enlisted, what they expected of the Army, and what they thought of the experience when it was all over. It is necessary therefore to reconstruct the circumstances in which a man would enlist from a general examination of the lives of those men who came from the class of the labouring poor, because it was very largely from that section of society that soldiers were drawn. Comment will also be made on the effects of military service in an age when medicine was primitive and when rehabilitation after injury or amputation was non-existent. Explanations will be given as to how those fortunate enough to receive a recommendation to The Royal Hospital, Chelsea were discharged, examined, and accepted onto the pension and how they might have been able to live out the rest of their days considering that the out-pension was not enough for a single man to live on. It will also detail the other sources of support that disabled or decrepit former soldiers could call upon for support. The size of the sample examined is amply sufficient to illustrate the general conditions that applied to all of the other ranks of the early-Georgian Army whether or not they received pensions at the time of their discharges.[1]

It is necessary to start with some background. The Royal Hospital was the brainchild of King Charles II who gave orders for its establishment in 1682. A hospital for

---

1 A.E. Cormack, *These Meritorious Objects of the Royal Bounty - The Chelsea Out-pensioners in the Early Eighteenth Century* (London: Published by the Author, 2017).

soldiers of the British Army serving in Ireland had been founded, under the King's name, by James Butler, 1st Duke of Ormonde in 1679, and a building had been constructed at Kilmainham on the outskirts of Dublin.[2] It may safely be assumed, however, that the examples of beneficence on the part of the state set up within the British Isles took their inspiration from the inauguration of Louis XIV's foundation of the *Hotel Royal des Invalides* near Paris in 1674. It is also not unlikely that His Majesty was drawing on lessons from his own past and from that of his father, which indicated that soldiers who became dissatisfied with the way the government treated them, such as trying to disband them without arrears of pay, could become extremely disruptive and dangerous. The New Model Army had shown how unwise it was to attempt such proceedings and had purged Parliament in 1648 and subsequently abolished the monarchy and effectively taken over the government of the country for most of the 1650s. Charles' exile had also doubtless impressed upon him how miserable a servant of the state could be if the body from which he expected support and succour provided none of these aids. In addition, the example set by the French king demonstrated what praise and glory might be showered upon a monarch who took such loving care of those subjects who had assisted him to defend, maintain, and transform his kingdom in accordance with the policies that he had chosen. The fully gilded, bronze statue of Charles II that still graces the main courtyard of the Hospital today radiates exactly the aura of splendour, generosity, power and benevolence that would be attributed to the founder of such an institution.

When the Hospital first opened its doors in 1692 after a ten-year building period, it could accommodate 472 soldiers. It was not, however, a barracks with dormitories, as each man was lodged in his own booth six feet square. Most of the life of the In-pensioners would be spent in the common parts of the building – the long wards with the booths arranged down one side, the large dining hall or the chapel – or in the extensive grounds. The garrison of the hospital, whose residents were organised into companies with drummers, manned its guardroom and the sentry posts at its entrances and they also undertook patrolling duties on the road to Knightsbridge in an effort to deter highwaymen. However, even at the very beginning there were more than 500 additional old soldiers who were entitled to the shelter of the Hospital but who could not be accommodated within it, so from early on in its history there were those who were sent home to wherever they had originally come from and who received a pension. These men were designated the Out-pensioners.[3]

It is clear from the admissions registers of the hospital that when examined and accepted for pension by the Hospital Commissioners men were not graded at that time as In- or Out- pensioners, and there appears to have been no real difference in terms of severity of disablement or length of service, rank, or any other factor

---

2   E.S.E. Childers & R. Stewart, *The Story of the Royal Hospital, Kilmainham* (London: Hutchinson & Co., 1921).
3   G. Hutt, *Papers Illustrative of the Origin and Early History of the Royal Hospital at Chelsea* (London: Eyre & Spottiswoode, 1872). This volume contains transcripts of many original documents of relevance to the Hospital and the Out-pension but very little analysis as to why and how the institution was administered.

that differentiated the one from the other.[4] All successful candidates were taken on as Out-pensioners and some of them found their way into the hospital either immediately, if there were vacancies, or eventually if, by some unknown means, they indicated that they wished to be admitted. Those who did so must have been living in London or at least within the 25-mile radius that obliged them to collect their pensions in person from the hospital. No systematic records appear to exist to explain how men switched their status from Out-pensioner to In-pensioner. Those who were already married or who hoped to marry in the future had to remain outside, as there was no question of accommodation for spouses, let alone children.

In actuality Out-pensioners had existed even while the hospital was being built, because in 1686 King James II had instituted pensions as an interim measure for those old soldiers who would otherwise have had no means of support before they could be allotted a booth. These pensions were paid at varying rates according to the branch of service and the rank of the recipient.[5] When the Out-pension came to be recognised as an indispensable part of the system, payments according to this scale were continued until towards the end of the War of the Spanish Succession.

Infantry Private	5d
Corporals and Drummers	7d
Infantry Sergeant	11d
Trooper of the Horse Guards	18d
Trooper of Light Horse	12d
Corporal of Light Horse	18d
Private of Dragoons	6d
Corporal of Dragoons	8d
Master Gunner	14d
Gunner	7d

It is interesting to note that the cavalry was referred to after the manner of the French army as light horse and that artillery personnel were included in the provision. The latter were excluded at some time before 1712, probably earlier, and the Royal Artillery, which was not established as a regiment until 1716, did not regain its entitlement to the benefit of Chelsea until 1833. No research has been conducted on what pension provision was made for troops of the Board of Ordnance – artillerymen and engineers – but it is hard to believe that they were not assisted in a similar way to their infantry and cavalry colleagues.[6]

Although it is convenient to write of men as having an entitlement to pension, such a right did not, of course, apply to all soldiers discharged from the Army. With

---

4   The Chelsea Examinations Registers, which were effectively the Admissions Registers because few men were rejected, are to be found at The National Archives (United Kingdom) (hereafter TNA) in the War Office collection under reference WO 116. Various other versions of the registers exist, but WO 120, which is arranged by regiment, contains only a sub-set of the records in WO 116.
5   Hutt, *Origin and Early History*, p.146.
6   A history of the Royal Regiment of Artillery in the eighteenth century dealing not only with personnel matters but equipment, methodology and capabilities is sorely needed.

very little variation throughout the whole of the eighteenth century, the qualifications that soldiers had to show were that they had been 'disabled by wounds in fight or other accidents in the service of the Crown'[7] or that they had become unfit after having served 20 years continuously. During the period before the Glorious Revolution when a standing army was viewed with great suspicion by Parliament on the grounds that it constituted a constant threat to the liberties of the people, 20 years' continuous service was highly unlikely to apply to more than a very small number of soldiers.[8] However, after the arrival of William III, whose foreign policy tied Great Britain into a pattern of alliances with mainland European powers in the struggle against French hegemony, extended service without a break became much more possible, indeed likely.[9] At the same time, the Army increased enormously in size from the handful of regiments that had existed in Charles II's time, and overall the number of men who might qualify for the hospital's provision increased likewise. What was never stated clearly was that in order for his commanding officer to certify that any discharged man was entitled to an examination by the hospital's commissioners, that man had to have a faultless disciplinary record. In consequence, there are no instances among the 25,000 men who were examined between 1715 and 1755 of soldiers who had been punished by flogging.

So why did men choose the Army as their principal employment? The early eighteenth century was a fairly prosperous era. There was no major economic slump nor periods of mass unemployment, though failures of the harvest occasionally led to rises in the price of basic foodstuffs that engendered civil unrest and 'tumultuous behaviour'. Nevertheless, work within the civilian sphere was constantly available. However, it is necessary to consider what work was like for the labouring and artisan classes. Firstly, everyone had to work or starve. There was no social welfare available for the physically fit, and children were put to work from a very early age – at 6 they might be scaring pigeons off the crops, gathering firewood or doing any odd chore of which they were capable. From 14 years old, it would be normal for a boy to be put to an apprenticeship, and if the child's parents could not afford the fees to settle him with a master to learn a trade, then the authorities in his parish would find a place for him with a master in another parish so that the child did not become a burden on their part of the Poor Law if his parents died. If the master was good and willing to teach the lad, then all might be well, but if he was unskilled, indifferent, abusive, or had insufficient work for himself, then the child was unlikely to learn and would be unable to earn. As apprenticeship lasted for seven years, a good deal of patience would be required to stick with a process that might be disagreeable and which promised very little at the end of it. Secondly, it is necessary to forget about the availability of education or training from any source other than an apprenticeship and

---

[7] ESTABLISHMENT and REGULATION of REWARDS and other PROVISIONS to be made to HIS MAJESTIES LAND FORCES, 1st January 1685/86, quoted in Hutt, *Origin and Early History*, p.146.

[8] The best accounts of the armies of Charles II and James II available are still those written by John Childs in the 1970s and 1980s.

[9] See J. Childs, *The Nine Years War and the British Army 1688-1697, the operations in the Low Countries* (Manchester: Manchester University Press, 1991).

equally inapplicable is the concept of social mobility, because that did not exist for the working classes at the time. Once set to a trade therefore, it was likely to be the occupation that the lad remained in for the rest of his life. If he was well-instructed, enjoyed it, and was good at it, then his future might be prosperous and he could take on apprentices of his own, but if he hated it, was not well taught, or simply could not pick up the skills or did not have the strength or the application, then he was unlikely to be successful.[10] However, the possibilities for change were extremely limited and the opportunity of learning a different trade – re-skilling – during which time the operative would not be productive and therefore not earning, were extremely scarce. There were also, of course, fluctuations in the economic cycle if not periods of outright slump, and there was, in small communities, the problem of having too many people doing the same activity. As towns and villages were small, they could only viably sustain so many tailors, shoe makers, carpenters or blacksmiths and there would not necessarily be enough work to go round.

There was, however, always the Army, and although at the end of every war the number of regiments was drastically reduced, as was the number of men per company or troop within each regiment, the force was constantly in search of men to fill its ranks. It is true that it struck a pretty hard bargain, but joining a regiment provided stability and certain advantages that would not invariably have been available in civilian life. Military life was not subject to economic cycles or underemployment. Pay was guaranteed, albeit that the soldier's own management of his finances was, by and large, taken away from him, because his subsistence – food money – was managed within his company or troop, and there were stoppages for his small clothing and necessaries. However, housing was provided essentially free of charge and the infantryman was guaranteed a new set of outer clothes every year. For the cavalry, replacement of clothing was spread across a two-year cycle because all mounted troops had cloaks with which to protect their garments from the worst of the weather, and because horsemen had a greater quantity of kit, both for themselves and their mounts, that needed to be replaced according to the rate at which, with careful management, garments, accoutrements and saddlery could be expected to wear out. Another great attraction was that a soldier's life was infinitely more varied than that of a labouring civilian. That variety was more evident for regiments serving in Great Britain or Ireland, because they moved around in those countries in response to requirements for assistance in the maintenance of law and order, to perform the 'coast duty' – the suppression of smuggling – to take their turn in the garrison of Scotland, or simply to relieve the public house keepers, in whose premises they lived, of the burden of quartering soldiers. However, for those regiments serving overseas doing garrison duty on Minorca, at Gibraltar, in the West Indies or manning the North American outposts of Annapolis Royal and Placentia, life must have been deadly dull, as the men were very much confined to post, and in the first half of the century there was no regular rotation of regiments through the overseas

---

10 M.D. George, *London Life in the XVIIIth Century* (London: Kegan Paul, Trench, Trubner & Co. Ltd., 1930). What applied in London with regard to apprenticeships applied throughout the country.

garrisons, so it was very hard on those units that were sent overseas. That burden was not shared evenly.[11]

Motivation is very difficult to discern in men who were overwhelmingly illiterate and who left no record of why they joined up. In wartime the possibility of excitement, plunder, comradeship and, in some cases, a certain patriotic feeling undoubtedly played a part, though it is impossible to quantify which of these factors was the most operative. In peacetime, under-employment, the stagnation of civilian life, the desire to escape from boredom and a yearning after something different may well have accounted for much recruitment.[12] When signing up for the second time in Bristol in 1727 John Mills told the recruiting officer that he wanted to become a soldier again 'because the masters were so severe and the wages so low that he could not live by his trade and he would rather be a soldier again than starve or steal'.[13] He had evidently served in the Army during the War of the Spanish Succession and, as he was not his own master, he was hard put to it to make ends meet. It is rare, however, to find such a cogent statement of why a man joined up. Some men found themselves in the Army whether they wanted to be soldiers or not as, at the beginning of all wars, impressment of 'sturdy beggars' or those deemed to have no visible means of supporting themselves was permitted.[14] According to their statements of service, James Earl spent 22 years in the Royal Fusiliers having been 'listed at Derby by the Grand Jurie';[15] John Parford was noted as 'a prestman' when examined for pension, unsuccessfully, after breaking his leg, in 1748. He was clearly thought to have recovered sufficiently because he was ordered back to Cholmondeley's 34th Foot to serve on.[16]

It seems extraordinary to us today, but in the early eighteenth century there was no maximum or minimum recruiting age. The Chelsea records show that some men, who were eventually pensioned, had joined up as children, though it is clear in most cases that they were the sons of soldiers and had probably known no other life, so the regiment was their home and family and their natural employer. Robert Pepper, whose father was a lieutenant in Pearce's 5th Foot, was taken on at the age of 10, presumably as a fifer.[17] Eight men who had joined up as 11-year-olds appear in the pension lists of the Marching Foot and the Foot Guards and a further 11 boys had joined up at 12 years of age. From the entire sample, 2,516 men had enlisted before they were 20 years old and apart from those 'born in the Regiment' most

---

11 The rotation of regiments through the various garrisons is dealt with in detail by J.A. Houlding in *Fit for Service - The Training of the British Army, 1715-1795* (Oxford: The Clarendon Press, 1981) in Appendix B p.409 et seq. This work is by far the best book on the British Army of the eighteenth century published in the last century.
12 I. Berkovich, *Motivation in War - The Experience of Common Soldiers in Old-Regime Europe* (Cambridge: Cambridge University Press, 2017) tackles this subject, though dealing with most European armies rather than particularly the British Army.
13 TNA, Secretary-at-War Out-letter Books, WO 4/28, f.334.
14 G. Davies, 'Recruiting in the Reign of Queen Anne', *Journal of the Society for Army Historical Research*, Vol. XXVIII, 1950, pp. 146-159. For later reigns, see Cormack, *These Meritorious Objects* p.29.
15 TNA, Admissions Registers, WO 116/2, 19.6.1728.
16 TNA, Admissions Registers, WO 116/3, 4.4.1748.
17 TNA, Admissions Registers, WO 116/2, 9.12.1730.

either declared no trade at all or they must have abandoned their apprenticeships and escaped to the Army. Conversely, many men entered the service at an age at which physical fitness might be thought to be on the decline, though for the infantry the continual requirement for manual labour, either on the King's Works or just loading and unloading baggage wagons, and the necessity to march everywhere would certainly have kept men fitter than modern-day men of the same age group. The same would have been true of the cavalry because of the necessity for suppleness and muscle control when riding and the work associated with looking after horses would have contributed significantly to the maintenance of physical fitness. Twelve hundred and thirty-eight men enlisted at or after their 40th year and evidently had much experience of work before joining the Army, but they were still acceptable as recruits. Private John Jeffries enlisted in the Royal Welch Fusiliers in 1713 at the age of 48[18] and Bartholomew Dowdall joined up aged 46, though his service in the Royal Fusiliers was ended by his descent into lunacy.[19]

Another aspect of this disregard of age is that men served for much longer than would be thought reasonable today. In four years chosen across the period covered by the database – 1725, 1735, 1745 and 1755 – the following numbers of men had served for 30 years or more.

Year	Cavalry	Foot Guards	Marching Foot	Total	Total examined in Year	Percentage of Year's Total
1725	7	18	10	35	240	14.5
1735	11	9	99	119	256	33.4
1745	13	5	65	83	1,033	8.0
1755	7	1	10	18	324	5.5

Notes to Table: The second, third and fourth columns show the numbers of men with 30 or more years' service in each arm examined in each of the chosen years. The fifth column shows the total within all arms. Column 6 shows the total of all men examined in that year and Column 7 shows the percentage of the whole annual batch who had served for 30 years or more.

It is clear from these figures and percentages that in the years before the War of the Austrian Succession, by and large years of peace, the Army retained a significant percentage of men who had served at least 30 years. Naturally, after the start of the War of Jenkin's Ear in 1739, men who were thought unlikely to be able to sustain the demands of active campaigning were discharged because they could easily be replaced, but even in the middle of the Austrian Succession War eight percent of those discharged to pension had actually joined the Army in or before 1715. The discharge of very large numbers of men in 1748-1749 brought the percentage down significantly, but at the start of the Seven Years War at least five percent of soldiers had more than 30 years' service. As there was no official age of discharge, men served on for as long as they could and the pension records indicate that 186 men attained 40 years of service and 31 men reached 45 years of service. Thereafter the figures

---

18 TNA, Admissions Registers, WO 116/3, 15.2.1722.
19 TNA, Admissions Registers, WO 116/4, 23.2.1749.

decrease notably, though 10 men soldiered on for up to 50 years and Drummer Alexander Main claimed 60 years continuous service in the Independent Company that garrisoned Stirling Castle when he was pensioned in 1747.[20] He was buried as an In-pensioner of the Hospital aged 87 in 1751.

Soldiering for many men therefore was in reality a job for life and they continued in that work for as long as they possibly could. This was indeed the same for all members of the labouring classes because there was no such thing as retirement and until complete decrepitude was reached there was no respite from labour. Being a soldier was, however, an occupation not without its dangers. Clearly, during a war, the efforts of the King's enemies might disable a man at any time, but even in peacetime circumstances arose that could terminate a man's service almost before it had begun. Three hundred and eighty-eight men who received out-pensions each served for less than 24 months and some for only a handful of months. Discounting the 102 who were disabled by combat wounds, accidental injury with weapons accounted for 29 of the remainder but others were caused by horses falling on, throwing off, or kicking their riders (17 instances) or falls on shipboard, particularly among the Marine Regiments of Foot raised in 1739 (26 instances). Eighty men simply became ill within a short time of joining the Army. Clearly in these latter cases the ailments were considered to have derived from their service rather than being pre-existing conditions at the time of their recruitment.

Despite the fact that the vast majority of soldiers served for much longer periods – between 20 and 29 years – the brevity of service highlighted above nevertheless indicates that the government recognised the fact that soldiers disabled at a young age were likely to continue claiming their pensions for decades and, by implication, accepted the duty of care over them. William Shaw of Bragg's 28th Foot, who lost his left arm at Fontenoy aged 17, may well have been claiming pension until after the French Revolutionary War, though he had only been in the Army six months.[21] Thomas Garnet of Fleming's 36th Foot, also aged 17, was wounded at Falkirk in both wrists and may not have been able to return to his trade of weaving, though he may well have survived for many years after his encounter with the Highlanders.[22] As no registers recording the deaths of Out-pensioners exist, it is impossible to assess the number of years for which pensioners survived after becoming recipients of 'the Royal Bounty'.

As the majority of soldiers enlisted during their twenties or later, it is not surprising that almost all of them declared that they had a trade. Whether they were actively employed in it at the time of their enlistment is not known, but many were artisans who had passed through some period of training and were either unable to establish themselves in their calling thereafter, or had undertaken the instruction unwillingly and wished to avoid being tied to that daily occupation for the rest of their lives. Out of the entire Out-pensioner sample of 25,000, 14,100 declared their occupations prior to having enlisted – 3,010 stated that they were labourers but most of the rest came from the artisan group, though their levels of skill and the quality of their work doubtless

---

20   TNA, Admissions Registers, WO 116/4, 21.1.1747.
21   TNA, Admissions Registers, WO 116/3, 12.11.1745.
22   TNA, Admissions Registers, WO 116/4, 2.6.1746.

varied. There were 1,652 weavers, 1,316 husbandmen, 924 shoe makers, 697 tailors, 557 farmers, and 404 servants, but there were blacksmiths, farriers, carpenters, clothiers, leather workers and butchers by the hundreds as well as musical instrument makers, goldsmiths, sculptors and school masters in lesser numbers. It was clearly not the case that the Army took only those who had nothing to offer but brawn.

Soldiers were discharged from the Army for various reasons and many, at the end of a war, were unscathed and had not acquired enough service to qualify for a pension. They were simply released with a small bounty to take them home and the infantry received three shillings for their swords. Those cavalrymen who wished to do so could take their horses, but received a lower bounty. It was assumed that these men would re-integrate themselves into civilian life. Those soldiers having a spotless disciplinary record qualified for the Out-pension either on the basis of long service, for which the minimum required was 20 years, or, more usually a combination of long-service and disability/incapacity of some sort. Reasons for discharge are complex and they are set out in detail in my book. In the table below, taking the same years as in the previous example, the reasons for discharge are shown in the first column. They have been compiled from the Admissions Registers and have been kept within a reasonable number of permutations, though some men presented themselves suffering from multiple complaints, medical and traumatic, originating from combat as well as accident. Soldiers received injuries during battles as well as wounds and, for instance, Drummer Robert Collins 'ruptured right side at Preston',[23] has been categorized as Injured not Wounded, as have men who were hurt by earth, stones or debris from fortifications thrown up by the near strike of an artillery projectile, though they were not hit by the ball itself. Analysis of the cavalry, the Foot Guards, the Marching Foot and the Marines has been undertaken year by year, but for the purposes of this essay only the Marching Foot, which constituted the majority of those examined for pension, is shown. The number of men discharged for each reason is given against the total of the Marching Foot examined in that year.

Reason for Discharge	1725	1735	1745	1755
Ill	6	23	185	88
Wounded and Ill	2	0	11	5
Injured and Ill	6	8	16	2
Injured only	15	52	140	41
Wounded only	32	57	319	16
Wounded and Injured	10	15	11	4
Wounded and Decayed	2	3	1	0
Decayed	1	10	4	5
Superannuated	6	19	26	2
Worn Out	11	41	53	31
Dismissed	12	2	9	0
Total for year	**103**	**230**	**775**	**194**

---

23   TNA, Admissions Registers, WO 116/2, 3.2.1732.

Even in years of peace, men cited wounds as being the only cause of disablement despite the fact that they had been received several, perhaps many, years before. The wounds cited in 1725 must have been acquired mostly in the War of the Spanish Succession or the Jacobite rebellions of 1715 and 1719. Injuries, such as ruptures from loading baggage wagons, being beaten by smugglers, accidents with vehicles or animals always accounted for between 15 and 20 percent of all discharges even during a war-year such as 1745. Illness increased during wartime when men were obliged to camp in all weathers and were deprived of the comfort of warm public houses, but it is noticeable that the numbers of men rejected for pension were generally very small indeed. It is clear that officers recommending the men they discharged to Chelsea were aware of the rules and adhered to them closely, thereby ensuring that their deserving soldiers were accepted onto the pension.

Examination for pension always took place in London before the Commissioners of the Royal Hospital and their surgeon at premises in Whitehall, initially in the old War Office building and later in Killigrew Court. Discharged soldiers had to get themselves to London from wherever their regiments were stationed, and were maintained by their regiments until the Board sat and they could be examined. The Commissioners' meetings were irregular, though the first item of business was always the examination of any invalids who had been called to attend. In some years, 1725 for instance, the Board sat only six times, but in 1748 it held 33 meetings and dealt with a total of 2,674 men. The procedure was that the men's discharge papers would be looked at and the regimental agent, who was required to attend the meeting, was requested to verify that the handwriting of the man's captain was genuine. The soldier's physical condition was examined by the Hospital's own surgeon to see that he agreed with the comments of the regimental surgeon who had also signed the certificate: if he did, the man would be admitted. In 1732, during a parliamentary debate that sought to limit the funds available for pensions and which questioned why so many men were being admitted, the Secretary-at-War defended the scrupulousness of the Commissioners' examinations and declared that:

> We have been so cautious, that we have made the fellows strip to the skin, that we might examine them the more narrowly, and might be better able to judge whether they were actually disabled ... after such a strict enquiry, we could not in conscience, we could not in humanity, refuse to admit them.[24]

The pension, delivered supposedly every six months and in arrears, amounted to 5d per day – £7 and 12 shillings a year. However, as most men had a considerable distance to travel back to their homes and would have had very little, if any, of their own money to support them on their journey, a solution to this problem had to be found. Private enterprise took advantage of this difficulty and men known as dealers – money-lenders – provided ready funds in return for a legal document endorsed by the pensioner allowing them to collect the former soldier's money at the Hospital whenever it was issued. Clearly this means of receiving their money persisted after

---

24 W. Cobbett, *Cobbett's Parliamentary History of England* (London: Hansard, 1811), Vol.VIII 1722-1732, Columns 930-936.

the Out-pensioner had reached his home and credit arrangements were set up with a local shop-keeper to hand over the pension in cash or in kind in the future. In return, the latter was credited with a sum of money with which he could purchase imported goods only available in London – tea, wine, tobacco – and have them carted into the country for sale to his customers. Regrettably no shop-keepers' ledgers or financial papers are known to this author that might provide evidence of the link between a particular dealer and the man in the country many miles from London who actually paid the Out-pensioner. Those Out-pensioners who lived within 20 miles of London were expected to attend the hospital to collect their own money when it was issued. This perimeter was extended to 25 miles in 1735.

Until almost the end of the period dealt with here – 1755 – unless the pensioner was able to collect his money in person from the Royal Hospital, he therefore received a good deal less than the full amount, because the money-lenders took a substantial cut of the pension for the service they provided. It is recorded that in general men received 6 guineas – £6 and 6 shillings – so they lost 17 percent of the value of the pension by this arrangement. However, there was no real alternative as there was no Civil Service in the provinces to undertake the task of paying the pensioners. This system persisted from the institution of the Out-pension up to 1754, though it was widely recognised as being an abuse. In that year, the method of payment was reformed by William Pitt who was the Paymaster General. Thereafter out-pensions were paid in advance and the money was made available from the funds collected by Excise officers to whom the duties levied on manufactured goods made in Great Britain were paid. Each county had at least one collection area and as the officer rode round it collecting revenue, he was instructed to divert some of these funds to the Out-pensioners living in his area. He was provided with lists of men who would be entitled to call upon him after they had verified their entitlement to pension by visiting a Justice of the Peace. This official reported each such visit to Chelsea, certifying in a document that the former soldier had shown his discharge papers and his acceptance certificate from the Hospital and was therefore due his next payment.

The fundamental question, however, is, was the pension in total or in its discounted form, sufficient to live on? The answer to that question is 'No'. The pension was never intended to leave the old or disabled soldier in comfort for the rest of his life; it was a slight safety net that would assist in keeping him out of absolute poverty, but it was not enough for him to live on. That was particularly the case if he had a family. Men were not encouraged to marry while in the Army, but a handful in each company or troop did so with permission from their commanding officers, and some acquired women without permission and maintained them as best they could when in Great Britain, but were obliged to abandon them if they were sent overseas. Some Out-pensioners married after discharge and produced children, but the pension was never intended to assist in the maintenance of a family because that was not its purpose. It is the case nevertheless that in the eighteenth century the family constituted the most effective economic unit, with all of its members contributing to its collective income through cottage industry, husbandry in its own patch of garden, or labouring within the community in which it lived. Living alone was scarcely a viable option either on an economic level or from a social point of view, particularly to men who had spent so much of their lives within the regimental community and had benefitted from the advantages of mess comrades.

If at all possible, therefore, Out-pensioners had to work in order to keep a roof over their heads, clothes on their backs and food in their bellies. This seems a harsh fate, but it was exactly the same for all members of the labouring classes, whether male or female. Only in extreme old age or when utterly decrepit was it possible to apply to the parish for relief.[25] The provisions of the Poor Law went back to Elizabethan times and it was only from the parish in which the subject had been born or had acquired a right of settlement in some other way – by marriage or long-term residence and payment of the local taxes – that he or she had any right of assistance. While a former soldier could maintain himself, and any family he may have had, by his own labour, he was entitled to work anywhere in the country, and legislation at the ends of the various wars specifically gave discharged soldiers that right, but if their businesses failed or they became incapable of continuing them, they were obliged to return to their parish of settlement in order to claim relief.

The case was much harder for those incapable of working because of the injuries or wounds that they had received during their service. Some men found themselves in this very difficult predicament. John Yarwood, who had served in Lee's 55th Foot for only six months, was never going to return to blacksmithing having lost his right thumb in a firearms accident;[26] Jeremiah Osborn's ability to take up weaving again would have been severely compromised by the loss of fingers and his thumb from his right hand by a cannon shot at Boca Chica in Central America;[27] stone masonry was probably no longer practicable for Thomas Griffith of Wolfe's 8th Foot who lost four fingers from his right hand at Fontenoy.[28] John Dayley of St. George's 8th Dragoons would make no more barrels after his horse disabled his right hand by a kick;[29] managing a needle and thread was probably no longer practical for James Ellis, a tailor, who had lost two fingers from his right hand at Fontenoy,[30] but blindness must have been the worst affliction. Corporal Edward Guy of the 3rd Foot Guards lost his left eye and the use of both hands in an accident making up cartridges.[31] William Phillips had been struck blind by lightning when serving in Anstruther's 26th Foot on Gibraltar,[32] and no return to joinery and cabinet-making was possible for Jeremiah Hollis who had lost his right eye completely and was almost blind in his

---

25 S. Ottaway, *The Decline of Life: Old Age in Eighteenth Century England* (Cambridge: Cambridge University Press, 2004) deals with the general conditions that applied to the aged in the period. S. King, *Poverty and Welfare in England, a regional perspective, 1700-1850* (Manchester: Manchester University Press, 2000) provides detail of the variations in the application of the Poor Law around the country.
26 TNA, Admissions Registers, WO 116/4, 29.4.1747.
27 TNA, Admissions Registers, WO 116/3, 8.10.1741.
28 TNA, Admissions Registers, WO 116/3, 21.10.1745.
29 TNA, Admissions Registers, WO 116/4, 27.11.1747.
30 TNA, Admissions Registers, WO 116/3, 21.10.1745.
31 TNA, Admissions Registers, WO 116/2, 30.7.1745.
32 TNA, Admissions Registers, WO 116/2, 13.10.1730.

left when he was discharged from the Royal Irish Regiment.[33] Such men must have found it extremely hard to make ends meet.

Some towns still operated a system of relief dating back to the Maimed Soldiers and Mariners Funds established in 1593. I have found them still operating in Norfolk in the 1730s, but it is unlikely that they were widespread, as the legislation that underpinned them had lapsed before the end of the seventeenth century.[34] For men utterly incapable of work, the Poor Law was their only other resource unless they could find a place in an almshouse, such as the Lord Leyster Hospital for Old Soldiers in Warwick. Receipt of the Chelsea pension did not disbar a man from receiving assistance from any other source.

This essay is a brief survey of the complexities of the Out-pension and the factors that drew men into the Army and those that obliged them to leave the Army. Pensions did not exist for any other section of the labouring population, apart from Royal Navy sailors. So, it was an extraordinary recognition on the part of government that men from the humblest class of society should receive regular assistance from the state. This financial commitment was significant because although quite a lot of men were discharged at an advanced age – such as Trumpeter John Wood of Wade's 4th Horse who was pensioned at the age of 80 with 50 years' service in 1729,[35] and it seems unlikely that he would claim pension for very many years – there were also raw recruits of 16 who were disabled by accident or injury and were no use any longer as soldiers, but who could reasonably expect to live for decades during which time they would continue to be entitled to pension.

The examination of the records that form the basis of *These Meritorious Objects* provides an extraordinary picture of a section of the labouring class that was drawn into the Army. A great deal is known about officers because they were literate and a lot of background can be found out about them even if they left no writings of their own. Yet we know little of the other ranks and the individual details of their service. The Chelsea examination records provide a means of gaining an insight into their working lives as soldiers, and although only a minority of all soldiers were examined for pension, the experiences of those who were not must have been very similar to those who were. These records provide a very clear and rare window through which we can observe the life of the other ranks in the British Army of the eighteenth century.

The Act of Parliament of 1754 that reformed the method of paying the Out-pension referred to them as 'These Meritorious Objects of the Royal Bounty' and the descriptions of their service, the hardships they went through and the wounds, injuries and ailments that they suffered amply prove that they were indeed deserving of the state's care and support.

---

33 TNA, Admissions Registers, WO 116/3, 23.12.1745.
34 Norfolk County Record Office, Maimed Soldiers and Mariners Fund Accounts 1738 & 1739, BUL 4/12.
35 TNA, Admissions Registers, WO 116/2, 18.7.1729.

Bibliography

The following are recommended as further reading on this topic:

Cormack, Andrew, *'These Meritorious Objects of the Royal Bounty' The Chelsea Out-Pensioners in the Early Eighteenth Century* (London: Published by the Author, 2017). [available via www.andrewcormack.com]

Dean, C.G.T., *The Royal Hospital Chelsea* (London: Hutchinson & Co. Ltd, 1950).

Hutt, G., *Papers Illustrative of the Origin and Early History of the Royal Hospital at Chelsea* (London: Eyre & Spottiswoode, 1872).

In addition, the following were consulted in preparation of this chapter:

Archival Sources
The National Archives, Kew
    WO 116 - Chelsea Examinations Registers
Norfolk County Record Office
    Maimed Soldiers and Mariners Fund Accounts 1738 & 1739, BUL 4/12.

Printed Sources
Berkovich, I., *Motivation in War - The Experience of Common Soldiers in Old-Regime Europe* (Cambridge: Cambridge University Press, 2017).

Childers, E.S.E., & Stewart, R., *The Story of the Royal Hospital, Kilmainham* (London: Hutchinson & Co., 1921).

Childs, J., *The Nine Years War and the British Army 1688-1697, the operations in the Low Countries* (Manchester: Manchester University Press, 1991).

Cobbett, W., *Cobbett's Parliamentary History of England* (London: Hansard, 1811).

Davies, G., 'Recruiting in the Reign of Queen Anne', *Journal of the Society for Army Historical Research*, Vol. XXVIII, 1950, pp.146-159.

George, M.D., *London Life in the XVIIIth Century* (London: Kegan Paul, Trench, Trubner & Co. Ltd., 1930).

Houlding, J.A., *Fit for Service - The Training of the British Army, 1715-1795* (Oxford: The Clarendon Press, 1981).

King, S., *Poverty and Welfare in England, a regional perspective, 1700-1850* (Manchester: Manchester University Press, 2000).

Ottaway, S., *The Decline of Life: Old Age in Eighteenth Century England* (Cambridge: Cambridge University Press, 2004).

2

The Rank and File of the British Army at Culloden

Jonathan Oates

There has been much work on the Battle of Culloden, fought on 16 April 1746, the Jacobite army of the '45, and of the leaders on both sides.[1] It is true that there has been a book specifically on Cumberland's army, but it was short and was very much an overview, concerned with tactics, equipment, organisation and officers without recourse to the existing primary sources for the study of the actual men in the ranks of the British Army.[2] They will be the subject of this chapter.

Books studying the men in the Jacobite ranks include the work on the prisoners taken, which also consider the regiments or battalions in which they served.[3] More recently, there has been an attempt to list those men in the units of the same army, whether captured, killed or survived.[4] Currently there is an online resource to list all known Jacobites, military and otherwise.[5] Yet there has been a neglect of their opponents. In part this can be attributed to the general pro-Jacobite bias among many authors. However, it can also be seen to be due to the great mass of documentation created both by the state and its opponents about the Jacobites, especially when it came to prisoners taken, tried, and disposed of. For officers of the British Army, War Office records at the National Archives and published army lists chart their careers. Records of the rank and file are fewer and less accessible, because they have not been published.

Many academic historians, in otherwise very original works, make no reference to the men in the ranks of the British Army. They are seemingly taken for granted;

---

1   John Prebble, *Culloden* (London: Secker and Warburg, 1961); Stuart Reid, *Like Hungry Wolves: Culloden Moor, the 16th of April, 1746* (London: Windrow and Greene, 1994); Stuart Reid, *Culloden* (Barnsley: Pen and Sword, 2005).
2   Stuart Reid, *Cumberland's Culloden Army, 1745-6* (London: Osprey Publishing, 2012).
3   J.G. Arnot And B.S. Seton (eds.), 'The Prisoners of the '45', *Scottish History Society*, 3rd Series, vols.13-15 (Edinburgh: 1928-1929); Maggie Craig, *Bare Arsed Banditti: The Men of the '45* (London: Mainstream Publishing, 2014).
4   Alistair Livingstone, Christian Aikman and Betty Hart (eds.), A *Muster Roll of Prince Charles Edward Stuart's Army, 1745-46* (Aberdeen: Aberdeen University Press, 1984).
5   Jacobite Rebelion of 1745 <www.jacobites.net> viewed 3 March 2020.

yet without them there would have been no campaign or battles.[6] McLynn has a chapter on the Jacobite army but oddly enough nothing equivalent on their opponents, who are but fleetingly noted. Often the men in the ranks have been dealt with in a derogatory offhand manner, with Michael Barthorp writing, 'The better type of man was loath to enlist, so that recourse had to be made to the poorest and often criminal classes of society'.[7] Reid discusses the British Army in his several books on Culloden and the campaign. He cites a company roll of 1775 (albeit nearly three decades later) to show that many of the men in the ranks had been agricultural labourers, tailors, cloth makers, gardeners, shoemakers and others. He also introduced the notion that some of the troops had only recently been recruited by the parishes being paid a bonus for men employed as soldiers for a short period of time, naming them 'Vestry men' and alleging they dealt with wounded Jacobites and prisoners in a most murderous manner.[8] In a later book, Reid adds to this thesis:

> Most of those who joined the army were young and footloose agricultural labourers attracted by the notion of seeing a bit of the world, rather than working themselves to death in the same parish in which they had been born. Weavers and other cloth workers were equally common, either because they were thrown out of work by the industry's periodical slumps or else because the sheer boredom of sitting at a loom all day long proved too much for them. Other trades were represented too, but between the two of them countrymen and weavers accounted for most of King George's recruits.[9]

There are three longstanding myths about the British army at Culloden that need recalling at the outset; that this was an English army (the opening words of the film *Culloden* (1965) by Peter Watkins, states, 'This was an English government army'), that it was 9,000 men strong (repeated in the same film and in many books) and, in contradiction to the first assertion, that there were more Scots in the army than in the Jacobite army. A Scottish character in the third series of the television drama *Outlander* (2018) is shocked that there could even be one Scot in the British Army.

I will be using three main sources here; pension records of the rank and file, comments by their officers and finally those letters and memoirs written by those handful of rankers who were both literate and there, including Scottish privates Alexander Taylor of the Royals and Edward Linn of Campbell's (a former porter from Leith); English volunteer Michael Hughes; dragoon Enoch Bradshaw of Cirencester,

---

6   Jeremy Black, *Culloden and the Forty Five* (Stroud: Sutton, 1997); William Speck, *The Butcher: The Duke of Cumberland and the suppression of the '45* (Cardiff: Welsh Academic Press, 1995); Frank McLynn, *The Final Campaign: The Jacobite Army in England* (Edinburgh: John Donald Publishers, 1983); Jonathan Oates, *Sweet William or the Butcher: The Duke of Cumberland and the '45* (Barnsley: Pen and Sword, 2008), Jacqueline Riding, *Jacobites: A New History of the '45 Rebellion* (London: Bloomsbury Publishing, 2016).
7   Michael Barthorp, *Jacobite Rebellions, 1689-1745* (London: Osprey, 1982), p.23.
8   Reid, *1745: A Military History of the last Jacobite Rising* (Spellmount: Staplehurst, 1995), pp.183-186.
9   Reid, *Culloden*, pp.114-115.

a 40 year old former tailor; and William Oman, rank unknown. Reference will also be made to other individuals.[10]

Pension records for the rank and file of the British army are to be found at The National Archives, in the War Office papers, Royal Hospital Chelsea Disability and Out-Patients' Admissions Books, covering 1746-1774, WO116/4-6, for infantry and cavalry and can be viewed electronically. These list in chronological order, usually month by month, lists of men who were awarded pensions due to disability and age. The man's name, age (at the time the pension was awarded), parish of origin, former occupation, length of military service, regiment(s) served in, and the reason for the pension are recorded. In case of disabilities, these are recorded, along with the action in which they happened. For many men, the phrase 'worn out' is used, to show that they were elderly and so past active service. The methodology used here is to read through these books and note the relevant details of the men who served in the regiments present at Culloden until men who could have been present at the battle are no longer listed. This is the only source for the systematic recording of rank and file at this period of time.

The figure of 9,000 men in Cumberland's army has been generally accepted, but is based on a misconception originally taken from the reported numbers of the army. This source states that there were 2,400 dragoons, artillerymen and militia along with the infantry, but the vast majority of the militia was not present on the battlefield but were kept to the rear, as they had been at Falkirk.[11]

The strength of the army is easy to ascertain by examining official battalion returns. There were 15 battalions of foot and three regiments of dragoons or light horse in Cumberland's army at Culloden; numbering respectively 6,410 and 842 men. Together with the artillery and staff there were, then, just over 7,500 men in all, together with four companies of Highland irregulars, 140 strong, as noted below. Rather less than usually asserted. To learn about the men in the ranks, the prime sources are the pension records showing a man's parish and county of origin, his former occupation, age and years of military experience. Not all men received pensions; many were killed or deserted, but 3,213 men from the battalions which fought at Culloden and whose service dates from 1745, were awarded them in the half century after Culloden. This is almost 50 percent so is a reasonable sample of the whole.

However, not all these men were necessarily at Culloden, some would have been on detachment or ill; Cumberland described Bligh's 20th Foot as having 573 rank and file in March 1746, but only 447 were present at Culloden as noted below.[12] Yet there is no way to separate these men from the rest of the sample.

---

10   Anon. (ed.), 'Battle of Culloden', *Journal of the Society for Army Historical Research*, 36 (1957) (Taylor); W.H. Anderson (ed.), 'The Battle of Culloden', *Journal of the Society for Army Historical Research*, 1 (1921) (Linn); Michael Hughes, *A Plain Narrative or Journal of the Late Rebellion begun in 1745* (London: Henry Whitridge 1746); Royal Archives, CP14/385, Enoch Bradshaw to brother, 11 May 1746; London Metropolitan Archives, WJ/SP/1746/06/12, Letter of Mr Forbes enclosing papers for William Oman, June 1746.
11   *Gentleman's Magazine*, 16 (1746), p.239.
12   Royal Archives (RA), Cumberland Papers, 12/353, Cumberland to Newcastle, 26 March 1746.

34 LIFE IN THE RED COAT

Infantry Unit Strengths

Unit	Field Officers	Captains	Subalterns	Sergeants	Drummers	Rank and file	Total
2/Royals*	2	5	19	29	25	401	481
Howard's 3rd*	2	4	10	21	14	413	464
Barrell's 4th	2	5	13	18	10	325	373
Wolfe's 8th*	1	7	14	17	11	324	374
Pulteney's 13th*	2	6	14	23	19	410	474
Price's 14th	2	7	14	21	11	304	359
Bligh's 20th*	2	5	13	22	13	412	467
Campbell's 21st*	1	5	13	21	14	358	412
Sempill's 25th*	2	5	15	20	14	420	476
Blakeney's 27th+	2	4	14	24	12	300	361
Cholmondeley's 34th*	2	7	15	21	15	399	459
Fleming's 36th	2	6	18	25	14	350	415
Dejean's 37th	2	6	15	23	19	426	491
Conway's 59th	3	5	16	21	16	325	386
Battereau's 62nd++	1	7	19	24	18	345	4,218
Total	28	84	222	330	225	5,512	6,410

*Indicated unit served at Fontenoy
+/++ 5/4 staff officers
Argyllshire Militia: 140 men in four companies on the field; another eight companies (361 and officers) in reserve/baggage guard.
Company of Murray's 43rd Highlanders: strength unknown.

Cavalry Unit Strengths

Unit	Field Officers	Captains	Subalterns	Others*	Sergeants	Drummers	Troopers	Total
Kingston's 10th Light Horse	1	4	10	8		7	183	211
Cobham's 10th Dragoons	1	3	4	3	15	8	241	276
Kerr's 11th Dragoons	2	2	11	6	12	11	255	255
Total	4	9	25	17	27	26	679	787

*indicates adjutants, surgeons and quartermasters: none had a chaplain
Total cavalry strength: 55 officers and 787 men (842)

Royal Artillery Strength

Major William Belford and Captain John Godwin
2 lieutenants, 2 sergeants, 2 corporals, 1 fireworker, 21 gunners, 47 matrosses and 7 bombardiers.

Total strength: 7,476, plus company of Murray's 43rd and staff.[13]

---

13   RA, CP14/7, Strength of English at Culloden.

So, having established its numbers, the next question to pose is whether this was an English army or were there more Scots in it than with the Jacobites at Culloden? The latter, for comparison, numbered about 5,000, with about 4,400 being Scottish? In the 3,213 men sampled from the British Army at Culloden, there were, 1,145 Scots, (34 percent), 1,745 English, (52 percent), 77 Welsh, (2 percent) and 246 Irish (7 percent). This was indeed a British army, with men from all around Great Britain. Doubling these numbers to reach a rough figure for the army as a whole, we can see that there were almost 2,300 Scots in the British army, so about half the number fighting for the Jacobites. Given that the Scots formed only about 10 percent of Great Britain's population, they were represented in Cumberland's regular forces far beyond the expected proportion, which would be about 700. The numbers cited above also exclude the militia companies, which can be assumed to have been wholly Scots. Therefore, more Scots fought for the Jacobites at Culloden, but many fought against them.

Three battalions were overwhelmingly Scottish; Sempill's 25th (long associated with Edinburgh), with 163 out of 201 sampled (81 percent), 2/Royals (later the Royal Scots), with 205 out of 265 sampled (77 percent) and Campbell's 21st (Royal North British Fusiliers), with 314 out of 367 sampled (86 percent).

A very small number of men had been born overseas; one from Switzerland, one from Hanover and one from another German state. James Duckveller, a 33-year-old former stocking weaver from Zurich was in the Royals. Christopher Hamborough of Barrell's was a 45-year-old former tailor born in Brandenburg-Prussia. Another man was born in Ghent. One man had been born in Gibraltar, probably to a member of the garrison there.

Regiments were made up of men from extremely diverse parts of the country. For example, in Barrell's 4th, of the 259 rank and field that we know of, men had come from 186 different parishes. There was a preponderance of men in this battalion from south west England; 14 from Exeter, eight from Taunton and seven from Somerset. Yet in most cases for each battalion, a parish might yield one or two men. Most of the recruits were from villages and small towns, which is no surprise since Britain was predominantly rural. Relatively few men came from cities. London had a population of about 600,000 in 1750 (10 percent of that of Britain), yet only 40 of our sample, when one might expect about 300, named London as a parish of origin. Possibly this was because average wages for labourers were nine shillings per week, compared to five elsewhere, creating less incentive to seek an alternative life in the army. Liverpool, Bristol and Norwich each all provided 10 or less men. Birmingham, Manchester and Newcastle all supplied 20 or more men each.

Other cities supplied more men; 67 men from Glasgow (population 31,700 in 1755) and 51 from Dublin (about 60,000 population). This suggests that non-monetary motivations played a part, as Glasgow was staunchly anti-Jacobite in 1715 and 1745 and Dublin was mostly Protestant in a predominantly Catholic Ireland.[14] Victoria Henshaw has suggested that Scots may have joined for religious reasons;

---

14 William A. Speck, *Stability and Stride, 1714-1760* (London: Arnold, 1977), p.298; Geoffrey Holmes and Daniel Szechi, *The Age of Oligarchy: Pre-Industrial England, 1722-1783* (London: Longman, 1993), pp.346-351.

Presbyterians fearful of a Catholic or Episcopalian restoration. The examples of friends and neighbours may have played a part, too.[15]

The men were taken from a diverse range of backgrounds, mostly of humble origins. Of their former occupations, 1,399 (44 percent) were labourers, 320 were weavers (11 percent), 188 had been shoemakers (6 percent), 147 (5 percent) had been tailors, 109 had been husbandmen (3 percent) and 75 had been butchers (2 percent). There were men from over 50 other skilled or semi-skilled occupations. A more detailed breakdown is as follows:[16]

Occupation	Number	Percentage
Baker	32	1
Barber	28	1
Bricklayer	29	1
Butcher	75	3
Carpenter	59	2
Clothier	47	1
Cordwainer	18	1
Cutler	23	1
Farmer	40	1
Gardener	54	2
Husbandman	109	3
Labourer	1,296	38
Nailor	34	1
Servant	48	1
Shoemaker	188	6
Smith	81	2
Soldier's son	33	1
Stocking maker	22	1
Tailor	147	4
Tanner	20	1
Unknown	96	3
Weaver	320	9
Woolcomber	47	1
Others	538	15
Total	3,384	100

Some of those who enlisted were not from professions usually associated with the army's rank and file. What possessed those five surgeons and four officers' sons to enlist? Did the sword cutler and gunsmiths find their former professions of use when serving in the army? Brickmakers could earn up to 22 shillings a week and

---

15 Victoria Henshaw, *Scotland and the British Army, 1700-1750: Defending the Union* (University of Birmingham, 2014), pp.60, 116.
16 The National Archives (TNA), WO116/4-6, RoyaL Hospital Chelsea, Disability and Out Pensions Admission Books, 1746-1774.

other skilled workers a similar wage. This was far more than they would receive in the army, so men simply were not leaving their profession for the army for monetary reasons unless they were facing long term unemployment.[17]

It is worth noting that common soldiers and sailors were near the bottom of the social scale; only cottagers, small ale house keepers, paupers and gypsies were below them. Even labourers were above soldiers; manufacturers, craftsmen, artisans and lesser merchants were above all of these. Clearly members of these groups were falling down the social ladder when they entered the army, and so business failure may have led to this.[18]

Rates of daily pay in the army were not extravagant, as the table below demonstrates:[19]

Rank	Dragoons	Infantry
Sergeant	2s 6d	18d
Corporal	2s	1s
Drummer	n/a	1s
Trumpeter	2s	n/a
Private	1s 6d	8d

It is, of course, impossible to know why individual men joined the army. None left records to explain why they did so. Most were illiterate. The reasons usually stated are unemployment, poverty, boredom, escaping family responsibilities and a desire for variety in life. Poverty could well have been one recruiter. The years 1739 and 1740 were those of a deficient harvest followed by a dearth and so in the latter year there were a number of grain riots throughout England.[20] These years were when 20 percent of those who were at Culloden enlisted, these being the highest level of any years for men joining up. Whether this is a coincidence or not is impossible to know with any certainty, particularly since these were the years at the outbreak of the war when one would expect recruiting to be stepped up, yet it is suggestive, at least.

Some of the men were newly recruited. Due to the emergency posed by the Jacobite insurrection, special measures were taken to raise men for the army. One method was to encourage men to join the existing units returning from the Continent. On 19 October and 16 December 1745, the following proclamation was issued:

> His Majesty's service requiring at this time a speedy augmentation of his forces, it is this day ordered in council that Sir Dudley Ryder, His Majesty's Attorney General do forthwith prepare the draught a proclamation for encouraging able bodied men to inlist into Hs Majesty's Land service and for that purpose to declare His Majesty's Royal Pleasure that all such as shall inlist in His Majesty's service before the 25th of December next shall

---

17 Speck, *Stability and Strife*, p.55.
18 Holmes and Szechi, *The Age of Oligarchy*, pp.352-353.
19 TNA, WO24/95, Regiments moved from Ireland, 1719.
20 Holmes and Szechi, *The Age of Oligarchy*, p.384.

upon their request be discharged accordingly at the end of six months from the time of their inlisting in case the rebellion be extinguished within that time and if not then as soon as the rebellion shall be extinguished.[21]

A bounty of £6 was paid to each recruit joining the Foot Guards and £4 for any other unit.

Another method was to create new regiments from scratch; noblemen were given commissions to raise forces. Only one of these units fought at Culloden; Kingston's Light Horse, raised from Nottinghamshire in October 1745.

We now turn to the ages of men serving at Culloden, again using pensions records to do so. At the time of the battle, the average mean age of the men sampled was 33 and the average mean length of service in the army was eight years. Most of the men were in their twenties and thirties. The youngest was Henry Knowles, of Wakefield, of Sempill's 25th Foot, aged 11; there was a 12-year-old and two 13-year-olds. The oldest was George Harding of Dejean's 37th Foot, aged 73. Only 106 (3 percent) were in their teens, with 631 (19 percent) in their 40s and 226 (7 percent) over 50. The breakdown of ages across the sample as a whole is shown in the table below:[22]

Age	Number	Percentage
11-15	9	under 1 percent
16-20	179	5 percent
21-25	600	17 percent
26-30	682	19 percent
31-35	713	21 percent
36-40	456	13 percent
41-45	345	10 percent
46-50	257	7 percent
51-55	143	4 percent
56-60	47	2 percent
61-65	17	under 1 percent
66-70	1	under 1 percent
71-75	1	under 1 percent
Unknown	10	under 1 percent

The levels of military experience, as seen by the number of years a man had served in the army at the time of Culloden was also varied as seen in the table below:[23]

---

21 *London Gazette,* 1 October 1745.
22 TNA, WO116/4-6, Royal Hospital Chelsea Disability Out Pensions Admission Books, 1746-1774.
23 TNA, WO116/4-6, Royal Hospital Chelsea Disability Out Pensions Admission Books, 1746-1774.

Years	Number of men	Percentage
0-5	1,459	43 percent
6-10	988	29 percent
11-15	412	12 percent
16-20	269	8 percent
21-25	158	5 percent
26-30	57	2 percent
31-35	28	1 percent
36-40	6	under 1 percent
41-45	4	under 1 percent
Unknown	10	under 1 percent

One of the regiments consisted of men who had virtually no military experience, having been recruited as recently as October 1745. This was Kingston's 10th Light Horse. Unlike most of the army, none of these soldiers had experienced a battle before. They arrived in Scotland in February 1746 and had taken part in this month and in March in scouting expeditions. Cumberland was enthusiastic about their worth, for having heard of the surprise attack at Keith where 70 loyalist Highlanders and 30 men of Kingston's were lost, he wrote to Newcastle thus, 'I should have had little Concern about this Accident, if it had not been for the loss of some of Kingston's People. For, I cannot sufficiently commend the behaviour of that Regiment upon all occasions, or the Readiness with which they undergo all the Service & Fatigues they are employed in'.[24]

Most of the men had fought in battle in recent years. Of the infantry, seven of the 15 battalions had fought at Fontenoy and 12 at Falkirk; defeats both. One of the dragoon regiments had also seen action at Falkirk. Of those who had served at Falkirk, the majority had run away rather than having stood and fought, but men from four regiments, including Barrell's 4th, had stood their ground and repelled Jacobite troops, before making an orderly withdrawal. Yet some of the men were new recruits, who had never seen a battle previously. Experience rates were mixed. For 263 men (8 percent) it was almost nil having joined the army in the previous 12 months. Most had between one and seven years of soldiering behind them; 1,895 or 59 percent, but 520 (16 percent) had served between 20-30 years and 42 men (1 percent) had served for over three decades, so probably served in the War of the Spanish Succession.

It is not certain how many of the men in the ranks were married. Generally speaking, marriage was not encouraged and many senior officers were unwed (Cumberland and Hawley included). Linn and Taylor wrote letters to their wives, indicative of the fact that they did not follow the army but remained at home. Apart from these two literate men, the only other married men we know of were those who were killed and whose wives were assisted financially.[25]

---

24 RA, CP12/353, Cumberland to Newcastle, 26 March 1746.
25 W.B. Blaikie (ed.), 'Origins of the Forty Five', *Scottish History Society*, Series 2, 2 (1916), p.433.

There were seven married men in Dejean's 37th Foot. This represented half of the total fatalities that that battalion took at Culloden, but this cannot imply that nearly half of the men were married because a further 40 men were injured and of these at least some would have died shortly afterwards. The youngest wife, now widow, was aged 25 and the oldest aged 46. The latter had two daughters, the eldest of whom was 10 and, unlike the case with Linn and Taylor, his family went with him. Another man was a widower; his 15-year-old son William accompanied the army (presumably in a military capacity) but his 10-year-old daughter Sarah was living in London. Another man left a wife and four children, but two, perhaps newly wed, were childless. In Barrell's 4th Foot there were also seven married men among the 16 rank and file fatalities. Of these seven, all had children, numbering from one to five and whose wives were aged between 30 and 46, though one man was a widower.[26]

We now turn to the day of the battle and the period leading up to it. Morale among the men was high, as frequently noted by Cumberland. On 1 February he wrote they were 'in the highest spirits'. Two weeks later, they were 'all in great health & spirits'. Later that month he told Lord Granville of, 'The good spirits I found His Majesty's Troops in'. On crossing the Spey on 12 April, Cumberland wrote 'they all went on with great Chearfulness, which they have shewn ever since our setting out'.[27]

It is fortunate that some of the rank and file wrote down their experiences of the battle. It was not a prepossessing day as Private Alexander Taylor of the Royals later wrote:

> It was a very cold, rainy Morning, and nothing to buy to comfort us. But we had the Ammunition loaf, thank God; but not a dram of Brandy or Spirits, had you given a Crown for a gill, nor, nothing but the Loaf and the water. We had also great Difficulty in keeping the Locks of our firelocks dry; which was absolutely necessary.[28]

Fellow Scot, the 51-year-old Private Edward Linn of Campbell's 21st, also wrote of the dispiriting march to Culloden, 'We waded to our knees in mud & dirt through the Moor Severall times that day with a good will to be att them, & no Wonder, considering the fatigues we have undergone this Winter by hunger & Cold & Marching, Night & Day, after them'.[29]

It was an unsettling march for the men. Taylor wrote:

> We marched but four miles till we were alarmed by their Out-parties and drew up in order of battle, and marched that way for two miles with our arms secured and Bayonets fixed (a very uneasy way of marching.[30]

---

26 Blaikie (ed.), 'Origins', p.433.
27 TNA, SP54/28, 1B, Cumberland to Andrew Fletcher, 1 Feb. 1746; CP10/233, Cumberland to Newcastle, 14 Feb. 1746; 11/15, Cumberland to Granville, 20 Feb.1746; TNA, SP54/30/16, Cumberland to Newcastle, 15 April 1746.
28 Anon. (ed.), 'Battle of Culloden', p.184.
29 Anderson (ed.), 'The Battle of Culloden', p.21.
30 Anon (ed.), 'Culloden', p.184.

The weather continued to be dull, with Linn writing 'it was a very bad day both for Wind & Rain, But thank God it was straight upon our backs'.[31]

Before hostilities commenced, Cumberland made a speech to the troops. Michael Hughes, a volunteer in the ranks, later wrote that it was 'followed by a full acclamation of all the soldiers, testifying their intire satisfaction and loyalty'. Apparently, he spoke to each battalion and platoon, 'Had you seen him as I did, you could never forget him. His presence and intrepid Behaviour was enough to inspire the most pusillanimous with courage' and he told them to 'Depend my lads on your Bayonets: let them mingle with you; let them know the Men they have to deal with'.[32] Cumberland was convinced that the infantry held the key to success, 'by all accounts the rebels don't fear that [the cavalry] as they do our fire & on that alone I must depend'.[33]

The battle began with an exchange of artillery fire; though the effect has been exaggerated, it was much to the Royal Artillery's advantage. Hughes wrote of 'the great Execution performed with our Cannon' and of 'our Cannon began to play so very briskly upon them, and their Lines were formed so thick and deep, that the Grapeshot made open Lanes quite through them, the Men dropping down by Wholesale'.[34] This was clearly when the Jacobites were at close range when canister was used.

This was followed by the centre and right of the Jacobite line advancing to charge. Taylor referred to their charge at Culloden thus, 'they betook them to their small Arms, Sword and Pistol, and came running on our Front-Line like Troops of Hungry Wolves, and fought with intrepidity'.[35] Likewise, Hughes wrote of the enemy as being 'like Wildcats their Men came down in swarms'.[36] Linn wrote 'they came up very boldly & very fast all in a Cloud together, Sword in hand'.[37]

A letter from a contemporary newspaper reported, 'the fire from the King's Troops was so hot, quick, regular and well aim'd, that they [the Jacobites] fell with incredible Slaughter'.[38] George Brereton of Cholmondeley's 34th Foot wrote 'our men kept their fire till within four paces of us then poured ball into their very bosoms and cut them down like grapeshot from a cannon'.[39]

Despite the musketry volleys poured on them, many Jacobites reached the left of the British line, where there were two battalions, both predominantly made up of Englishmen. What was crucial was that unlike the case at Falkirk, the men all stood and fought, whereas one of these regiments, Dejean's 37th, had run away at Falkirk. There were several comments on this melee. It was reported, 'There was scarce a soldier or officer in Barrell's or Munro's [Dejean's]which engaged, who did

---

31 Anderson (ed.), 'The Battle of Culloden', p.22.
32 Michael Hughes, *Plain Narrative*, p.40.
33 TNA, SP54/27, 55A, Cumberland to Newcastle, 30 January 1746.
34 Hughes, *Plain Narrative*, p.26.
35 Anon (ed.), 'Culloden', p.184.
36 Hughes, *Plain Narrative*, p.26.
37 Anderson (ed.), 'Battle of Culloden', p.22.
38 *General Advertiser*, 1 May 1746.
39 Alan W. Robertson, The Jacobite Rising of 1745: The Battle of Culloden from the PRONI Archives', *History Scotland* XVI, no.2 (2016), pp.42-45.

not kill one or two men each with their bayonets or spontoons'. Of Barrell's 4th it was alleged, 'After the battle there was not a bayonet in this regiment but was either bloody or bent'.[40] A soldier from Barrell's later wrote, 'the old Tangerines bravely repulse those Boarders with a dreadful slaughter, and convinced them that their Broadswords and Target is unequal to the Musket and Bayonet, when in the hands of Veterans who are determined to use them'. [41] An officer of Dejean's 37th attested, 'Our lads fought more like Devils then Men'.[42]

The might of Jacobite numbers told, as several battalions descended against these two, made up of 864 men in total, and the colours of Barrell's were at risk. It could have been then that David Robertson, a private from Sempill's 25th, came forward to aid the wounded ensign (either Brown or Campbell) and guard the colour.[43]

Those Jacobites breaking through the first line were met by a number of battalions from the second. William Oman was in the ranks of one of these, his account does not make it clear which one, and wrote, 'The perpetual fire of our troops made for five minutes...which beat them off, and obliged them to turn their backs and run away'.[44] The men of Wolfe's 8th Foot 'soon made the place too hot for them and retook the cannon'. [45]

Several of the rank and file captured Jacobite standards at this point. These men were Edward Patridge from Bligh's 20th, Sergeant Dunn, Charles Robinson, and John Brown (a 42-year-old former weaver from Glasgow); the latter three from Sempill's. Later Patridge was rewarded with £16 and the other three shared £50 18s with Robertson, who had saved one of Barrell's colours.[46]

Once the Jacobite infantry began to falter and turn tail, they were fired on by the artillery again, as Linn wrote, 'our cannon & a few royalls [mortars] sent them a few small bomb shells & cannon balls to their farewell'. [47]

It was then that the cavalry was unleashed to deadly effect. Cumberland urged Cobham's 10th Dragoons, 'Brush, my lads, for the honour of Old Cobham' and to others, 'Cut hard, pay 'em home'.[48] Three former Nottinghamshire butchers in Kingston's Horse later bragged of having killed 14 Jacobites each. Enoch Bradshaw of Cobham's narrowly missed being shot but as he told his brother 'a miss is as good as a mile as we say in Gloucestershire'. He undoubtedly relished the work of cutting down fleeing Jacobites, referring to them as 'these rapacious villains' and 'barbarous villains'.[49]

The soldiers cheered their leader, 'Flanders! Flanders! We'll follow your Highness against any enemy'. Linn wrote, 'We lost very few men of our Army, only a few

---

40   *Gentleman's Magazine*, 16 (1746), p.220.
41   *The Oxford Gazette or Reading Mercury*, 24 & 28 April 1746.
42   *The Newcastle Courant*, 2731, 19-26 April 1746.
43   RA, CP14/11, List of men of Sempill's regiment who took colours, 16 April 1746
44   London Metropolitan Archives, WJ/SP/1746/06/12, Letter of Mr Forbes enclosing papers for William Oman, June 1746.
45   *General Advertiser*, 1 May 1746.
46   RA, CP14/10, Note of payment to a man taking a standard, 16 April 1746.
47   Anderson (ed.), 'Battle of Culloden', p.22.
48   *General Advertiser*, 1 May 1746.
49   RA, CP14/385, Enoch Bradshaw to brother, 11 May 1746.

wounded; our loss is about 200 men Wounded & Killed. Thank God we lost not one man of our Regiment, only a few wounded, we never had such good Luck befor'.[50]

The majority of soldiers had not taken part in the desperate melee outlined above; only men from two battalions of infantry to the left of the front line had done so. Some men, from the battalions on the right of the second line, had not even fired a shot. Most of the cavalry had the bloody task of pursuing fugitives. Therefore, experiences of men on the same side in the same battle were very variable, ranging from those involved in life and death hand to hand fighting to those who were essentially spectators.

The battle had not been a painless experience for the victors; 50 men were killed outright and of the 259 listed as wounded many undoubtedly did not survive. The bulk of these (176) were from the two battalions who had borne the brunt of the melee; Barrell's and Dejean's. Of those who were wounded, some received disabling injuries, entitling them to pensions. John Adams of Barrell's lost the use of his right hand and Thomas Appleton of the same regiment lost the use of his left arm. Some of those killed were married with children and their widows received cash sums.[51]

Infantry Casualties

Battalion	Killed	Wounded
2/Royals	0	4
Howard's 3rd	1	2
Barrell's 4th	17*	108*****
Wolfe's 8th	0	1*
Pulteney's 13th	0	0
Price's 14th	1*	9*
Bligh's 20th	4	17*
Campbell's 21st	0	13
Sempill's 25th	1	7
Blakeney's 27th	0	13
Cholmondeley's 34th	1	2
Fleming's 36th	0	6
Dejean's 37th	14	68*****
Conway's 59th	1	5*
Battereau's 62nd	0	3*
Total	40	245

*denotes number of officer casualties.

---

50 Anderson (ed.), 'Battle of Culloden', p.23.
51 *Gentleman's Magazine*, 16 (1746), pp.239-240; TNA, SP54/29/32d; List of killed and wounded at Culloden, WO10/30, Artillery Muster and Pay Book, 1746.

44 LIFE IN THE RED COAT

Artillery, Cavalry, and Highland Casualties

Unit	Killed	Wounded
Gunners	0	1
Other artillerymen	0	5
Loudon's 64th Highlanders	6	3*
Argyllshire Militia	0	1*
Kingston's 10th Light Horse	0	1
Cobham's 10th Dragoons	1	0
Kerr's 11th Dragoons	3	3
Total	10	14

*denotes one wounded man subsequently died thereof.

Equine Casualties

Unit	Killed	Wounded
Kingston's 10th Light Horse	2	1
Cobham's 10th Dragoons	4	5
Kerr's 11th Dragoons	4	15
Total	10	21

In summary, 50 men were killed, 259 wounded and 1 was reported missing, or about 3 percent of the whole. Comparing this to the battle of Fontenoy, where 4,041 British soldiers were casualties, this is a very small number. One dead and seven injured at Culloden from Sempill's 25th compares favourably to the same regiment's 32 dead and 91 wounded at Fontenoy.[52]

For the victors, the Guildhall Fund paid out sums to all the rank and file survivors; for sergeants this was 19s 1½d, corporals, 12s 9½d and privates and drummers, 9s 6½d. For the artillerymen, sergeants received £1 18s 3s, bombardiers, £1 11s 11d, gunners £1 5s 7d each and the others, 19s 1½d. The subalterns were given £1,000 between them; so about £4 apiece. Widows and orphans of soldiers having been killed were also given sums varying from £10-30. Widows of officers killed received higher sums.[53]

Looking beyond these statistics, we need to note the injuries actually inflicted. These are recorded in the pension records which list those men who received such wounds. The majority of wounds, were, of course, inflicted on those men from the two regiments that were most involved in the melee; Barrell's 4th and Dejean's 37th.[54]

---

52   *Gentleman's Magazine*, 15, 1745, pp.248-249.
53   Blaikie (ed.), 'Origins', pp.432-434.
54   TNA, WO116/4, Royal Hospital Chelsea: Disability Out Pensions Admission Book, 1746-1754.

Name of Man	Regiment	Wound
Adams, John	Barrell's	Lost use of right hand
Alexander, William	Barrell's	Wounded
Appleton, Thomas	Barrell's	Lost use of left arm
Barnsfeather, David	Barrell's	Wounded in right leg
Buller, James	Barrell's	Lost left leg
Burford, Peter	Barrell's	Disabled in left hand
Caw, John	Barrell's	Shot through left leg and thigh
Chambers, John	Barrell's	Wounded in left hand
Chapington, Mathais	Barrell's	Lost right arm
Checke, John	Barrell's	Wounded in left arm
Clarke, John	Barrell's	Wounded
Clarke, Robert	Barrell's	Wounded in head
Crocker, Simon	Barrell's	Lost use of right hand
Dent, Samuel	Barrell's	Wounded in left heel
Dills, John	Barrell's	Wounded
Griffith, John	Barrell's	Lost use of left leg
Hant, James	Barrell's	Wounded in head and right hand
Harris, Thomas	Barrell's	Wounded in left leg
Hobbs, John	Barrell's	Wounded
Hockley, John	Barrell's	Wounded
Holt, John	Barrell's	Wounded in head and side
Jackson, Ralph	Barrell's	Disabled in left hand
Jenkins, John	Barrell's	Lost use of left arm
Kelly, Joseph	Barrell's	Lost use of left leg
Johnson, William	Barrell's	Wounded in head and left arm
Knight, Thomas	Barrell's	Disabled in right leg
Leatherbarrow, John	Barrell's	Lost use of right leg
Lee, John	Barrell's	Lost right arm
Lotty, David	Barrell's	Shot through right arm
Messinger, John	Barrell's	Wounded
Midgeley, Isaac	Barrell's	Disabled in left hand and arm
Openan, David	Barrell's	Disabled in right thigh
Parker, Richard	Barrell's	Wounded in the head
Pretty, John	Barrell's	Lost use of left leg
Rowland, Evan	Barrell's	Wounded in head
Scoon, Jonathan	Barrell's	Wounded in head
Scott, John	Barrell's	Wounded in head and side
Telford, John	Barrell's	Wounded
Tinlins John	Barrell's	Disabled in right hand and shoulder
Truscott, John	Barrell's	Wounded
Webb, George	Barrell's	Shot through the legs
Weedons, Francis	Barrell's	Disabled in left hand and arm
Wilson, Robert	Barrell's	Wounded

Name of Man	Regiment	Wound
Whitehead, Mark	Campbell's	Wounded in right thigh
Byram, John	Bligh's	Disabled in left foot
Forkes, George	Bligh's	Disabled in right leg
Smith, Archibald	Bligh's	Wounded in side
Spencer, Robert	Bligh's	Lost right arm
Summer, Joseph/John	Bligh's	Head wound
Wilkie, Joseph	Battereau's	Wounded in breast
Forsham, Robert	Cobham's Dragoons	Wounded in pursuit
Ashmore, William	Dejean's	Disabled in left hand and shoulder
Barlow, Samuel	Dejean's	Wounded in right thigh
Bohannon, Arthur	Dejean's	Disabled in right thigh
Cunningham, Luke	Dejean's	Shot through the body
Dalloway, John	Dejean's	Disabled in left thigh
Davidson, John	Dejean's	Disabled in left hand and shoulder
Gill, William	Dejean's	Shot in right elbow
Grant, Thomas	Dejean's	Disabled in both thighs
Gregg, Isaac	Dejean's	Disabled in right foot
Griffith, Thomas	Dejean's	Shot in right knee
Guest, John	Dejean's	Disabled in right arm
Harrison, John	Dejean's	Shot in left knee
Irwin, William	Dejean's	Lost use of left leg
Lowne, Thomas	Dejean's	Disabled in left leg
McLelland, Charles	Dejean's	Shot through right arm
McMullin, Edward	Dejean's	Disabled in several parts of body
Moulson, Richard	Dejean's	Disabled by being shot in right leg
Perry, John	Dejean's	Disabled in right leg
Tovey, John	Dejean's	Jaw shot off
Wheeler, Edward	Dejean's	Cut in skull and shoulder
Millross, Nicholas	Dejean's	Stabbed by bayonet
Bull, John	Kerr's Dragoons	Bruised by horse
Brodie, Daniel	Price's	Wounded
Denninson, Richard	Price's	Lost left leg
Lemmon, John	Sempill's	Disabled in left arm

Unfortunately, we do not know which weapons made the bulk of these wounds. We can, however, be fairly certain that most were caused in melee, by swords cutting and stabbing, and bayonet thrusts. It is interesting to note that a few were caused by musketry. Five of Dejean's men and two of Barrell's were shot, presumably by Jacobite highlanders as they fired before the final rush to contact.

Where the location of the wound is known, 17 were to the arm, 23 were to the leg, nine were on the hand, three were on the foot, 10 were to the head, and two were to the body. Two men lost a leg and three men lost an arm, presumably due to amputation. It is likely that most head and body wounds were fatal or resulted in the man dying after the battle. Limb wounds were less often deadly, but could lead to a man being permanently disabled. Unable to serve or to work, these men left the army and became recipients of disability pensions. They probably returned to their parish of origin as ordained by the Old Poor Law and many have received parish funds from the overseers.

Dr John Pringle, an army physician, wrote that, after the battle, two malt barns near Inverness were used as hospitals for the wounded, which he recorded as being 270 rather than 259 as cited above. He recorded:

> There were several who had cuts of the broadsword, till then uncommon wounds in our hospitals; but these were easily healed, as the openings were large in proportion to the depth, as they bled much at first, and as there were no contusions and eschars, as in gunshot wounds, and to obstruct good digestion.[55]

Some men were treated elsewhere by the regimental surgeons, who had orders to provide quarters for the men in their units, but the worst injured were sent to the malt barns. Due to observations of prison inmates, Pringle took care that there was no crowding which led to contagions spreading. Regular cleaning was also essential. Most of the men on campaign were actually injured by falling ill, largely due to the temperature – about 2,000 in all – and had they been fit then Cumberland's army would have been substantially numerically stronger.

For those not killed, the victory was sweet. Bradshaw wrote after the battle, 'No history of battles can brag of so singular a victory and so few of our own men lost'.[56] Linn was more modest, 'I give you the trouble of these to acquaint you what great things God almighty hath done for us'.[57] Bradshaw told his brother, 'In short, tis mine and every bodies' opinion no history can brag of so singular a victory'.[58] Finally Private Taylor wrote that it was: 'so compleat a victory…We are now here encampd and I hope soon to be south again, most of our work now been over, except among the Highlands and taking them that have escaped'.[59]

Much of this success was due to the behaviour of the rank and file, who stood and fought, which had not always been the case in the previous battles of the campaign. An anonymous observer noted 'Not a man in the whole army behaved ill. On the contrary an uncommon spirit appeared through the whole of them'. Campbell of Airds wrote, 'The Troops all behaved remarkably well, and what I believe is very singular, not a single man turned his back or came off from the line. Even the few wounded men came off in spirits'.[60] The Royal North British Fusiliers 'had the Duke's

---

55 John Pringle, *Observations on The Diseases of the Army* (London: A Millar, 1765), pp.44-45, 52.
56 RA CP14/385, Bradshaw to brother, 11 May 1746.
57 Anderson (ed.), 'Battle of Culloden', p.24.
58 RA, CP14/385, Bradshaw to brother, 11 May 1746.
59 Anon (ed.), 'Culloden', p.185.
60 National Library of Scotland (NLS), MS3735, f.190, Campbell of Airds to unknown, 22 April 1746.

Particular thanks, saying it was owing to them the victory was so cheap', but he also singled out the men from Barrell's 4th and Dejean's 37th, too.[61]

Linn made great emphasis on his belief that God was on the side of the British army. In an age of near universal Christian belief, reinforced from the pulpits and presumably by the army chaplains, this should come as no surprise. His letter to his wife is full of references to the deity, though how widespread this view was among his comrades is impossible to discern, but it seems reasonable to assume that he was not alone in his views. He wrote 'what great things God almighty hath done for us' and 'I desire you would give thanks and praise to Almighty God and desire the Minister to remember me in his Prayers to God for so great a deliverance'.[62]

After the fighting was over, many British soldiers took the opportunity to avenge themselves against their enemies. For some, this was a personal matter. A letter in one newspaper claimed, 'The regiment, late Monroe's [Dejean's], remembered the villainous cruelty committed on their colonel in cold blood, and amply avenged it'.[63] At the Battle of Falkirk on 17 January 1746, the same regiment had, in contrast to their behaviour at Culloden, ignominiously fled the Jacobite advance; the colonel and his brother remained on the field and were cut down by the Jacobites. At Culloden, the regiment also also captured three Jacobite standards.[64]

More recent Jacobite behaviour also provoked vengeance, it being reported that 'Our men have really been pretty severe, and gave little quarter, being exasperated at the treatment our prisoners met with, they been [sic] found in dark dungeons at Inverness, almost naked and eat up with vermin'.[65]

The controversy over this battle is not the actual fighting but its aftermath. Jacobite accounts talk of great severity on the behalf of the victors, Lord Elcho noting 'Every body that fell into their hands gott no quarters, except a few who they resrv'd for publick punishment'.[66] Andrew Henderson noted in the aftermath of the battle:

> The Field was clear, and the Victory being compleat, the soldiers, warm in their Resentment, did Things hardly to be accounted for; several of their wounded Men were stabb'd, yea some who were lurking in houses, were taken out and shot upon the Field, tho' others were sav'd, by those whose Compassion was raised at the sight of so many victims.[67]

Henderson then went on to explain why such behaviour happened:

> the rebels had enraged the Troops, their Habit was strange, their Language still stranger, and their way of fighting was shocking to the Utmost degree: The Rebellion was unprovoked and the King's Troops had greatly suffered

---

61 NLS, MS. 3735, 190, Campbell of Airds to unknown, 22 April 1746.
62 Anderson (ed.), 'Battle of Culloden', p.2.
63 *Penny London Post*, 28 April 1746.
64 *General Advertiser*, 1 May 1746.
65 *General Advertiser*, 1 May 1746.
66 Lord Elcho, *A Short Account of the Affairs of Scotland in the Years 1744-1746* (Edinburgh: John Douglas Publishing, 1907), p.434.
67 Andrew Henderson, *A History of the Rebellion* (London: R. Griffiths 1748), p.116.

by it: the fields of Preston [pans] and Falkirk, were fresh in their Memory, they had lost a Gardner, a Whitney, a Munro besides other officers... their mangled corpses could not but stir up the soldiers to revenge. Therefore, if they found Vengeance in their Power, they violated the stricter rules of Humanity, some allowance ought to be made for the Passions they were inspired with at that time.[68]

Apparently the Earl of Kilmarnock begged for mercy, 'which was granted him with difficulty'.[69] This unwillingness to give quarter may have been because when a Jacobite officer had earlier in the battle being taken prisoner by Captain Alexander Grossett of Price's 14th Foot, the man had, when Grossett fell off his horse, snatched one of his pistols and shot Grossett dead before being killed by the dead man's companions.[70]

As with other battles, spectators came along to view this one, some with the desire to take what spoils they could from it, and were caught up in the killing, as at Sheriffmuir three decades previously. For example, as Hughes explained, 'many of the inhabitants, not doubting of success, who came out of curiosity to see the Action, or perhaps to get plunder, never went home again to tell the story: for their being mixt up with their own people, we could not know one from another'.[71]

One story that has received much credence is that related by the Chevalier de Johnstone, who was not an eye witness:

> He [Cumberland] ordered a barn, which contained many of the wounded Highlanders, to be set on fire and the soldiers stationed round it drove back with fixed bayonets the unfortunate men who attempted to save themselves into the flames, burning them alive in this horrible manner.[72]

Others who were there contradict the story. Captain Kinnier of Dejean's 37th:

> [A]vers that to his certain knowledge none of the wounded rebels were carried to that house, that only a few of the common soldiers of the Rebels were there and two sergeants, but not one ensign, nor any of the superior rank. He adds that not one of these had received any hurt and that they did not remain in the house above two hours.[73]

---

68 Henderson, *History*, p.117.
69 P.C. Yorke (ed.), *The Life and Correspondence of Phillip Yorke, Earl of Hardwicke, Lord Chancellor of Great Britain* (Cambridge: Cambridge University Press, 1913), Vol.I, p.514.
70 *Stamford Mercury*, 4 Sept. 1746.
71 Hughes, *Plain Account*, p.44.
72 James Johnstone, *Memoir of the Chevalier de Johnstone* (London: Folio Society, 1958), p.237.
73 Yorke (ed.), *The Life and Correspondence*, Vol.I, p.553.

In any case, the house where this massacre was alleged to have occurred was not built until after the battle and there is no archaeological evidence to support the atrocity story.[74]

After the battle a note was found on the corpse of a dead Jacobite which included the following ominous phrase:

> It is His Majesty's orders, that every person attach himself to some Corps of the Army and remain with the Corps Night and Day, until the Battle and Pursuit be finally over, and to give no Quarter to any of the Elector's Troops on any account whatsoever. This regards the Foot as well as the Horse. Sign'd George Murray, Lieutenant General.[75]

One soldier later wrote, of this, that it was not known about until after the battle, 'so that many were saved by our Army', implying that if it had been known about then the body count would have been higher. Some Jacobites claimed that this order was a forgery. The Earl of Balmerino attested, 'I do declare that it is without all manner of foundation…I believe rather that this report was spread to palliate and excuse the murders they themselves committed in cold blood after the battle of Culloden'.[76] Yet fellow Jacobite Lord Kilmarnock thought otherwise, 'I have had all reason in the world to believe that there was such an order'.[77] In fact, it is possible that the order refers to the previous night's planned attack on Cumberland's camp at Nairn, where no quarter could be granted when sleeping troops were to be killed.

During the pursuit by the dragoons, 'there was much knapping of Noddles' and 500 Jacobites were slain 'and a great many officers and soldiers were taken prisoner'. Yet not all pursuers were so ruthless. James Ray, a volunteer who had attached himself to the dragoons, recorded:

> In their Flight, I came up with a pretty young Highlander, who call'd out to me, Hold your Hand, I'm a Campbell. On which I asked him, Where's your Bonnet? He reply'd, Someone snatched it off my head [loyalist Highlanders had red or yellow crosses in their bonnets, Jacobites white]…He having neither of these Distinctions, I desired him, if he were a Campbell, to follow men, and I would have him taken Care of, being slightly wounded, which he promised, but on the first Opportunity, gave me the slip.[78]

Troops also sought to profit from the battle. Plunder was seen as an occasional perk of the job. The goods of the dead enemy were fair game. A contemporary historian noted that the clothing of Jacobite officers and gentlemen was particularly attractive

---

74 Tony Pollard and Neil Oliver, *Two Men in a Trench: Battlefield Archaeology* (London: Michael Joseph, 2002), pp.263, 285.
75 James Ray, *History of the Rebellion* (Bristol: S Farley, 1752), pp.343-344.
76 Henry Paton (ed.), 'Lyon in Mourning', I, *Scottish History Society*, 20 (1895), pp.32-33.
77 W.S. Lewis (ed.), *Correspondence of Horace Walpole* (Yale University Press, 1955), Vol.19, p.299.
78 Ray, *History*, p.337.

to the victorious soldiery, as the latter were seen 'strutting about in rich lac'd waistcoats, hats, etc.'[79] It was not only dead Jacobites who were robbed. Prince Charles's cook, fleeing from the stricken field was overtaken by his pursuers. They 'tore the lace off his hat and cloathing and took everything valuable from him'. One sergeant 'more cunning than the rest' gave the man a crown for his horse and saddle; these were worth 34 and four guineas respectively.[80]

Michael Hughes, having signed on for only a limited duration, left the army shortly after the battle and went on to write a book of his military memoirs. He was alone in the latter. For most of his fellows, the battle was another milestone in their military careers as they soldiered on. As the years after the battle passed, many of the veterans went onto fight in the Seven Years War and some in the American War of Independence. Some of those mentioned here are noted as receiving their pensions. Linn was discharged from the army in 1748 after 27 years of service, aged 55, and Enoch Bradshaw, aged 48, after 28 years in 1754. The last survivor who is thought to have served in the British Army at the battle was John Salter, who died at Chelsea Hospital in October 1827, aged 107. It is regretted that no one recorded his experiences of military life, which included fighting in America in the 1770s before being discharged in the next decade.[81] The 111-year-old Patrick Grant died in 1824, perhaps the last known Jacobite to have fought at Culloden.[82]

Cumberland's army at Culloden was thus predominantly English and Scottish. It was largely made up of veterans, some of longstanding, but for some it was their first battle. They had come from a multitude of parishes throughout the British Isles and from very many professions taken from among the skilled, unskilled and semi-skilled workers. Contrary to the previous battle, the men performed very well, standing to fire short range volleys and then fight in a hand to hand melee. Cumberland attested to this and later wrote, 'All the Generals, Officers and soldiers did their utmost in His Majesty's service and shewed the greatest zeal and Bravery on this occasion'.[83] Leadership was good and the enemy had weakened itself, it is true, but the battle restored the reputation of the British soldier, whose fighting qualities were once again demonstrated.

Bibliography

Archival Sources
Royal Archives
    Cumberland Papers, 10-12, 14
London Metropolitan Archives
    WJ/SP/1746/06/15.

---

79 John Marchant, *History of the Present Rebellion* (London: Published by the Author, 1746), p.395.
80 *Caledonian Mercury*, 10 June 1746.
81 *The Times*, 4 October 1827.
82 *The Times*, 27 February 1824.
83 TNA, SP54/30, 21a, Cumberland to Newcastle, 18 April 1746.

The National Archives
> SP54/27, 28-30
> WO 24/295
> WO30/10
> WO 116/4-6

National Library of Scotland
> MS3735

Printed Primary Sources

Anon. (ed.), 'Battle of Culloden', *Journal of the Society for Army Historical Research*, 36 (1957), pp.183-185.

Anderson, W.H., (ed.), 'The Battle of Culloden', *Journal of the Society for Army Historical Research*, 1 (1921), pp.21-24.

Blaikie, W.B., (ed.), 'Origins of the Forty Five', *Scottish History Society*, series 2, 2, (1916).

Elcho, Lord, *A Short Account of the Affairs of Scotland in the Years 1744-1746* (Edinburgh: John Douglas Publishing, 1907).

Henderson, Andrew, *A History of the Rebellion* (London: R. Griffiths 1748).

Hughes, Michael, *A Plain Narrative or Journal of the Late Rebellion begun in 1745* (London: Henry Whitridge 1746).

Johnstone, James, *Memoir of the Chevalier de Johnstone* (London: Folio Society, 1958).

Lewis, W.S., (ed.), *Correspondence of Horace Walpole* (Yale University Press, 1955).

Marchant, John, *History of the Present Rebellion* (London: Published by the Author, 1746).

Pringle, John, *Observations on The Diseases of the Army* (London: A. Millar, 1765).

Ray, James, *History of the Rebellion* (Bristol: S. Farley, 1752).

Robertson, Alan W., The Jacobite Rising of 1745: The Battle of Culloden from the PRONI Archives', *History Scotland* XVI, no.2, (2016).

Yorke, P.C., (ed.), *The Life and Correspondence of Phillip Yorke, Earl of Hardwicke, Lord Chancellor of Great Britain* (Cambridge: Cambridge University Press, 1913).

Newspapers

Caledonian Mercury, 10 June 1746.
General Advertiser, 1746.
Gentleman's Magazine, 15-16 (1745-1746).
London Gazette, 1745.
The Newcastle Courant, 2731, 19-26 April 1746.
The Oxford Gazette or Reading Mercury, 24, 28 April 1746.
Penny London Post, 1746.
Stamford Mercury, 1746.
The Times, 1824, 1827.

Secondary Sources

Barthorp, Michael, *Jacobite Rebellions, 1689-1745* (London: Osprey, 1982).

Black, Jeremy, *Culloden and the Forty Five* (Stroud: Sutton, 1997).

Craig, Maggie, *Bare Arsed Banditti: The men of the '45* (London: Mainstream Publishing, 2014).

Henshaw, Victoria, *Scotland and the British Army 1700-1750: Defending the Union* (University of Birmingham, 2014).

Holmes, Geoffrey, and Szechi, Daniel, *The Age of Oligarchy: Ore-Industrial England, 1722-1783* (London: Longman, 1993).

McLynn, Frank, *The Final Campaign: The Jacobite Army in England* (Edinburgh: John Donald Publishers, 1983).

Oates, Jonathan, *Sweet William or the Butcher: The Duke of Cumberland and the '45* (Barnsley: Pen and Sword, 2008).

Paton, Henry (ed.), 'Lyon in Mourning', I, *Scottish History Society*, 20 (1895).

Pollard, Tony and Oliver, Neil, *Two Men in a Trench: Battlefield Archaeology* (London: Michael Joseph, 2002).

Prebble, John, *Culloden* (London: Secker and Warburg, 1961).

Reid, Stuart, *Like Hungry Wolves: Culloden Moor, the 16th of April, 1746* (London: Windrow and Greene, 1994).

Reid, Stuart, *Culloden* (Barnsley: Pen and Sword, 2005).

Reid, Stuart, *Cumberland's Culloden Army, 1745-6* (London: Osprey Publishing, 2012).

Riding, Jacqueline, *Jacobites: A New History of the '45 Rebellion* (London: Bloomsbury Publishing, 2016).

Speck, William A., *Stability and Strife, England, 1714-1760* (London: Arnold, 1977).

Speck, William A., The *Butcher: The Duke of Cumberland and the suppression of the '45* (Cardiff: Welsh Academic Press, 1995).

3

A Serious Inconvenience? Foreign Prisoners of War and Deserters in Wellington's Peninsular Army 1808-1814

Robert Griffith

In September 1811 Viscount Wellington wrote to Lord Liverpool, Secretary of State for War, regarding a battalion of foreign recruits at Cadiz:

> I am not at all anxious to have any of them with this Army. The number of foreigners with this army is a serious inconvenience; as they not only convey intelligence to the enemy, which they could acquire in no other manner, but they have nearly put a stop to desertion from the Enemy's ranks by their accounts, unfounded or exaggerated, of the manner in which Deserters are treated and disposed of in the British Service.[1]

It was not the first time that Wellington had commented on the subject of foreign troops to his superiors, nor would it be the last.

In September 1811 foreign corps constituted 13 percent of the British Army's troops with Wellington; 7,504 rank and file out of a total of 56,297.[2] These were distributed between 12 units: the 5/60th; the 1st & 2nd KGL Hussars; the KGL Artillery; the 1st & 2nd KGL Light Infantry; the 1st, 2nd, and 5th KGL Line Infantry; the KGL Garrison Company; the Chasseurs Britanniques; and the Duke of Brunswick's Light Infantry. In September 1810 the proportion of foreign corps had been 12 percent, it rose to 15 percent in September 1812, and then fell back to 12 percent in September 1813. Whilst all these units had been formed from a core of volunteers from the European armies

---

1 TNA, WO 1/250, pp.469-71, Wellington to Liverpool, 18 September 1811.
2 A. Bamford, 'British Army Theatre Returns: 1808-1815', at <https://www.napoleon-series.org/military/organization/Britain/Strength/Bamford/c_BritishArmyStrengthStudyIntroduction.html> accessed 2 April 2019. In all cases the 'total other ranks' figures have been used rather than 'effectives'. The returns were completed on the 25th of each month and cover from the 25th day of preceding month, but for brevity are referred to by the month the return is completed.

fighting against the French, and in most cases had then recruited directly from the continent, by 1811 they had been forced to rely upon deserters from the French armies, and from the ever increasing number of prisoners of war, to maintain their numbers. This chapter will examine the extent to which foreign troops were a 'serious inconvenience' for Wellington. It will examine why foreign corps were employed by Britain, the issues surrounding the methods and systems of recruitment employed, their desertion rates, and also any positive contributions that they made to Wellington's forces.

The Foreign Corps

Foreign recruitment had long been a key component of British military policy. With a small volunteer army that was usually underfunded in peace time, Britain had often relied on foreign troops to bolster its forces on the outbreak of war. For example, during the American War of Independence between one-third and one-half of the British forces in North America were German.[3] When France declared war on Britain in 1793 the regular Army numbered just 38,945, with another 8,450 Militia. Only half the regular troops were in Britain and Ireland though, with the remainder distributed around the colonies.[4] Initially, foreign regiments were hired from some of the many small German states and these quickly contributed 20,000 men by the summer of 1794.[5] Foreign regiments directly in British pay also began to be raised. These units were often filled with experienced soldiers from continental armies and officered by émigrés who had been in French service. By 1795 these émigré corps numbered 14,832 infantry and 5,057 cavalry, or over 15 percent of the British Army's infantry and over 33 percent of its cavalry.[6]

Europe at this time was a continent with many small states and even in the larger entities, such as France, people often identified more with their locality than their nationality. The stronger sense of nationalism that emerged later in the nineteenth century was often a function of the wars of unification in Germany and Italy, other conflicts or societal changes, and deliberate policies by governments. Even today Britain still relies on foreign-born troops to make up for a failure to recruit sufficient Britons. In 2012 12 percent of the armed forces came from the Republic of Ireland, Commonwealth countries and Nepal.[7] Recent policy changes have made it easier for foreigners to join,[8] and a new battalion of Nepalese Gurkhas is being raised.[9]

---

3   M. Wishon, *German Forces and the British Army; Interactions and Perceptions 1742-1815* (Basingstoke: Palgrave Macmillan, 2013), p.15.
4   Return of the Effective Men in the British Army 1793-1806, TNA, WO 1/903, p.33.
5   P. Demet, *We Are Accustomed to do Our Duty* (Warwick: Helion & Company, 2018), p.223.
6   N. Arielli & B. Collins (eds.), *Transnational Soldiers – Foreign Military Enlistment in the Modern Era* (Basingstoke: Palgrave Macmillan, 2013), p.54.
7   <https://www.telegraph.co.uk/news/uknews/defence/9577167/One-in-ten-members-of-Armed-Forces-was-born-abroad.html> Accessed 8 April 2019.
8   <https://www.theguardian.com/uk-news/2018/nov/05/foreign-nationals-to-be-allowed-to-join-british-army> Accessed 8 April 2019.
9   <https://www.gov.uk/government/news/new-gurkha-battalion-to-be-established-as-brigade-grows> Accessed 8 April 2019.

By 1808 the number of foreign troops in British service stood at 31,891 and rose to a peak of 52,416 in 1813, growing from approximately one man in seven to one man in five of the British Army's strength. Between November 1811 and November 1812 the foreign corps would grow from 30,935 to 39,124 – a 26 percent increase.[10] In October 1813 the Duke of York, the Commander-in-Chief, wrote to Earl Bathurst, the Secretary of State for War, stating the need for 'extraordinary measures for increase of the Disposable Force'.[11] The Duke of York was clear that Britain had gained many advantages from the foreign corps, especially the German units, and was an advocate of increasing their numbers.[12] In 1812 Lord Palmerston, Secretary at War, said to parliament:

> If any man would look at the map of Europe, and see what a proportion of its population the enemy had forced into hostility against this country, if he were also to consider the limited population of these two islands, and the extensive colonies we had to defend, and the navy we had to support, it appeared to him hardly possible that such a man could now adhere to the idea of not employing foreigners in our service.[13]

With the war in the Peninsula reaching its culmination, the desperate need for troops in North America after the declaration of war by the United States, plus the requirements of defending the colonies and keeping order at home, the Army was at full stretch. Recruiting was barely keeping up with casualties. Transfers from the Militia were well below target. Without the contribution of the foreign corps Britain would not have had enough troops.

Recruitment

The Foreign Depot, at the small port of Lymington near the New Forest on the south coast of England, served all of the foreign corps, including the KGL which had its own depots at Bexhill for infantry and Ipswich for cavalry, plus a depot company on the Isle of Wight. The Foreign Depot had its own staff made up of the commandant, a staff captain, three subalterns, an adjutant, a paymaster, a storekeeper, a clerk, a sergeant major, quarter master sergeant, and 12 staff sergeants.[14] The depot processed recruits from the continent, from prisoner of war depots in Britain, and from deserters and prisoners from Spain and Portugal. They were assessed, clothed, equipped, and partially trained before being sent in drafts to their units. The depot had its own hospital, staffed by a surgeon and two hospital mates, plus another for

---

10 Effective Strength of the Foreign and Provincial Corps 25th November 1811 and 25th November 1812, TNA, WO 25/3225.
11 York to Bathurst, 20 October 1813, TNA WO 25/3225.
12 York to Liverpool, 4 September 1811, TNA, WO 1/648, p.37.
13 R. Knight, Britain *Against Napoleon: The Organisation of Victory 1793-1815* (London: Penguin, 2013) p.440.
14 Establishment of the Staff of the Foreign Depot, TNA WO 7/81 p.190.

invalids at Eling, near Southampton. Soldiers discharged as invalids, those whose service had expired, and rejected recruits, were sent back to the continent via the depot.

Most of the foreign corps raised in the 1790s began with cores of experienced volunteers from the armies fighting on the continent against France. With many of the corps being posted to the West Indies constant wastage from disease, both deaths and those discharged as invalids, meant that new recruits were frequently needed. However, Napoleon's victories made recruitment on the continent increasingly difficult and other sources had to be found.

Early in the war many regiments began to recruit from the prisoner war depots, and not just the foreign corps. The 23rd Fusiliers recruited Dutch prisoners taken at the Battle of Camperdown in 1797 to such an extent that their participation in an expedition to Ostend was cast into doubt.[15] The visits of recruiting parties from British regiments struggling to get enough native born recruits are evident in the records of many of the prisoner of war depots, for example in 1807 the 5th and 87th Foot recruited small numbers from Plymouth.[16] Many foreigners also served in the Royal Navy and Royal Marines.

Conditions for prisoners of war in Britain were quite good. The men were generally fed, housed and clothed adequately, often far better than they were used to on campaign. Inmates could even earn money through handicrafts such as carving wood or bone. Traditionally prisoners of war had been exchanged with those held by the enemy but this system broke down during the Napoleonic Wars, partly due to the great disparity in the large number of prisoners held by Britain compared with France, and partly due to a lack of trust between the two governments. The British government built new prison depots at Dartmoor and Norman Cross, and improved others. There were issues with corruption and poor-quality rations from contractors but the system was generally well managed. Prison hulks at ports like Chatham and Portsmouth were overcrowded and squalid, but prisoners were not generally housed in them for long periods.

No matter how good their subsequent treatment, the circumstances of their capture, often in battle, could have been traumatic. French prisoners shipped back to Britain had no idea when they would see their homes again and often felt very isolated, with their futures very uncertain.[17] Lieutenant Moyle Sherer, 34th Foot, recalled in his memoir that his first sight of French soldiers was a party of German prisoners:

> The prisoners were marched past our ground to headquarters. I had never as yet, though upwards of a year in the country, seen a French soldier; and I walked out alone to meet the escort. I know not how it was, but I had certainly connected very strange ideas with the appearance of the French soldiery. What I expected to see I cannot at all define; not, certainly, men of fair, fresh complexions, tall, well made, and handsome. Such, however, were

---

15   D.E Graves, *Fix Bayonets!* (Stroud: Spellmount, 2007) p.45.
16   Register of Prisoners of War, Plymouth, TNA, ADM 103/286.
17   Forrest, *Napoleon's Men*, p.159.

the prisoners: they were chasseurs, about sixty in number, clothed in neat green uniforms, with very becoming forage-caps. Some of them seemed cast down and depressed, a few irritated and indignant; but the greater part gazed around them with fearless and careless curiosity, while their laughing blue eyes certainly indicated any thing rather than cruelty. It is true these men were very few of them natives of France; but although Germans, they were soldiers of the French army – marched with it, fought with it, and were enemies whom we often encountered.[18]

It was thought, and often proven, that Germans made obedient, steadfast, sober and professional soldiers.[19] The Foreign Depot sent recruiting officers over to Germany and operated a recruiting station at Straslund on the Baltic coast, until the area came under French control and forced it to move to Gothenburg in Sweden in 1807. Direct recruitment in the German states was suspended, although there was some continued presence by recruiting officers and agents on the British occupied island of Heligoland on the North Sea coast, where efforts were made to direct Hanoverian recruits to the KGL and Brunswickers to the Duke of Brunswick's corps. 'Bringers-in' were paid bounties for the recruits they gathered from within the German states but the numbers of recruits that travelled from Heligoland to Harwich did not keep pace with demand from the foreign corps.

The opportunity presented by the large numbers of Germans amongst the French deserters and prisoners of war being held by the British in the Peninsula was quickly recognised and Baron Ferdinand Hompesch, who had raised troops for Britain during the 1790s, wrote to the Duke of York offering to recruit 'natives of the banks of the Rhine' from amongst those held, arguing that 'a very large proportion of these unfortunate people are every day forced away from their homes and marched, in most cases handcuffed, as conscripts to the armies' and he claimed many would be willing to serve in a legion under a leader whose name was already familiar to them. His offer was declined.[20]

However, in June 1810 General Merck, a German officer formerly in French service, made a similar offer and wrote to Horse Guards proposing that he travel to Spain and contact colleagues still in the French army and encourage them to desert. His proposal was accepted but Wellington was of the opinion that any such scheme would soon be discovered and countered by the French.[21] Merck instead recruited from the French deserters and prisoners already collected at the coast, and from the late summer of 1810 to the spring of 1811 he enlisted hundreds of men. However, he did not restrict himself to just Germans and many of the surnames listed in his records appear to be French or Italian. A large portion of his correspondence with

---

18 M. Sherer, *Recollections of the Peninsula* (London: Longman, Rees, Orme, Brown, & Green, 1827) pp.139-40.
19 Wishon, *German Forces*, p.27.
20 Hompesch to York, undated, TNA, WO 1/237, p.327.
21 Wellington to Liverpool, 1 May 1810, quoted in Gurwood, *Dispatches* Vol.VI, pp.78-80.

Horse Guards relates to the bounties he received for each recruit, which may have been an incentive not to be that discriminating.[22]

Germans and other northern Europeans were preferred to French and Italians, who were seen as far less reliable and more prone to desertion. The majority of French and Italians were posted to the battalions of the 60th, the York Light Infantry Volunteers, and other units serving in the West Indies. However, there were occasions that recruits, on learning of their destination, had second thoughts about British service and had to be returned to confinement.[23]

The impact of overenthusiastic recruiting was born by Colonel Lewis von Mosheim, commandant of the Foreign Depot, who wrote to Horse Guards to complain about the quality of the recruits coming from the Peninsula, 982 of whom had arrived in five transports from Gibraltar:

> I think it my duty to State, that by far the greatest Proportion of those Recruits are Frenchmen by Birth, those not French are Italians and only 84 men are natives of such countries as may be considered properly calculated to furnish Recruits for His Majesty's Service.[24]

Despite this 575 were enlisted into the KGL cavalry, the 60th, and York Light Infantry Volunteers. Mosheim awaited instructions for the remainder, but he did query if all the French were to be allowed to enlist.

To encourage good quality, experienced, men to volunteer for British service NCOs were allowed to retain their French ranks. All the foreign corps were allocated some of these men and they were to be borne as supernumeraries if there were no vacancies for corporals or sergeants in the units.[25] Having NCOs imposed upon them could prove a headache for commanders of the foreign corps as the men would be unfamiliar with British service and the culture of the unit.

The men chosen from deserters and prisoners of war may not have always been that carefully selected at the point of recruitment, but any men deemed physically unfit were weeded out at the Foreign Depot and then returned to the continent. For some, though, this was not the end of their military service. Jean Marc Bussy was serving in the French 3e Régiment Suisse when he was captured in 1810. After enduring the squalid conditions on a hulk at Corunna and refusing offers Spanish enlistment he entered British service, meeting many former comrades at Lymington. He was discharged as unfit due to a hernia, but was arrested on his return to the continent and had to serve two more years for the French.[26]

Almost two-thirds of the soldiers in foreign corps with Wellington's army belonged to the KGL, which contained infantry, both line and light, cavalry and artillery. The legion was formed from the remnants of the Hanoverian army following the French

---

22 General Merck's mission (1810-1811) to win over German deserters from the French forces in Spain, and subsequent correspondence, TNA, WO 1/413.
23 Mosheim to Torrens, 24 September 1811, TNA, WO 1/648, p.205.
24 Mosheim to Torrens, 4 September 1811, TNA, WO 1/648, p.61.
25 Mosheim to Williams, 27 July 1811, TNA, WO 7/84, p.26.
26 Nichols, *They Turned Out So Ill!*, pp.20-21.

occupation in 1803, with the initial recruits being bolstered by an expedition to northern Germany in 1805. However, from 1807 the Hanoverian core of the legion began to be diluted by recruits from other northern and central European states. Wastage of around 3,000 men since 1807 meant that by 1810 the KGL was in dire need of recruits and was allowed to start recruiting prisoners of war, both from prison depots in Britain and directly in the Peninsula. However, men of the latter category were not meant to be posted to KGL units in Spain and Portugal, but to other KGL units elsewhere.[27] The KGL's numbers peaked in 1812 at 14,000,[28] and the legion was generally very well thought of by their British comrades. Wellington was keen to keep the KGL as Hanoverian as possible, writing to the Duke of York in June 1811: 'It is impossible to have better soldiers than the real Hanoverians; and it would be very desirable that the 1st, 2d, and 5th line battalions of the Legion, should be reinforced by any men of that description who may be in the depots'.[29]

In September 1811, at around the same time that Wellington was writing his letter complaining about the number of foreigners in his army, plans were being made in Whitehall to increase the establishments of the KGL and the 60th, partly to relieve the pressure of prisoner numbers in Britain. In total 3,308 men would be added to the KGL and 1,643 to the 60th.[30] The scheme came with comprehensive instructions to limit recruitment to those deemed most reliable.[31] In a letter to the Duke of Cambridge, colonel-in-chief of the legion, Henry Calvert, the Adjutant General, stipulated that only Germans, Austrians, Prussians, Flemings, Dutch, Poles and Swiss be recruited and that 3,180 prisoners that fit that description were present across nine prison depots. German speakers from territories recently incorporated into France were allowed, but those from traditional areas of France plus Italians, Danes, Swedes, Russians, Spaniards and Portuguese were prohibited. The depots were split into four divisions and a KGL major appointed as the recruiting officer for each division. The instructions for the recruiting officers included:

> The greatest Circumspection will be required on the part of the Field Officers employed on this duty, to detect the impositions, which may be attempted by the Prisoners of War as to their Country, Age, & Former Service, & to prevent as far as possible, the very serious Consequences, which may in some Cases arise, from returning to the Ship or Depot such Men as may be rejected.[32]

There was a fear that rejected men might face reprisals from other prisoners if they were sent back into the depots or hulks. Using a broad term like 'Germans' before

---

27 D.S. Gray, 'Prisoners, Wanderers, and Deserters: Recruiting for the King's German Legion, 1803-1815', *Journal of the Society of Army Historical Research*, Vol.LII, pp.152-3.
28 A. Bamford, *Sickness, Suffering and the Sword* (Norman: University of Oklahoma Press, 2013), p.18.
29 Wellington to York, 27 June 1811, quoted in J. Gurwood, *The Dispatches of Field Marshal the Duke of Wellington*, (London: John Murray, 1835), Vol.VIII, p.56.
30 York to Liverpool, 4 September 1811, TNA, WO 1/648, p.37.
31 York to Liverpool, 17 October 1811, TNA, WO 1/648 pp.369-70.
32 Calvert to Duke of Cambridge 6 December 1811, TNA, WO 3/54, pp.459-61.

such a country existed did lead to complications and one of the KGL recruiters had to query if he could recruit German-speaking Danes from Holstein.[33]

In 1813 after the Duke of Cambridge asked to recruit from prisoners of war at Plymouth into the KGL, Colonel Henry Bunbury, the military undersecretary, wrote to Colonel Henry Torrens, military secretary to the Duke of York, that the Secretary at War, Lord Bathurst, objected to such a proposal, especially as direct recruitment from Germany was again possible, and that previous permission for such recruitment had concerned a particular group of prisoners likely to make good recruits.[34] The *History of the King's German Legion* lists the number of recruits in 1811 as 2,242, in 1812 as 3,438 and 1813, up to September, as 521. It is noted that deserters and prisoners of war were the only source of recruits in those years. Recruits were still being taken from prison depots across Britain up to the spring of 1814.[35] The demand for replacements from the KGL units with Wellington meant that rules on where prisoners or deserters from the Peninsula could serve had to be relaxed during 1811, but the subsequent rise in desertions meant that restrictions were reintroduced in August 1812.[36] The care that the KGL took over recruiting no doubt contributed to the Legion's relatively lower desertion rates.

Integrating a wide spread of nationalities had its own problems, of course. The surgeon of the 7th KGL Line Battalion, which was withdrawn from the Peninsula in 1811 to recruit, recalled:

> Our Battalion had, by this, increased to 800 men, in consequence of the incorporation of numerous French deserters. This reinforcement was, in truth, necessary, since the English were now so completely blocked out from Germany that it was impracticable to obtain recruits from the natural source – Hanover. But it is inconceivable how much trouble was incurred in teaching these men the exercise, since they knew scarcely one word of German, and still less, if possible, of English.[37]

Elements of the KGL had arrived in Portugal just after the Battle of Vimeiro, which marked the end of the opening campaign of the Peninsular War, but the 5th Battalion of the 60th (Royal American) Regiment had been amongst the first troops ashore at Mondego Bay and were one of only three battalions to be present right through until 1814. The 5/60th had been formed in 1797 and was the first all-rifle armed battalion in the British Army. The 60th Regiment had been raised in North America during the Seven Years War and initially recruited from German and Swiss colonists, directly from the continent, and other British regiments. The regiment maintained a mix of British and foreign soldiers and varied in size from two to four battalions until the fully foreign fifth battalion was established. At the same time,

---

33 Decken to Legion Office, 26 March 1812, TNA, WO 1/651, p.21.
34 Bunbury to Torrens , 20 January 1813, TNA, WO 6/135, p.128-9.
35 N.L. Beamish, *History of the King's German Legion* (London: Thomas & William Boone, 1837). Vol.II Memorandum on recruiting in the appendices.
36 Gray, 'Prisoners, Wanderers, and Deserters', p.155.
37 J.F. Hering, *Journal of An Officer in the King's German Legion* (London: Colburn, 1827) p.259.

many of the other foreign corps were merged into the 1st-4th Battalions, and the proportion of British men much reduced. A further three battalions were added before the end of the Napoleonic Wars making the regiment the largest in the British Army.[38] To maintain their numbers the 60th also had to recruit from prisoners of war and foreign deserters. The 5/60th took part in the capture of the Dutch colony of Surinam in 1799 and subsequently recruited 133 men from the Walloon Guards, a Spanish regiment stationed at the colony.[39] The Walloon Guards had traditionally been recruited from Spanish possessions in the Low Countries but the men in Surinam were mostly German and Hungarian prisoners of war who had been given to Spain by France. Many of these men were still serving when the battalion landed in Mondego Bay and would go on to fight through the campaign. Another batch of prisoners of war joined the battalion in the autumn of 1806, following the capture of a French troop convoy on its way to the West Indies. The battalion was authorised to take 100 men from Germany and the low countries from the convoy, and another 113 were recruited from the prisoner of war depots along the south coast.[40]

With the potential dangers of employing former enemy troops there was often some resistance to their recruitment by senior officers. In September 1808 Major Davy, commanding the 5/60th, received a reply to a request he had made, via Sir Arthur Wellesley, to Sir Hew Dalrymple:

> I am desired by the Commander of the Forces to acknowledge your letter of yesterday's date, with an inclosure from Major Davy commanding the 5th Battalion of the 60th regiment desiring permission to enlist deserters, and I am to acquaint you that his Excellency does not approve of deserters from the enemy being enlisted in a corps destined to do the duty of advanced posts; nor does he think it expedient, at this moment, to allow Hanoverians to be enlisted by any other corps than those composing the infantry of the German Legion, for the recruiting of which instructions have been received from home.[41]

However, Davy was eventually allowed to recruit from Swiss regiments at Oporto that had been in French service, but the men went to the 2/60th.[42] Davy's successor, Lieutenant Colonel Williams, was reluctant to take former deserters from the French into the battalion and in February 1811 Colonel Mosheim had to reassure him:

> The men posted to the 5th Batt. 60th Regt. I beg to assure you are very carefully selected by me, for you aught to have lusty Men but if none from the Germans who have deserted from the Enemy are to be posted to the Battn.

---

38 R. Burnham & R. McGuigan, *The British Army against Napoleon, Facts, Lists, and Trivia 1805-1815* (Barnsley: Frontline Books, 2010), p.88.
39 5/60th September 1799 Pay List, TNA, WO 12/7066.
40 5/60th Lists of Recruits December 1806, TNA, WO 12/7072 & WO 2/54 p.22.
41 Clinton to Wellesley, 16 September 1808, quoted in G. Rigaud, *Celer et Audax* (Oxford: Hall & Stacy, 1879) p.62.
42 Davy to Bathurst, 13 September 1809, quoted in Rigaud, *Celer et Audax*, p.69.

under your Command, you cannot expect to receive any Recruits from this depot at present.[43]

Many of Mosheim's letters make it evident that he was taking a particular interest in the recruits that were selected at the depot for the 5/60th. Mosheim had briefly served with the battalion when it was formed and had gone on to command the 6/60th. His support helped to increase the quality of recruits and reduce the incidence of desertion from the battalion. Detached companies of the 5/60th were used by Wellington to bolster the light companies in many of his brigades and give them some rifle-armed troops.

The Duke of Brunswick's Light Infantry had arrived in Portugal in September 1810. The Duke had raised a corps of volunteers to fight with Austria against the French in the War of the Fifth Coalition in the summer of 1809. After the Austrian defeat at the Battle of Wagram, the Duke refused to surrender and led his men across Germany in a fighting retreat until they were evacuated by the Royal Navy. The remnants were organised into a light infantry regiment and one of hussars. The infantry regiment was comprised of one rifle company and 11 musket-armed light infantry companies. After some shifting between divisions the main body of nine companies were incorporated into the newly formed 7th Division. Two companies were detached to brigades in the 5th Division and the rifle company to the 4th Division, in a similar fashion to the companies of the 5/60th. An inspection report from April 1810 praised the regiment's 'extremely soldierlike' appearance and concluded with 'there appears throughout an Esprit de Corps which promises to render the Battalion highly Serviceable'.[44]

The initial core of volunteers in the Brunswick regiments was rapidly diluted by other recruits, but the Duke, with the help of Mosheim, did try and maintain both the national character of the unit and its quality. In December 1810, soon after the regiment was taken into British service, the Duke wrote to Mosheim complaining that he had heard that recruits that had been earmarked for his corps were being diverted into the 60th and Mosheim replied that on the contrary the Duke's corps 'has been the favoured one'.[45] In June of the following year Mosheim reassured the Duke that 'no Frenchmen, nor Italians, or any person of suspect character, shall be posted by me to your Serene Highness's Corps'.[46] He went on to say of 58 recruits that had recently arrived at the depot for the Duke's corps 13 were found to be French, and had been removed to other regiments.

The Chasseurs Britanniques arrived in the Peninsula at the start of the 1811. The Chasseurs had been raised from elements of the French Royalist armies in 1801. They fought in Egypt in 1801 and then served in the Mediterranean until being sent to Lisbon. The majority of the officers with the regiment were French or Swiss, but the rank and file came from a much wider range of nations with many from

---

43 Mosheim to Williams, 27 February 1811, TNA, WO 7/83, pp.206-7.
44 TNA, WO 27/99, Inspection of the Duke of Brunswick's Light Infantry.
45 Mosheim to Brunswick, 2 December 1810, TNA WO 7/82, pp.435-6.
46 Mosheim to Brunswick, 20 June 1811, TNA WO 7/84 p.148.

France and southern Europe, including Spain, so it was the one foreign corps in the Peninsula not to be of a Germanic character.

The way that officers treated their men differed both between the foreign corps and British regiments, but also within the foreign corps as the national make-up of their officers influenced the regimental culture. Almost all the officers of the KGL were German and discipline could be swift and informal with officers frequently hitting their men.[47] With units such as the 5/60th serving in the Peninsula for over five years, the inflow of different drafts, with recruits from various sources, and officers joining and leaving, could also change the character of a unit over time. For example, the 5/60th landed in Portugal in 1808 with mostly foreign officers but marched into France in 1814 with mostly British and Irish.

One foreign corps in Wellington's army chose a different source of recruits to the many enemy prisoners and deserters. The 97th (Queen's Own Germans) Regiment of Foot was created from mainly former Austrian troops captured on the island of Minorca in 1798 and at first called the Minorca Regiment. The Austrians had been captured in Italy, sold to Spain by the French, and placed in Swiss regiments in Spanish service. The regiment fought in Egypt in 1801 and arrived in the Peninsula in time to fight at the Battle of Vimeiro. By October 1811 its strength had dropped to less than 300 and it was sent back to Ireland to recruit.[48] It still had a large portion of foreigners but had been drawing recruits from the militia to the extent that in March 1811 it was removed from the list of foreign regiments and counted as a fully British one.[49]

Memoirs written by men who served in both the British and French armies are very rare, but two were published from men who served in the rifle company of the 7th Line Battalion of the KGL. Johann Christian Maempel was born in the Electorate of Mainz on the banks of the Rhine. He witnessed the aftermath of a battle between the Prussians and the French, but nevertheless succumbed to the patter of a recruiting officer for one of the Westphalian regiments serving with the French army. Maempel marched into Spain in the spring of 1808, just before the revolt against French rule. He fought the Spanish in the early part of the Peninsular War before being taken prisoner by the British in 1811:

> We were brought to Villa Formosa, where the English head-quarters were established under Lord Wellington. He came with a number of other generals to see us, and all reproached us, particularly those who were Germans by birth, for having so long served the usurper (for so they denominated the Emperor Napoleon). One general above all others, he was probably a German, abused us most unmercifully: this cruel treatment, as

---

47 C. Hibbert (ed.), *The Wheatley Diary* (Moreton-in-the-Marsh: Windrush, 1997) p.9.
48 Ray Foster, 'Notes on Wellington's Peninsular Regiments: 97th Regiment of Foot (Queens Own)' <https://www.napoleon-series.org/military/organization/Britain/Infantry/WellingtonsRegiments/c_97thFoot.html> Accessed 19 April 2019.
49 Army Estimates <https://api.parliament.uk/historic-hansard/commons/1811/mar/04/army-estimates> Accessed 19 April 2019.

we were already unhappy enough, made a very unfavourable impression upon us.[50]

Despite this first impression Maempel, and the prisoners with him, were treated well by their captors as they marched through Portugal. On his way to Lisbon Maempel saw some of the Brunswickers at Pinhel:

> Here I also saw, for the first time, the black Brunswick Oel troops. These had been described to us as warlike, fierce, and blood-thirsty; they did not, however, at all correspond to the description: they were discontented, and not at all pleased with the mode of living in Portugal. I even heard that in a short time a great number of the corps had deserted, on which account they had been disbanded, and a company placed with each division of the English army. The soldiers of the German Legion called them, in derision, 'The Brotherhood of Revenge'.[51]

Maempel is probably mistaken about the reason that some of the companies had been detached, but his statement is an example of how the KGL saw themselves as a cut above some of the other foreign units.

When Maempel's column reached Lisbon they were not fed for three days, either by mistake or by design. On the fourth day, recruiting officers from the British foreign corps arrived seeking German, Dutch or Polish recruits. Maempel and 400 others volunteered, somewhat reluctantly, and were immediately separated from the other prisoners. They sailed for the Isle of Wight, and were allowed time to recover their health and strength, helping the locals bring in the harvest and developing a taste for the local beer. Those deemed unfit were sent back their homes on the continent. In October Maempel formally enlisted in the British Army for seven years. He was sent to the KGL infantry depot at Bexhill and joined his battalion. The 7th KGL Line Battalion served in Malta, Sicily, Naples, and the east coast of Spain. In 1816 Maempel was discharged and returned to Mainz after a decade serving under two different flags. He seems to have been as happy in British service as in French, and wrote of his time in Malta:

> I enjoyed myself here very much, and often reflected with a thankful heart upon the happy turn in my destiny: a year before I had, in the most miserable condition and constant danger, been marching through the devastated provinces of Spain and Portugal, little dreaming of so pleasant a futurity. My being taken prisoner, therefore, which at that time I considered a misfortune, had proved my greatest benefit; had I remained with the French army, a hostile ball or an assassin's knife would probably ere this have deprived me of life; or if even my life had been spared, I should still have had to contend with hunger and thirst, and been exposed to dangers

---

50 J. Maempel, *Adventures of a Young Rifleman in the French and English Armies* (London: Colburn, 1826) p.205.
51 Maempel, *Adventures of a Young Rifleman*, p.209.

of every description. Now, on the contrary, I was well fed, well clothed, had no hard duty to perform, and was living in a beautiful country without any cares.[52]

Phillipe Schwein also came from the banks of the Rhine and was conscripted into the French Army in 1806. He was captured at the Battle of Bailén in July 1808. Some of those taken with him were brutally treated by the Spanish and many were killed. After a long, gruelling march the prisoners were thrown into prison hulks or dungeons at Cadiz. Rations were poor and the conditions unsanitary. Despite this Schwein refused many offers to enter Spanish service. He was transported to the island of Majorca, where Germans in the Swiss regiments there shared some of their rations with their compatriots amongst the prisoners. Unfortunately, the respite from starvation was brief as Schwein ended up on the small island of Cabrera where the prisoners were virtually abandoned, with rations only being delivered sporadically. Some of the men were driven to extreme measures to survive. Schwein wrote: 'A cuirassier was, in fact, killed, for the actual purpose of consuming his carcass, by a Pole, who was in the act of extracting the entrails, when he was discovered by the Spaniards, informed against, and shot'.[53]

Many of his fellow prisoners eventually succumbed to the entreaties of the recruiters from both Spanish and British regiments but Schwein held out longer than many until:

> Three years had passed, and yet no prospect of the recovery of our liberty. My old comrades, who had originally borne me company to Cabrera, were all dispersed. Many had died broken-hearted: others, tired of this monotonous life, had taken service in the ranks of the Spaniards or English. At length, my friend and I grew weary likewise of our protracted durance, and resolved to take the first opportunity of getting employment: we sickened, however, at the idea of taking part with the Spaniards, and therefore lay out for procuring an engagement in some English regiment, nor was it long before means presented themselves. We received four guineas earnest-money, with the stipulation that we should either serve seven years, or be discharged six months after the conclusion of peace.[54]

Schwein was taken on a Royal Navy frigate to Tarragona, on the eastern coast of Spain. He rejoiced at getting clean clothes and regular food. He joined the 7th KGL Line Battalion in Sicily and was welcomed to his new unit with courtesy and kindness. Like Maempel he found life with the battalion far easier than campaigning or captivity, but eventually grew homesick:

> Neither the esteem of my officers, nor the friendship of my comrades, both of which, I rejoice to say, I enjoyed, could repress my longing to change the

---

52 Maempel, *Adventures of a Young Rifleman*, pp.247-8.
53 P. Schwein, *The Young Rifleman's Comrade* (London: Colburn, 1826) p.72.
54 Schwein, *The Young Rifleman's Comrade*, p.81-2.

military for the domestic life; but it was necessary to exercise the quality of patience, as was confessed, in their despondence, by a number of other anxious hearts, who, like me, languished for home, and who cursed the day on which they left it to follow a life of toil and bloodshed. So powerful was this sentiment, that some amongst us sought to gratify it by desertion; others by mutilating themselves; but not one of these succeeded in accomplishing his object.[55]

Schwein however, did not succumb to the temptation to desert and remained with his battalion in Sicily, where the greatest danger appeared to come from jealous Sicilian husbands. He was discharged in 1816 at Portsmouth, engaged as a servant to a British officer, then shipwrecked on an island in the Indian Ocean, but did eventually make it back to his home town.

It was not only ordinary soldiers that deserted from the French Army and sought to enter British service; officers did so too. In June of 1811 Wellington reported that *Capitaine* Aconville, an aide-de-camp to *Général de Division* Montbrun, had deserted and desired to serve in the East Indies, or if not in the British Army then in Russian service.[56] In October of the same year Daniel Pedemonte, who described himself as 'Director of Hospitals & Captain of Ambulances' reported to the Foreign Depot.[57] A month earlier Colonel Mosheim had to enquire what to do with two other officers, one French and one Swiss, who had both been in King Joseph's Spanish Army.[58] The Duke of Brunswick warned Mosheim of his suspicions about another former French officer, *Capitaine* Gunther. Mosheim replied 'I am not aware what his intentions may be; but he certainly shall not be enlisted; as I consider him to be an Adventurer;' and carried on to assure the Duke he would not be recommended for a commission.[59] Frederick Seidel was another French officer who chose to serve the British, in his case as a sergeant in the 5/60th, which he joined in January 1812. However, his career as a rifleman was a short one as he was taken prisoner on the retreat from Burgos later that year. He was then discovered amongst the prisoners after the Battle of Vittoria in the uniform a French sergeant, court-martialled, and shot.[60]

Desertion

Desertion from the foreign corps was far higher than the British regiments in Wellington's army, in June 1811 he wrote to Lord Liverpool:

> I beg leave to inform your Lordship that, since the commencement of the siege of Badajoz, fifty-two of the Chasseurs Britanniques have deserted,

---

55 Schwein, *The Young Rifleman's Comrade*, p.135.
56 Wellington to Liverpool, 18 June 1811, TNA, WO 1/249, p.587.
57 Mosheim to Torrens, 16 October 1811, TNA, WO 1/648, p.381.
58 Mosheim to Torrens, 5 September 1811, TNA, WO 1/648, p.81.
59 Mosheim to Brunswick 26 September 1811, TNA WO 7/85, p.115.
60 Mosheim to Williams 18 April 1812, TNA, WO 7/86; November 1812 Casualty Return, WO 25/1923; Register of Courts Martial WO 90/1, p.86.

notwithstanding that we have with the army only a selection of that corps; 686 who are suspected being left behind at Lisbon. The inconvenience of the desertion of the soldiers of this army is very great, because it is almost the only mode by which the enemy can acquire intelligence; but, besides the inconvenience which all must feel, the disgrace is no trifle, and it would be very desirable if these corps could be relieved by others.

I much fear from all that I hear that the recruiting of these corps has not been conducted as Government intended, and that prisoners have been enlisted, as well as deserters, into the Chasseurs Britanniques and the Brunswick Legion.[61]

In September 1811, the month when Wellington again had to point out the 'serious inconvenience' of the number of foreigners in his army to his superiors, nine men from foreign corps deserted, compared to 10 from the British and Irish regiments, but of course there were far fewer foreign troops. The desertion rate for the foreign corps was 0.11 percent whereas the rate for the British troops was 0.02 percent.[62] Over the preceding six months the desertion rate for British troops varied from 0.02 percent to 0.05 percent but the foreign corps rate was always much higher, peaking at 1.18 percent in June 1811. The Chasseurs Britanniques and the Brunswick Light Infantry had the worst records for desertion, with the former regiment's desertion rate varying between 0.42 percent and 3.04 percent, and the latter varying between 0.24 percent and 1.56 percent, per month, from April to September 1811. The Chasseurs had a total of 103 desertions and the Brunswickers 42 during this period. The figures for the Chasseurs do, however, include detachments at Lisbon and Cadiz and do not relate solely to the troops in the field. Many of the initial men to run were Spaniards who took the opportunity to return home or join the less formal army of guerrillas. Wellington was forced to limit the outpost duties that the Chasseurs Britanniques could perform, something that did not endear them to the men of other regiments that they served alongside.[63] An 1812 inspection report on the regiment noted that the men who had recently deserted from the Chasseurs were principally those that had been recruited from prisoners of war.[64]

Desertions across the army spiked when the men were under duress from the weather, supply issues, or long forced marches – conditions that often coincided with a forced retreat, but the spike was always more pronounced amongst the foreign corps. During the retreat from Burgos in November 1812, desertion from British regiments rose to 0.26 percent, but in the foreign corps it was 2.25 percent. Similarly, in July 1813 when the French had driven Wellington's army from the passes of the Pyrenees, the rate rose for the British units to 0.11 percent and 1.47 percent for the foreign corps. In August 1813 the rates generally dropped back down

---

61 Wellington to Liverpool, 13 June 1811, quoted in Gurwood, *Wellington's Dispatches*, Vol.VIII, pp.11-2.
62 Bamford, 'Theatre Returns'. Figures calculated from the number of deserters and total other ranks.
63 A. Nichols, *Wellington's Mongrel Regiment* (Staplehurst: Spellmount, 2005), pp.68-72.
64 Nichols, *Wellington's Mongrel Regiment*, p.226.

but the Chasseurs Britanniques surpassed themselves with a rate 21.8 percent with 165 desertions, including 136 men deserting on one day. Some of the Chasseurs had been kept on after their term of service had expired and told they had to serve until six months after the end of the war: this was obviously deeply unpopular with those that had served their time and wanted to go home. The French had also been actively encouraging desertions from the foreign corps as Wellington's army neared France. Leaflets were printed and left in the path of the allied advance:

> Advice
> The soldiers of all Nations, French Italian, German, Polanders, English, Spaniards and Portuguese who are in English service are advised that the deserters coming to the French imperial Army are perfectly well received; they are paid for the arms and the horses they bring with; none of them is obliged to serve; pass-ports are delivered to them to return to their native country, if they chuse, or go to inner parts of France where they may freely exercise their professions; they are moreover treated with all sort of regard. They are warned that the whole French Nation is armed, and that in the case of the English, Spaniard and Portuguese army should treat his territory, they would not find any where but death and destruction.[65]

Wellington too saw the advantage of encouraging desertion from the enemy's ranks. In April 1810 he wrote to the governor of Almeida:

> I request you to pay Señior Echcvarria all the expenses which he has incurred for the encouragement of desertion from the French army, and for the support of deserters, and to tell him that I request him to encourage desertion by the following measures. Let him send trusty persons to assure soldiers in the French army, induced to desert, that they shall be received here and treated in every respect as British soldiers; that their arms and horses, if they should bring them, shall be bought from them and paid for; that they shall have their option of enlisting into the British service or not; that if they choose to enlist they shall receive a bounty and shall have the choice of enlisting into any of the foreign corps with this army, or in England; and that, if they do not choose to enlist, measures shall be taken to send them out of the Peninsula, and to facilitate their return to their own country.[66]

Wellington specified that deserters enlisting in regiments with his army should be known to the officers, NCOs, or men already in the regiments. Foreign deserters from the French army were paid the same as British soldiers and transported to their home countries if they did not wish to enlist. To dissuade the Spanish peasants

---

65　I.C. Robertson, *Wellington Invades France* (London: Greenhill, 2003), p.161.
66　Wellington to Cox, 1 April 1810, quoted in Gurwood, *Dispatches,* Vol.VI, p.1.

from murdering any French deserters, rewards were offered for any brought into allied lines.[67]

How the British treated French deserters had an impact on how many men chose to come over from the French. The Royal Navy adopted a policy of not allowing French deserters to be shipped back to Britain and so large numbers built up around Lisbon. Those that were allowed to leave were enlisted in regiments in the West Indies and Wellington was of the opinion that such treatment dissuaded the French from deserting.[68] A return of 560 deserters enlisted into British service from 1810 shows that 355 were sent to the York Light Infantry Volunteers, serving in the West Indies, and 205 to the King's German Legion.[69] In 1811 desertion amongst the French foreign regiments reached a level high enough for Napoleon to restrict any more such units being sent to Spain.[70]

The 5/60th suffered their worst episode of mass desertion as they marched into Spain from Portugal for the first time as part of Lieutenant General Sir John Moore's army in the autumn of 1808. The battalion was divided into two wings. The wing marching through central Portugal and then into Spain and Salamanca suffered 26 desertions in the three months from October to December, with 19 of those returning to the ranks. The wing marching a longer route via Badajoz and then up to Salamanca suffered 98 desertions with 23 men returning.[71] The battalion was sent back to Portugal after the commanders of each wing had written to Moore to say that they could not trust their men. Moore was scathing of their behaviour: 'They would desert if they had stayed here, and are of so bad a Composition that if not disbanded they should be sent to the Colonies'.[72] After being reunited in early 1809, the battalion weeded out those that had deserted and other 'suspected men' and they were transferred to the 2/60th, which was serving in the West Indies. While many former prisoners were amongst those that were transferred many others remained and served loyally through the rest of the campaign.

KGL units generally had relatively low rates of desertion compared to the other foreign corps, but even they were not immune to the problem. In October 1813 Ensign Edmund Wheatly, serving with the 5th KGL Line Battalion wrote in his diary:

> Four Germans deserted an hour ago. It is matter of astonishment what can induce these men to run over to the French, above all when so many months' pay is due to them. The only reason I can suppose for the frequency of the practice is the inclemency of the season, the harassing duty just now, and the badness of our tents.

---

67 Wellington to Liverpool, 1 May 1810, quoted in Gurwood, *Dispatches*, Vol.VI, pp.78-80.
68 Wellington to Liverpool, 15 May 1811, TNA, WO 1/249 pp.277-8.
69 'Return of Deserters from French Army Enlisted in Portugal for the undermentioned Corps to the 4th of July 1810', TNA, WO 1/245.
70 E. Costa de Serda, *Opérations des Troupes Allemandes en Espagne de 1808 a 1813* (Paris: Dumaine, 1874) p.93.
71 September to December Pay Lists, & TNA, WO 17/179, March 1809 Return, TNA WO 12/7073.
72 Moore to Craddock, 10 December 1808, TNA, WO 1/232 pp.89-90.

> Perhaps these traitors imagine that should they reach the French outposts they will be instantly forwarded to some depot where [they will be] fed without labour and sheltered from the merciless weather.[73]

In May 1810 Captain William Warre, 23rd Light Dragoons, wrote to his father of the French:

> Their troops are also much dissatisfied, particularly the Germans and Italians, who compose the chief part, and those desert very fast, and would much more, if they were not exposed to be murdered by the Peasantry, whether deserters or prisoners. It is really horrible, and defeats the exertions which are making to entice them to fly from their oppressors, and they are willing enough but for these difficulties. Some have come over horses and all. I never saw handsomer or finer looking men. They all agree in complaining that they are never paid, and but indifferently fed, and that they are constantly harassed and marched about.[74]

Of course, the men could come to regret their decision if they found that they were equally likely to be paid late, fed badly and marched about in British service. Soldiers, from any source, chose to desert for many reasons. Often it was from an inability or unwillingness to adjust to army life, a specific issue such as pay being in arrears or being the victim of an unjust punishment, the grass seeming to be greener elsewhere, or simply reaching their limit of the danger and hardship of campaigning. In addition, soldiers recruited from foreign deserters and prisoners of war in Wellington's army had the added temptations of re-joining their old comrades, or attempting to get closer to their homes. Whereas British soldiers feared what fate would befall them if they went over to the French, those men that had already been in French ranks had less need to be afraid of the unknown. The lawlessness and lack of civil government in large areas of the Peninsula also meant that it was likely that deserters would seldom be caught.

The decision to desert was always a very personal one, and often involved emotional elements more than any rational weighing up of the risks. During the siege of Ciudad Rodrigo in 1812 two men of the 5/60th, Privates Joseph Lambrecht and Francis Schoen, made the curious choice to desert from a working party into the French held fortress, which was surrounded by the allied army. Lambrecht had been with the battalion since 1799, so one has to wonder what made him run after serving for so long. Schoen had joined more recently at the end of 1810. After the fortress was taken, a total of 18 deserters were found amongst the garrison; three from the 95th, one from the Royal Horse Artillery, five from the 52nd, two from the 88th, one from the 23rd, one from the 43rd, one from the 7th, one from the KGL, and three

---

73 Hibbert, *The Wheatley Diary*, p.9.
74 W. Warre, *Letters from the Peninsula* (London: Murray, 1909) p.127.

from 5/60th, including Lambrecht, but not Schoen. All 18 were tried, found guilty and ordered to be shot.[75]

The foreign corps are rightly singled out for their poor desertion record in the Peninsula but one statistical analysis of the British Army as a whole between 1803 and 1812, published in 1856, found that the overall desertion rate was marginally higher amongst British and Irish troops; the rate for foreign and colonial troops was 9.32 percent, but for British troops it was 10.37 percent.[76] For example, the monthly return for the army garrisoned in Ireland for September 1811 shows an average desertion rate of 0.52 percent across all 26 regiments, but the three foreign corps, the 1st and 2nd KGL Dragoons and the Duke of Brunswick's Hussars, only had one desertion between them whereas the 37th Foot alone had 17 and a rate of 2.02 percent.[77]

During the War of 1812 in North America the foreign corps also generally had high rates of desertion with the September 1814 return showing an average desertion rate of 9.37 percent for the two foreign corps (72 men from de Meuron's Regiment and 70 from de Watteville's) and 0.99 percent for the British regiments. However, the 1/27th Foot also lost 70 men to desertion (8.02 percent), and the 13th Foot lost 38 (7.85 percent).[78] British regiments could suffer from similar high desertion rates to the foreign corps, given the right combination of privations, temptations, and opportunities.

Any close examination of regimental records from the units serving with Wellington's army often reveals inconsistencies between pay-lists, monthly returns, and casualty returns. Men are sometimes marked as missing on one form and deserted on another. Many were lost in the network of general hospitals and could turn up long after they were assumed to be dead or having had deserted. For example, Private Francis Roer of the 5/60th was washed away during a river crossing in the mountains of Portugal during the pursuit of the French after the Battle of Oporto. He was listed as dead but this was later amended to deserted, so it seems likely that he survived, and equally likely that he had no intention at the time to absent himself from his unit – even if he subsequently made no attempt to return.[79]

It is also common for men to be marked as having returned from desertion or having been retaken. In 1810 43 percent of deserters from British regiments in the Peninsula returned, but only 23 percent of those from foreign corps came back. By 1812, a year of harder campaigning and possibly less reliable foreign recruits, these figures had dropped to 23 percent for the British units and 10 percent for the foreign.[80]

---

75 J. Gurwood, *The General Orders of Field Marshal The Duke of Wellington K. G. in Spain, Portugal & France* (London: Egerton, 1837), Vol.IV, pp.30-32; Register of Courts Martial, TNA, WO 90/1 p.73.
76 W.B. Hodge, 'On the Mortality Arising from Military Operations', *Journal of the Statistical Society of London*, Vol.XIX, p.239.
77 Monthly Returns for the Cavalry and Infantry in Ireland September 1811, TNA, WO 17/1082.
78 Bamford, 'Theatre Returns'.
79 5/60th June 1809 Pay List, TNA, WO 12/7073.
80 Bamford, *Sickness, Suffering and the Sword*, p.248.

Some of the deserters from the British regiments would also have been foreign. A soldier of the 71st Highland Light Infantry recalled:

> Among the French prisoners taken at Fuentes, we recognised a Swiss who had deserted from us at the retreat of Corunna, and who, it appears, had gone back to the French again. One of our sergeants had the cold blooded cruelty to go up to the colonel, and inquire if he might be allowed to shoot the man; but this brutal proposal was rejected with abhorrence.[81]

There are other cases where a portion of the desertion of British units can be blamed on foreign recruits in their ranks.[82]

As well as the sheer number of deserters from the foreign corps being a bad example to British regiments, Wellington also objected to them subsequently giving intelligence to the enemy. Writing to Major General Campbell in 1813 Wellington stated:

> The foreign troops are so much addicted to desertion that they are very unfit for our armies, of which they necessarily form too large a proportion to the native troops. The evil is aggravated by the practice which prevails of enlisting prisoners as well as deserters, and Frenchmen as well as other foreigners, notwithstanding the repeated orders of government upon the subject. The consequence is therefore that a foreign regiment cannot be placed in a situation in which the soldiers can desert from it, that they do not go off in hundreds; and in the Peninsula they convey to the enemy the only intelligence which he can acquire.[83]

Both Wellington and Napoleon often made a clear distinction between recruiting from enemy troops taken prisoner and those that chose to desert. Deserters who had chosen to leave the enemy's ranks were seen as more reliable recruits. Specific examples of the passing of intelligence by deserters are hard to come by, but one involves three men who left the 5/60th during Moore's advance to Salamanca in 1808. They were taken by a patrol of French dragoons and *Général de Division* Armand Lebrun de la Houssaye informed Napoleon:

> Monseigneur, I have the honour to report to your Most Serene Highness that one of my patrols met today on the road to Guadarrama three deserters from the British army who were brought to me and whom I questioned. These deserters, one of whom is a corporal, are French; they had been captured by the English in the battle of Trafalgar, and left the English army on the 13th of this month at Sotrico, the frontier of Portugal. It follows from their report that General Moore occupies Salamanca with 16,000 men,

---

81 Anon., *Vicissitudes in the Life of a Scottish Soldier* (London: Colburn, 1827), pp.165-6.
82 Bamford, *Sickness, Suffering and the Sword*, p.254.
83 Wellington to Campbell, 25 Feb 1813, quoted in W.F.P. Napier, *History of the War in the Peninsula* (London: Warne, 1892), Vol.V, p.428.

including two squadrons of cavalry. The first posts of the Spanish army are, they say, in Alva, where they saw 300 insurgents. The English army was still making no provision for its retirement to Portugal. The battalion of which these deserters were part, which is the 5th of the 60th regiment of infantry of line, is composed largely of Germans who seize every day the opportunity to pass into our ranks. I will conduct these three deserters tomorrow to your Highness' headquarters.[84]

Napoleon interviewed the men and rewarded them for telling him Moore was at Salamanca. However, by the time the men had told their tale Moore had already left the town to march north before falling back on Corunna. Another case of intelligence being passed on to the enemy was during the unsuccessful siege of Badajoz in 1811. Several deserters from the Chasseurs Britanniques and Brunswickers gave the French commandant the news that there was no sign of a relief column approaching.[85]

Wellington had an extensive network of agents in French held territory, received intercepted French communications via the numerous bands of guerrillas, and also sent out exploring officers ranging far and wide across the Peninsula. For Wellington, information from French deserters would have merely added to the wider picture he had of French movements and intentions. In contrast, French intelligence gathering was hampered by the largely hostile populace and the same guerrilla bands. Deserters from the British were one of the few sources that they had, but even so it is likely that much of the information garnered from deserters was limited to where the individual's unit had been and the morale within it, rather than a wider strategic perspective that could give a French commander an idea as to what Wellington would do next.

Benefits

There were advantages as well as disadvantages to the employment of foreign troops. On average the foreign corps had lower sickness rates than the British regiments, this could partly be explained by their greater sobriety, but also that so many had already served at least one campaign in French ranks, and so were less raw than the recruits or volunteers from the Militia that made up the British replacements. James McGrigor, Wellington's chief surgeon was clear why he thought the KGL had lower sickness rates: 'The temperance, steadiness, and regular habits of the German legion, kept them always in a state of health.'[86]

Several sources also mention the foreign troops' ability to get the most from their rations, which could also have contributed to their health. Captain James Campbell, who served in the 3rd Division with companies of the 5/60th noted:

---

[84] D. Balagny, *Campaign de l'Empereur Napoléon en Espagne 1808-1809* (Paris: Berger-Levraut, 1903) Vol.III, p.392.
[85] C. Oman, *A History of the Peninsular War* (Oxford: Clarendon Press, 1902), Vol.IV, p.430.
[86] Quoted in Bamford, *Sickness*, p.224.

> It seemed to be settled amongst themselves, that every man of the mess of the 5th Battalion 60th, had to carry something, that is say – highly-spiced meats, such as sausages, cheese, onions, garlic, lard, pepper, salt, vinegar, mustard, sugar, coffee, &c.; in short, whatever could add to or make their meals more palatable, nourishing, or conducive to health. As soon as the daily allowance of beef was issued, they set to work and soon produced a first-rate dinner or supper, which were often improved by certain wild herbs which they knew where to look for, whereas, in attempting this, I have known instances of our men poisoning themselves; and what a contrast to this were the ways of our too often thoughtless beings who rarely had any of the above articles – day after day they boiled their beef, just killed, in the lump, in water, which they seldom contrived to make deserving the name of soup or broth. This and their bread or biscuit was what they usually lived upon.[87]

John Malcolm of the 42nd Foot, which was also brigaded with a company of the 5/60th, had a similar high opinion of them:

> The most picturesque scene that our camp exhibited, was the space occupied by the German light troops, who, during the twilight, sat in groups before the doors of their tents, canopied in clouds of tobacco smoke, chanting together their native airs and anthems. They seemed to be more at home in the field than our soldiers, and had the art of making up a very palatable mess out of the simplest materials.[88]

Wellington too had a high opinion of the 5/60th. He replied to a report from one of his brigade commanders in 1809 with: 'I am delighted with your account of the 5th battalion 60th regiment. Indeed every thing that I have seen and known of that excellent corps has borne the same stamp'.[89]

Many journals from the Peninsula also note the differences between the British and German national characters. Ensign Edmund Wheatley, a rare British officer serving with the KGL, wrote:

> The Germans bear excessive fatigues wonderfully well, and a German will march over six leagues while an Englishman pants and perspires beneath the labour of twelve miles; but before the enemy a German moves on silent but mechanically, whilst an Englishman is all sarcasm, laughter and indifference.[90]

---

87   J. Campbell, *A British Army As It Was, – Is, – and Ought to Be* (London: T & W Boone, 1840), pp.105-6.
88   Anon. *Memorials of the Late War* (Edinburgh: Constable, 1828), Vol.I, p.263.
89   Wellesley to Donkin, 23 June 1809, quoted in Gurwood, *Wellington's Dispatches*, Vol.IV, p.431.
90   Hibbert, *The Wheatley Diary*, p.8.

Captain John Patterson, 50th Foot, likewise praised the German troops he served alongside:

> The German troops are superior to any I ever met with for strict attention to duty. They are determined, brave, and cool in the hour of battle; and, should they be entrusted with the out-posts, the camp may sleep in safety and in full assurance of being vigilantly watched. – Hardy and inflexible, they conform under any state of things to their commanders, at whose will they move with the regularity of a piece of mechanism.[91]

German troops were very widely acknowledged to be highly skilled light cavalry and light infantry. The British light cavalry regiments sent to the Peninsular had little knowledge or experience of outpost duties, one of their primary roles. Captain William Tomkinson of the 16th Light Dragoons admitted: 'And here I beg frankly to say, that the German Hussars in the Peninsula army were our first masters in outpost duties.'[92] Major Edward Cocks, who also served in the 16th, was equally complimentary of the KGL cavalry, but less admiring of the KGL infantry:

> Though I have not a very high opinion of the infantry belonging to the German Legion, yet I must bear the most unqualified testimony to the courage, skill, zeal and marked good conduct of the cavalry – the fact is, the first are foreigners of all descriptions and exactly the same species of troops except being finer men, as the French armies – the cavalry are old Hussars, almost all Hanoverians, and many of them men of great respectability. These men are perfectly to be depended on and understand outpost duty better, and take more care of their horses, than British dragoons.[93]

The 5/60th, the KGL Light Battalions, the rifle companies of the KGL line battalions, and the Brunswickers provided a large portion of the specialist light infantry and rifle troops with Wellington's army. Harry Ross-Lewin of the 32nd Foot, who also served alongside a company of the 5/60th, highlighted the beneficial effect of the German troops on the British infantry, and their differences in attitude:

> Our German sharpshooters improved them considerably in the several duties of light troops; still they never attained to such a degree of perfection as might have been expected from a consideration of their natural qualifications. Our men, particularly in the beginning of the war, entertained very generally the absurd notion that the taking advantage of any sort of cover which lay in their way, when skirmishing, was an act of cowardice, and some of our commanders, strangely as the assertion may sound, seemed desirous to encourage them in this way of thinking. When we consider our soldiers, as such, we cannot approve of their yielding to this sense of shame;

---

91 J. Paterson, *The Adventures of Captain John Patterson* (London: T & W Boone, 1837) pp.356-7.
92 W. Tomkinson, *The Diary of a Cavalry Officer* (London: Swan, Sonnenschein; 1894) p.216.
93 J. Page, *Intelligence Officer in the Peninsula* (Staplehurst: Spellmount, 1986) p.63.

but we cannot fail to admire them, as men, for preferring danger to what they considered dishonour. How differently the old Germans thought! They were always to be seen dodging from tree to tree, or ensconcing themselves between rocks and fences, with admirable method and steadiness, while the British skirmisher would step out sturdily on the open space, and make a target of himself for the enemy.[94]

Malcolm, of the 42nd, also rated them highly as skirmishers, whilst noting their difference in character to British troops:

> In this species of warfare, the German troops appeared to me to excel all others, advancing upon the enemy with what seemed to be a kind of dogged and phlegmatic courage, and in the most galling fire, neither quickening nor relaxing their jog-trot pace. One cannot help wondering how such troops should ever have been beaten. It would seem, however, that the courage of British troops, which seems to be a happy combination of the impetuosity of the French, and the stubbornness of the Germans, is of a more effective description.[95]

The combat records of the foreign corps in the Peninsula contain some of hardest won and most notable victories over the French: the 1st and 2nd KGL Dragoons excelled themselves at Garcia Hernandez; the 1st and 2nd KGL Light Battalions proved themselves to be very steady at Venta del Pozo and held the village of Albuera against superior odds. In general, the KGL were seen as every bit as dependable in action as British regiments. The 5/60th, spread across five of Wellington's eight divisions, were at the forefront of most of the battles of the campaign, winning 16 battle honours and many mentions in Wellington's dispatches. They were an integral part of the light battalions formed from the light companies of the line regiments in each brigade. *Maréchal* Soult specifically blamed the 5/60th for the high casualty rate amongst his officers during the fighting in the Pyrenees:

> There is in the English army a battalion of the 60th consisting of ten companies – the regiment is composed of six battalions, the other five being in America or the West Indies. This battalion is never concentrated, but has a Company attached to each Infantry Division. It is armed with a short rifle; the men are selected for their marksmanship; they perform the duties of scouts, and in action are expressly ordered to pick off the officers, especially Field and General Officers. Thus it has been observed that whenever a superior officer goes to the front during an action, either for the purposes of observation or to lead and encourage his men, he is usually hit. This mode of making war and of injuring the enemy is very detrimental to us; our casualties in officers are so great that after a couple actions the whole number are usually disabled. I saw yesterday battalions whose officers had been disabled in the ratio of one officer to eight men; I also saw battalions

---

94 H. Ross-Lewin, *With the Thirty-Second* (Dublin: Hodges, Figgis & Co., 1904), pp.305-6.
95 Anon., *Memorials of the Late War*, Vol.I, p.272.

which were reduced to two or three officers, although less than one-sixth of their men had been disabled.[96]

Even the two most criticised foreign corps, the Chasseurs and the Brunswickers, proved themselves to be reliable in battle. In 1812, at the start of the withdrawal from Burgos, the Chasseurs defended a position at Olmos with determination and bravery, and following the Battle of Vittoria, where they took heavy casualties, the regiment was also praised. In his dispatch after the battle of Fuentes de Oñoro Wellington stated: 'I particularly observed the Chasseurs Britanniques under Lieut. Colonel Eustace, as behaving in the most steady manner; and Major General Houstoun mentions in high terms the conduct of a detachment of the Duke of Brunswick's light infantry.'[97]

An Inconvenience?

Would the Battalion of Foreign Recruits, that Wellington did not want with his army, have been an asset or an inconvenience? The battalion, commanded by Major Henry Fitzgerald, was inspected in November 1811 by Colonel Louis de Watteville. He found them to be 'a fine body of men and have acquired a very good state of discipline.' The vast majority of the battalion were German, with a small number of French, Dutch, Hungarians, Poles and Italians. Charles Leslie was one of the officers who, in the hope of a step up in rank, volunteered to join the battalion in 1813, when it was still at Cadiz:

> The men were supposed to be all Germans, but many entered as such were French, Italian, or Poles. They were a remarkably well-conducted set of men, no drunkards or idlers. The generality of them were always employed, when off duty, in making fancy-work of all descriptions, carving in bone, plaiting hair-chains, &c., repairing watches, making busts. They had great power in acquiring languages. My servant, although a German, talked French, Spanish, and Italian, and English at last, remarkably well. He had been servant to a French General who was killed at Barossa.[98]

At the end of his letter to Lord Liverpool quoted at the start of this chapter, Wellington recommended that the men of the Battalion of Foreign Detachments at Cadiz be formed into a battalion of the KGL or the 60th.[99] The battalion was eventually formed into the 8th Battalion of the 60th in 1814 and moved to Gibraltar, but it was disbanded in 1816 and the men either discharged or transferred to the 5/60th.

---

96   J.B. Dumas, *Neuf Mois de Campagnes à la suite du Maréchal Soult* (Paris: Henri Charles-La Vauzelle, 1907), pp.42-43.
97   Wellington to Liverpool, 8 May 1811, quoted in Gurwood, *Dispatches*, Vol.VII, p.516.
98   C. Leslie, *Military Journal of Colonel Leslie, K. H., of Balquhain* (Aberdeen: Aberdeen University Press, 1887) pp.232-3.
99   Wellington to Liverpool, 18 September 1811, TNA, WO 1/250 pp.469-71,

The final inspection report noted the battalion was still commanded by Fitzgerald and the 'present state of the Corps does great honour, and credit to that officer.'[100] The 8/60th were never tested on campaign but there is no reason to suspect that they would have performed any worse than other foreign corps, and as light infantry could well have proved a useful addition to Wellington's army.

The Chasseurs Britanniques had the worst record for desertion in Wellington's army, but were otherwise a well-disciplined unit that proved itself reliable under fire. The reasons for the high rate of desertions are unclear, but it is the case that it had a wider spread of nationalities than most of the foreign corps with only a third from the more 'reliable' areas of Germany, Austria-Hungary, the Low Countries, and Switzerland, around a third from Poland and Russia, and a third from France, Italy, Spain and Portugal.[101] The Duke of Brunswick's Light Infantry also had a poor record for desertions but they were trusted enough by Wellington to provide three detached companies and also proved themselves in battle. The foreign corps with Wellington's army did not have any episodes of collapses in unit cohesion in battle like some of the French foreign regiments did; for example the 4e Régiment Etranger at Almaraz.

Wellington could have lobbied harder for the Chasseurs and Brunswickers to be sent away from his army, but he did not. The 85th Light Infantry suffered the ignominy of having the majority of their officers dismissed and being sent home, but none of the foreign corps did. With British regiments struggling to recruit, and mostly taking inexperienced men from the militia, the foreign corps provided boots on the ground that Wellington sorely needed, and also helped to raise both the numbers and quality of his light cavalry and light infantry. If the two most problematic regiments, the Chasseurs and the Brunswickers, had been replaced then while the desertion rate of the foreign corps would still have been higher than British regiments, this would not have been to such an extent to elicit so many complaints from Wellington, nor comments from historians like Napier and Oman. There were many times during the Peninsular War when the situation hung in the balance and defeat for the allies was only narrowly avoided. The contributions of the men from many nations across Europe who chose, for whatever reason, to fight for Britain helped Wellington win his many victories between Mondego Bay and Toulouse.

Bibliography

Archival Sources
The National Archives
    ADM 103/286 – Register of Prisoners of War, Plymouth.
    WO 1/232–50 – British Army in Spain, Portugal and France.
    WO 1/413 – General Merck's mission (1810–1811).
    WO 1/648–51 – War Department In–Letters.
    WO 1/903 – Papers on the recruiting and distribution of troops.

---

100 Inspection 8/60th May 1816, TNA, WO 27/137.
101 Nichols, *Wellington's Mongrel Regiment*, p.175-6.

WO 2/54 – Out Letters, Foreign Troops.
WO 3/54 – Commander-in-Chief General Letters.
WO 6/135 – Commander-in-Chief, letters to public departments.
WO 7/77–85 – Depot of Foreign Troops, out-letters.
WO 12/7066–73 – General Muster Books and Pay Lists, 60th Foot.
WO 17/179 – Monthly Returns, 60th Foot.
WO 17/1082 – Monthly Returns, Ireland.
WO 25/1923 – Casualty Returns, 60th Foot.
WO 25/3225 – Documents relating to Establishments and recruiting.
WO 27/99–137 – Inspection Returns.
WO 90/1 – General Courts Martial Registers, Abroad.

Books

Arielli, N., & Collins, B.(eds.), *Transnational Soldiers – Foreign Military Enlistment in the Modern Era* (Basingstoke: Palgrave Macmillan, 2013).
Bamford, A., *Sickness, Suffering and the Sword* (Norman: University of Oklahoma Press, 2013).
Beamish, N.L., *History of the King's German Legion* (London: Thomas & William Boone, 1837).
Bonaparte, J., *The Confidential Correspondence of Napoleon Bonaparte with his Brother Joseph* (New York: Appleton, 1856).
Burnham, R., & McGuigan, R., *The British Army against Napoleon, Facts, Lists, and Trivia 1805-1815* (Barnsley: Frontline Books, 2010).
Campbell, J., *A British Army As It Was, – Is, – and Ought to Be* (London: T & W Boone, 1840).
Chamberlain, P., *The Napoleonic Prison of Norman Cross* (Stroud: The History Press, 2018).
Costa de Serda, E., *Opérations des Troupes Allemandes en Espagne de 1808 a 1813* (Paris: Dumaine, 1874).
Demet, D., *We Are Accustomed to do Our Duty* (Warwick: Helion & Company, 2018).
Dempsey, G.C., *Napoleon's Mercenaries* (London: Greenhill, 2002).
Esdaile, C., *The Peninsular War* (London: Allen Lane, 2002).
Forrest, A., *Napoleon's Men* (London: Hambledon & London, 2002).
Graves, D.E., *Fix Bayonets!* (Stroud: Spellmount, 2007).
Gurwood, J., *The Dispatches of Field Marshal the Duke of Wellington* (London: John Murray, 1835).
Gurwood, J., *The General Orders of Field Marshal The Duke of Wellington K. G. in Spain, Portugal & France* (London: Egerton, 1837).
Hering, J.F., *Journal of An Officer in the King's German Legion* (London: Colburn, 1827).
Hibbert, C. (ed), *The Wheatley Diary* (Moreton-in-the-Marsh: Windrush, 1997) .
Knight, R., *Britain Against Napoleon: The Organisation of Victory 1793-1815* (London: Penguin, 2013).
Maempel, J.C., *Adventures of a Young Rifleman in the French and English Armies* (London: Colburn, 1826).
Napier, W.F.P., *History of the War in the Peninsula* (London: Warne, 1892).

Nichols, A., *Wellington's Mongrel Regiment* (Staplehurst: Spellmount, 2005).
Nichols, A., *They Turned Out So Ill!* (Peterborough: Fast Print, 2018).
Nichols, A., *Wellington's Switzers* (Godmanchester: Ken Trotman, 2015).
Oman, C., *A History of the Peninsular War* (Oxford: Clarendon Press, 1902).
Ompteda, C., *In the King's German Legion* (London: Grevel, 1894).
Page, J., *Intelligence Officer in the Peninsula* (Staplehurst: Spellmount, 1986).
Paterson, J., *The Adventures of Captain John Patterson* (London: T & W Boone, 1837).
Rigaud, G., *Celer et Audax* (Oxford: Hall & Stacy, 1879).
Robertson, I. C., *Wellington Invades France* (London: Greenhill, 2003).
Tomkinson, W., *The Diary of a Cavalry Officer* (London: Swan, Sonnenschein; 1894).
Schwein, P., *The Young Rifleman's Comrade* (London: Colburn, 1826).
Warre, W., *Letters from the Peninsula* (London: Murray, 1909).
Wishon, M., *German Forces and the British Army; Interactions and Perceptions 1742-1815* (Basingstoke: Palgrave Macmillan, 2013).
Anon., *Vicissitudes in the Life of a Scottish Soldier* (London: Colburn, 1827).
Anon., *Memorials of the Late War* (Edinburgh: Constable, 1828).

Journal Articles

Gray, D.S., 'Prisoners, Wanderers, and Deserters: Recruiting for the King's German Legion, 1803-1815', *Journal of the Society of Army Historical Research*, Vol. LII, pp.148-55.
Hodge, W.B., 'On the Mortality Arising from Military Operations', *Journal of the Statistical Society of London*, Vol. XIX.
Linch, Kevin, 'Desertion from the British Army during the Napoleonic Wars', *Journal of Social History*, Volume 49, Issue 4, 1 June 2016, pp.808–828, <https://doi.org/10.1093/jsh/shw007>.

4

John Wesley's War: Methodism off and on the Battlefield, 1739-1789

Alexander Burns

In early October 1739, John Nelson, a somewhat dissolute builder, was walking on the southern side of Hyde Park, when he heard an off-duty soldier begin to speak. This soldier, a private who had just come off of guard duty, spoke to a group of other soldiers and Welsh women about the new birth of religious transformation which was occurring in his life. While speaking, the soldier shared the story of his conversion experience. A growth of Christian faith had occurred as a result of the preaching of John Wesley. Whereas formerly, this soldier had embraced a harsh masculinity which he described as sinful, now, he had been changed by the transformative power of the blood of Jesus Christ. Nelson listened to the soldier's speech, and he recalled that it, 'sank deeply into my mind, and made me cry more earnestly that God would work the same change in my heart'.[1]

In Britain, the middle decades of the eighteenth century are not remembered as a particularly religious time. Rather, historians often frame this era as one of commerce and rationality in government and civil society, the paintings of Hogarth having replaced the religious hysteria of the previous century. Religion, it seems, fell more and more into the private sphere, as Britons became increasingly concerned with worldly concerns. More recent scholarship has tried to qualify this view, suggesting that religion was vital to the establishment of British identity. Together, these lines of inquiry have led to a vigorous debate about the nature of the eighteenth century: was it a time of religious renewal, or growing secularism?[2] This chapter seeks to examine a particular time and place where religion was vital to the private lives of ordinary people: among Methodist soldiers in the British Army between 1739 and 1789. As a

---

[1] John Telford, *Wesley's Veterans: Lives of Early Methodist Preachers* (Salem, OH: Schmul Publishers, 1912), Vol.III, p.15.
[2] For the broad outlines of this debate, see: Roy Porter, *English Society in the eighteenth century* (London: Allen Lane, 1982); Patricia U. Bonomi, *Under the Cope of Heaven* (New York: Oxford University Press, 1986); Paul Langford, *A Polite and Commercial People: England, 1727-1783* (Oxford, 1989: Oxford University Press, 1989); Jon Butler, *Awash in a Sea of Faith* (Cambridge: Harvard University Press, 1990); Linda Colley, *Britons: Forging the Nation, 1707-1837* (London: Pimlico, 2003).

Christian religious tradition, Methodism may bring to mind the conversion experience of John Wesley at Aldersgate, the earnest preaching of lay-ministers, and the hymns of Charles Wesley. Methodism is much less frequently remembered as part of the experience of soldiers in fighting in the British Army.

This chapter argues that Methodist soldiers were able to spread their movement across the Army as a result of two important factors. First, Methodists benefited from, and at times, even exploited, official indecision about their religious movement on the part of military authorities. Second, Methodists won converts by displaying a reckless fearlessness in the face of death, usually on the battlefield, but occasionally in judicial settings. The first thesis, that Methodists defied army leadership in order to embrace a civilian-led religious movement, challenges the idea that soldiers were developing an exclusive martial identity against civilians in the eighteenth century. The second thesis, that Methodist soldiers used the chaos of the battlefield to advance their religious cause, challenges the idea that soldiers were simply automata on the battlefield during the eighteenth century.

Methodism became part of an identity important sub-set of eighteenth century British soldiers. Rather grasping for the 'average' soldier, this chapter explicitly focuses on men whose military lives were touched by this Methodist wave. Methodist soldiers attempted to maintain a distinct religious identity and often defied military authorities in order to do so. These men were not developing a martial identity hostile to civilian society; by contrast, they were following the instructions of civilian religious leaders, and resist the efforts of military authorities to reform their religious sentiments. However, far from being disloyal, these soldiers claimed that they were intensely loyal and obedient to the ruling family of Great Britain even as they defied officers in the army.

In addition to archival reports and manuscripts which survive from identifiable Methodist soldiers, this chapter draws on accounts of Methodist soldiers from the War of the Austrian Succession era printed by Methodist magazines circa 1770-1800 and letters from Methodist soldiers written to John Wesley. As the readership of these Methodist magazines was primarily interested in the religious aspects of their stories, military details are often vague. The letters of Methodist soldiers only survive as a result of the preservation in the papers of John Wesley. Both the autobiographical articles and letters present problems to historians studying Methodist soldiers in the 1770s. Soldiers writing their autobiographies and letters to religious authorities have a vested interest in presenting themselves in a holy manner. Particularly in the case of the mini-autobiographies, their interest in weighty theological matters may have been added in at a later date. However, the sources are also remarkable in a number of ways. The letters come directly from the era in question, and while the memoirs are written approximately 30 years after the events they describe they were still, by and large, written before the onset of the French Revolution. With the types of sources used in this chapter described, the chapter will turn to the historiography of the War of the Austrian Succession and the eighteenth-century Methodist movement.

If historians have neglected the wars of the eighteenth century in comparison to scholarship on twentieth-century conflict, the War of the Austrian Succession stands out for its lack of scholarly attention in comparison with the rest of these wars. Reed Browning and M.S. Anderson attempted to fill this gap in the 1990s, but their scholarly overviews fail to provide the depth of coverage that is available for other mid-eighteenth century wars, such as the Seven Years War.[3] In a chapter covering the state of the field in 2014, Ciro Paoletti argues that the Seven Years War and American War of Independence continue to dominate the historiography of the eighteenth century wars, to the detriment of the War of the Austrian Succession, and earlier War of the Spanish Succession, to say nothing of the more minor conflicts in this period.[4] This general trend also proves true for the specific topic of this chapter: British enlisted men, or common soldiers. With the exception of Andrew Cormack's recent social history of the Chelsea Pensioners in the first half of the eighteenth century, and a chapter covering the entire eighteenth century in Michael Snape's *Religion and the Redcoat*, common British soldiers in the War of the Austrian Succession era have received much less attention than their counterparts in the Seven Years War or American War of Independence.[5]

By comparison, Methodism in Britain during the eighteenth century continues to develop a rich, if often popular, historiography. In 2017 Kenneth J. Collins, a professor of historical theology at Asbury Theological Seminary, published a comprehensive bibliography of works relating to Methodism and John Wesley, which ran to 313 pages.[6] There are numerous theological discourses on the particular doctrines of the Methodist faith, and even more numerous popular biographies of John Wesley. Tellingly, however, this bibliography did not contain any works on Methodism and the British Army. More broadly, historians have attempted to assess the impact of Methodism on British society. E.P. Thompson critically addressed the role of Methodism in combating working-class radicalism in his classic, *The Making of the English Working Class*, and historians continue to debate Thompson's contributions to understanding Methodism, and even his own personal experiences and opinions with regards to the subject.[7] When looking specifically at the history of the Methodist religious movement, the starting point for the serious researcher remains *The Oxford Handbook of Methodist Studies*.[8] David Hempton's study of Methodism

---

3 Reed Browning, *The War of the Austrian Succession* (St. Martin's Griffin, 1993); M.S. Anderson, *The War of Austrian Succession 1740–1748* (New York: Routledge, 1995).
4 Ciro Paoletti, 'War, 1688-1812', in Peter H. Wilson (ed.), *A Companion to Eighteenth Century Europe* (Oxford: Wiley Blackwell, 2014), pp.464-478.
5 Michael F. Snape, *The Redcoat and Religion: the Forgotten History of the British Soldier from the Age of Marlborough to the Eve of the First World War* (London: Routledge, 2008). Andrew Edward Cormack, *These Meritorious Objects of the Royal Bounty: The Chelsea Out-Pensioners in the Early Eighteenth Century* (London: Published by the Author, 2017).
6 Kenneth J. Collins, *A Wesley Bibliography* (Wilmore, KY: First Fruits Press, 2017).
7 E.P. Thompson, *Making of English Working Class* (London: Victor Gollancz Ltd, 1963); Stephen Heathorn, 'E.P. Thompson, Methodism, and the 'Culturalist' Approach To the Historical Study of Religion', *Method & Theory in the Study of Religion* 10, no. 2 (1998): pp.210-226; Roland Boer, 'E.P. Thompson and the Psychic Terror of Methodism', *Thesis Eleven* 110, no. 1 (2012): pp.54-67.
8 William J. Abraham and James E. Kirby (eds.), *The Oxford Handbook of Methodist Studies* (Oxford: Oxford University Press, 2009).

and politics is older but still highly instructive.[9] Methodism worked its way into the popular culture and army life during the eighteenth century, but in a military context that process has been largely left unexplored.

For converted soldiers, Methodism became an alternative identity to the rough masculinity of military life. These soldiers attempted to reconcile the harsh realities of their soldierly world with their new-found religious sentiments. In fusing these two aspects of their lives, they formed a new soldierly identity based both on military loyalty and religious purity. These men sought to deploy their Methodism as a pro-government ideology, where true adherents would, 'Fear God and Honour the King'. In doing so, they attempted to prove that they were both legitimate soldiers and subjects, indeed, that they were God's chosen people in a particularly British soldierly context. As these Methodist soldiers experienced new birth into a burgeoning religious movement, they also attempted to apply the effects of their new birth in a military setting.

At the outset, it is important to realise that Methodist soldiers only ever formed a vocal minority within the British Army of this period. Many soldiers in the British Army would have agreed with the sentiments expressed by an anonymous soldier, referred to as, 'Jack Careless', in Samuel Ancell's description of the great siege of Gibraltar:

> Fine talking of God with a soldier, whose trade and occupation is cutting throats: Divinity and slaughter sound very well together, they jingle like a crack'd bell in the hands of a noisy crier: Our King is answerable to God for us. I fight for him. My religion consists in a fire-lock, open touch-hole, good flint, well-rammed charge, and seventy rounds of powder and ball. This is my military creed. Come, comrade, drink Success to the British arms.[10]

Methodist soldiers were in contention with men like 'Jack Careless' over the heart and soul of the British Army. Methodist soldiers, though more numerous than it might first appear, were never the 'average' British soldier. In light of the sources available to historians working prior to the twentieth century, searching for an 'average' soldier is increasing difficult. Jason Phillips has suggested that as opposed to looking for an average soldier, military historians might be better served by examining groups of soldiers who formulated influential ideologies.[11] Philips followed this recommendation with his book, *Diehard Rebels,* which examined a group of soldiers who refused to accept defeat even as the American Civil War drew to a close.[12] In this line of thinking, Methodists soldiers become an important minority

---

9   David Hempton, *Methodism and Politics in British Society, 1750-1850* (London: Routledge, 1984).
10 Samuel Ancell, *A Circumstantial Journal of the Long and Tedious Blockade and Siege of Gibraltar from the 12th of September, 1779, to the 23d. of February, 1783, Etc.* (J. Schofield: Liverpool 1785), p.97.
11 Jason Phillips, 'Battling Stereotypes: A Taxonomy of Common Soldiers in Civil War History', *History Compass*, No. 6 (2008), pp.1417-1425
12 Jason Phillips, *Diehard Rebels: The Confederate Culture of Invincibility* (Athens: University of Georgia Press, 2010).

within the army, as they both attempted to evangelise their beliefs and formulated pro-government ideologies.

The Spread of Methodism and the Response of the Military Authorities

The Methodist movement grew out of meetings held by John and Charles Wesley at Lincoln College at the University of Oxford in the late 1720s and 1730s. After attempting missionary work among Native Americans in the colony of Georgia, John Wesley felt his 'heart strangely warmed', while attending a Moravian religious service at Aldersgate near London on 24 May 1738. This conversion based upon feeling was a key aspect in Methodist and future evangelical Christian faith. Charles Wesley reported a similar religious experience, and both began a program of openair preaching. While the first largescale Methodist societies cropped up during the 1744 campaign in Flanders, John and Charles Wesley's encounters with soldiers in Britain during 1738 and 1739 laid the groundwork for this spread of religious feeling.[13] Soldiers often flocked to the preaching of John and Charles, but they occasionally faced hostility from other soldiers, especially when these soldiers were led by anti-Methodist officers. Examining the journal of Charles Wesley in the year 1743, we find that he was accosted by a company of soldiers near Sheffield:

> The Captain laid hold on me, and began reviling. I gave him for answer, "A Word in season; or, Advice to a Soldier;" then prayed, particularly for His Majesty King George, and preached the Gospel with much contention. The stones often struck me in the face. After sermon I prayed for sinners, as servants of their master, the devil; upon which-the Captain ran at me with great fury, threatening revenge for my abusing, as he called it, "the King his master." He forced his way through the brethren, drew his sword, and presented it to my breast. My breast was immediately steeled. I threw it open, and, fixing mine eye on his, smiled in his face, and calmly said, "I fear God, and honour the King." His countenance fell in a moment, he fetched a deep sigh, put up his sword, and quietly left the place. To one of the company, who afterwards informed me, he had said, "You shall see, if I do but hold my sword to his breast, he will faint away." So perhaps I should, had I had only his principles to trust to; but if at that time I was not afraid, no thanks to my natural courage.[14]

---

13 John Telford, *Wesley's Veterans: Lives of Early Methodist Preachers* (Salem, OH: Schmul Publishers, 1912), Vol.III, p.13; John Wesley (ed. W. R. Ward and Richard P. Heitzenrater), *The Works of John Wesley* (Nashville, TN: Abingdon Press, 1990), Vol.XIX, Journals and Diaries II, p.19.
14 Charles Wesley (ed. Thomas Jackson), *The Journal of the Rev. Charles Wesley, M.A. To Which Are Appended Selections from His Correspondence and Poetry* (London: Methodist Press, 1849), entry for 25 May 1743.

Charles also had positive interactions with soldiers. During the height of the Jacobite Rebellion of 1745 he preached to an army camp on 8 November 1745:

> Fri., November 8th. I preached first in Bexley church, then in the front of the camp near Dartford. Many of the poor soldiers gave diligent heed to the word. One of the most reprobate was pricked at the heart, and entered the Society.
> Sat., November 9th. A regiment passing by our door, I took the opportunity of giving each soldier a book. All, excepting one, received them thankfully.[15]

Methodism was at its peak in the British Amy during the War of Jenkins Ear and War of the Austrian Succession, when lay preachers and common soldiers actively created Methodist societies throughout the British Army. Michael Snape studies the chronological progress of this revival in detail, in the first chapter of his work, *Religion and the Redcoat,* to such an extent that this chapter will only cover the revival briefly. Snape also points out that many of these soldiers were already formed into religious societies before Methodism took root, and those wartime deployments may actually have facilitated the spread of Methodism in the army.[16] These Methodist soldier-societies were made up of soldiers who attempted to reject their former way of life by abandoning desires they now considered sinful, such as gambling and sexual liaisons. One such soldier, often identified as one of the founding fathers of the 1740s Methodist army revival, John Haime, outlined the practices of Methodist societies in an angry confrontation with an officer: 'I preach against swearing, whoring, and drunkenness; and exhort men to repent of all their sins that they may not perish'.[17]

Methodist soldiers, perhaps unsurprisingly, viewed the Anglican chaplaincy in the British Army as both inadequate and an object of suspicion. Soldier Duncan Wright recalled that 'the care four or five regiments [were] left to an unhappy [chaplain] who was an object of common ridicule among the soldiers for his perpetual drunkenness'.[18] Wright continued, 'were the chaplains men of real piety, and courage, much good might be done in the army'.[19] Complaints about the chaplaincy by Methodist soldiers continued until the end of the century.[20] Lacking a dedicated chaplaincy, Methodist soldiers took it upon themselves to write to, and even meet with leading members of their religious movement, such as John Wesley. John Haime wrote to Wesley reporting the great success in increasing the number of Methodist soldiers with the army: 'Our Society has now increased to upwards of two hundred, and the hearers are frequently more than a thousand'.[21] Wesley was overjoyed at Haime's success and carried on a lively correspondence with numerous

---

15 Wesley, *Journal*, entry for 8-9 November 1745.
16 Snape, *The Redcoat and Religion*, p.43.
17 Thomas Jackson, *The Lives of Early Methodist Preachers: Chiefly Written by Themselves* (London: Wesleyan Conference Office, 1875), Vol.I, p.284.
18 Telford, *Wesley's Veterans*, Vol.II, p.33.
19 Telford, *Wesley's Veterans*, Vol.II, p.33.
20 National Army Museum, London (NAM), 2010-11-16, Roger Lamb's Scrapbook, p.128.
21 Wesley, *Journal*, p.455.

common soldiers in the 1740s. Their letters are full of theological discussions, as well as reports from the battlefield on the progress of the war.

British officers noticed Haime's religious revival and were not entirely impressed. He wrote John Wesley in May of 1744: 'many say I am mad[.] I have been sent for and examined several times; but, blessed be God, He has always delivered me'.[22] Some British officers often felt that their chaplaincy was not terribly effective in ministering to the spiritual needs of the men, and attended Haime's meetings to support his cause. Other officers considered Haime a dangerous religious radical who would undermine the authority of the command structure. In a stormy meeting with Lieutenant General James Sinclair, Haime was accused of a breach of military discipline for coming to Sinclair himself and not sending an officer to represent him. Sinclair then asked, 'How came you to preach?' To which Haime replied, 'The Spirit of God constrains me to call my fellow sinners to repentance'.[23] General Sinclair was not impressed and ordered Haime to stop preaching.

As Haime's story demonstrates, Methodists in the army found often found themselves in a strange no man's land between the official support and harsh censure of their officers. Methodist soldier Duncan Wright of the 10th Regiment of Foot captured this dilemma from the perspective of an officer in his regiment in the 1750s: 'Though he did not like Methodists… he wanted us all to be very good… therefore we had very strict orders against swearing, drunkenness, etc.'[24] Like many other Methodist soldiers, Wright noted that there was no official position held by officers toward Methodists in the ranks: 'Our lieutenant-colonel did not care was a soldier's religion was, provided he did his duty; but our major… to whom the command of the regiment was left for a time, thought it a disgrace to have a sergeant a preacher among them'.[25] Wright was eventually discharged during the reduction of the Army at the end of the Seven Years War, as a result of the machinations of this particular officer. Some officers attempted to intercede on his behalf, saying that they 'wished I could persuade all their men to be religious, for they had no trouble with the Methodist soldiers'.[26] Charles Wesley noted that he managed to convert an officer in 1745.[27] Methodist soldiers were able to use this discord among officers over the rise of their religious movement. While confusion reigned among officers, Methodists continued to attract new followers to their cause, and gain contacts with greater authority to safeguard them. Official indecision regarding Methodism allowed it to become part of the religious fixture of the British Army for the next century.

As a result of the deficiency of the chaplains, Methodists obtained the opportunity to gain the attention of a member of the British royal family. Haime began a campaign of open protest that chaplains were not administering the sacrament regularly. He recalled that, 'I complained aloud in the open camp… the chaplains

---

22 Wesley, *Journal*, p.455.
23 John Telford, *Wesley's Veterans*, Vol.I, p.31.
24 John Telford, *Wesley's Veterans*, Vol.II, p.27.
25 John Telford, *Wesley's Veterans*, Vol.II, p.31.
26 John Telford, *Wesley's Veterans*, Vol.II, p.32.
27 Wesley, *Journal*, entry for 10 November 1745.

were exceedingly displeased; but the Duke of Cumberland, hearing of it, ordered that it should be administered every Lord's day[.]'[28] This gained Haime notoriety, and eventually, Cumberland requested an interview with the cantankerous Methodist:

> The duke, hearing many complaints of me, inquired who I was; if I did my duty, if I would fight, and if I prayed for a blessing on the king and his arms: they told his royal highness, I did all this as well as any man in the regiment. He asked, "Then what have you to say against him?" Afterwards the duke talked with me himself, and asked me many questions. He seemed so well satisfied with my answers, that he bade me "go on;" and gave out a general order that I should preach anywhere, and no man should molest me.[29]

An examination of HRH the Duke of Cumberland's orderly book for this period does not bear out Haime's story but shows that there were indeed problems with the established chaplaincy. On 30 May 1745, Cumberland ordered, 'The commanding officers of the Regiments whose Chaplains are absent is ordered by H.R.H. to write immediately to those several Chaplains, to repair forthwith to their duty here; without the least delay or excuse'.[30] The Duke's troubles concerning Chaplains continued into the summer, and Methodists took advantage of this by showing their devotion both to God and the cause of their sovereign. Later in the year, Haime preached a sermon exhorting soldiers to be loyal to their king, a portion of which read:

> You fight for a good cause, and for a good king, and in defence of your country. And this is no way contrary to the tenderest conscience, as many of you found at the Battle of Fontenoy; when both you and I did our duty, and were all the time filled with love, and peace, and joy in the Holy Ghost.[31]

Unbeknownst to Haime, the Duke of Cumberland was present in the audience when he delivered this sermon. Although no formal patron-client relationship developed between Cumberland and the Methodist soldiers, Haime subsequently used Cumberland's name in arguments with his superiors, which opened doors which had previously been closed to him.[32] By exploiting friction between absentee chaplains and his army's commander, Haime had secured the Methodists' right to worship within the army. As a result, the Methodist movement continued to grow.

By the mid-1740s, Methodism had spread within the British Army to such an extent that British civilians began to associate the two subjects. The builder we met at the beginning of this chapter, John Nelson, after being converted by the preaching of the Methodist soldier in 1739, became an itinerant Methodist lay-preacher. He

---

28 Jackson, *Lives of the Early Methodist Preachers*, Vol.I, p.290.
29 Telford, *Wesley's Veterans*, Vol.I, p.291.
30 Society of the Cincinnati Library (SCL), MSS L2017F30, Duke of Cumberland's Orderly Book, p.54.
31 Telford, *Wesley's Veterans*, Vol.I, p.33.
32 Telford, *Wesley's Veterans*, Vol.I, p.37.

eventually ran afoul of townspeople and a recruiting party, which pressed him into military service in an infantry regiment. He was brought before a tribunal of local commissioners, who told him: 'You have no licence to preach, and you shall go for a soldier'. When Nelson protested this decision, one commissioner, laughingly said that he was, 'fit to go for a soldier, for there [Nelson] might have preaching enough'.[33]

Nelson's description of his imprisonment at the hands of military officials is decidedly biblical. His jailors are diabolical; his judges are described as 'Egyptians'. However, when he was actually sent to a marching regiment, his story begins to change: 'The officers bade them march us off to Hepworth Moor, to learn the exercise of a soldier; but Corporal W. seemed as tender to me as if he had been my own father'.[34] As it turned out, the corporal was a religious man himself. Nelson was sent to York, where he continued to preach as a soldier, and like the other Methodists we have encountered, found the military hierarchy divided on what to do with him. He reproved younger officers for swearing; in return, they had him confined and beaten. His major, however, found that his preaching was, 'no crime; for when you have done your [military] duty I do not care if you preach every night... you may go home to your quarters, and... I may send for you and hear you myself... for I wish all men were like you'.[35]

Nelson's fellow soldiers, whether from sincere religious feeling, or amusement that a meek Methodist preacher had been forced to join them in the army, often attempted to make life easier for him. While marching to Durham, he noted, 'I was much surprised at the good-nature of the soldiers in all this march; for I believe twenty offered to carry the gun for me, or anything else I had'.[36] Thanks to the intercession of Charles Wesley, the Earl of Stair obtained discharges papers for John Nelson. Charles noted in his diary: 'Toward the end of my discourse at the chapel, Mr. Erakine was sent to receive a soldier brought by William Shent, to redeem John Nelson. He immediately took him to Lord Stairs, and got a discharge for John Nelson'.[37] With his freedom secured by the patronage of Charles Wesley and Stair, Nelson preached to the officers and soldiers of his regiment one final time. Nelson's major told him that, 'I wish you well wherever you go: for I believe you Methodists are a well-meaning people'.[38] His fellow soldiers heard him preach one final time, and told him that, 'We are glad you are set at liberty, but sorry to part with you'.[39] As Methodist societies increased their following in the army, Britain was faced with its most dangerous foreign policy challenge of the mid-eighteenth century: the War of the Austrian Succession and Jacobite Rebellion of 1745.

---

33 Telford, *Wesley's Veterans*, Vol.III, p.106.
34 Telford, *Wesley's Veterans*, Vol.III, p.122.
35 Telford, *Wesley's Veterans*, Vol.III, pp.135-136.
36 Telford, *Wesley's Veterans*, Vol.III, p.140.
37 Jackson, *The Journal of Charles Wesley*, entry for 25 May 1743.
38 Telford, *Wesley's Veterans*, Vol.III, p.152.
39 Telford, *Wesley's Veterans*, Vol.III, p.152.

Methodist Soldiers in Battle

Methodist soldiers fought and died as soldiers on the battlefield, and experienced its full range of horrors. In order to understand their actions and performances on the battlefield, we must first turn to what combat was like during the War of the Austrian Succession. The wars of the eighteenth century have often been dismissed by historians of other eras as 'wars in lace' or a 'decorative interval'.[40] This view, often spawned by a reading of Voltaire's description of the Battle of Fontenoy in the War of the Austrian Succession, has officers doffing feathered cocked hats and amicably talking with the foe about how battles should be sequenced. Manuel de Landa has argued that soldiers were mere 'clockwork' instruments on the battlefields on the eighteenth century, that they had no loyalty, or drive, as the soldiers of Napoleon possessed.[41] Ilya Berkovich strongly challenged this argument with regards to motivation with his recent book, *Motivation in War*. However, many military historians still view combat in the eighteenth century as robotic, limited, and formalised.[42] This view needs to be complicated by the wealth of evidence that suggests eighteenth century soldiers reacted to the stress of battle in much the same way as soldiers in the modern world. In the eighteenth century, soldiers took cover, compensated for the stress of battle by firing as quickly as they could without orders, ran and moved at speed across the battlefield in order to avoid being shot, fled from combat, and experienced combat fatigue or what we today think of as Post-Traumatic Stress Disorder. The wars of the *Kabinettskriege* era may have been more limited than the conflicts of the twentieth century, but soldiers continued to experience battle in incredibly visceral and terrifying ways.

In the War of the Austrian Succession, British soldiers responded to the danger of combat by lying down, both with and without orders. At the Battle of Fontenoy in 1745, Sampson Staniforth described lying down under orders to avoid being shot by enemy artillery:

> We marched up boldly; but when we came close to the town of Fontenoy, we observed a large battery ready to be opened on us. And the cannon were loaded with small bullets, nails, and pieces of old iron. We had orders to lie down on the ground; but for all that, many were wounded, and some killed. Presently after the discharge we rose up, and marched to the first trench, still keeping up our fire.[43]

---

40 Alexander Martin, 'The Last 'War in Lace' or the First 'Total War'?' *Kritika: Explorations in Russian and Eurasian History*, Vol.15 No.2, 2014, pp.293-301; Duffy, *Military Experience in the Age of Reason*, p.3.

41 Manuel De Landa, *War in the Age of Intelligent Machines* (New York, NY: The MIT Press, 1991), pp.60-65.

42 For an example of this type of thinking among a prominent scholar in the field, see John Lynn, *The Bayonets of the Republic: Motivation and Tactics in the Army of Revolutionary France, 1791-94* (Urbana, IL: University of Illinois Press, 1984).

43 Telford, *Wesley's Veterans*, Vol.I, p.79.

Staniforth described another such encounter at the Battle of Lauffeld in 1745.[44] At the Battle of Fontenoy, the 43rd Highlanders fought in a similar manner. The regiment's commanding officer, Sir Robert Munro, order his men, 'to clap to the Ground on receiving the French Fire; and instantly, as soon as it was discharged, they sprung up, and coming close to the Enemy, poured in their Shot upon them'.[45] This system of alternatively taking cover and returning fire is similar to the tactics which modern armies use in the twenty-first century. Further evidence of this type of fighting comes from the letters of Lieutenant Colonel Russell of the British Guards. Russell observed the Battle of Dettingen in 1743, and described the infantry combat in a letter to his wife:

> That the Austrians behaved well also is true; that except one of their battalions which fired only once by platoons, they all fired as irregular as we did; that the English infantry behaved like heroes, and as they were the major part in the action to them the honor of the day is due; that they were under no command by way of Hide Park firing, but that the whole three ranks made a running fire of their own accord, and at the same time with great judgement and skill, stooping all as low as they could, making almost every ball take palce, is true, that the enemy, when expecting our fire, dropped down, which our men perceiving, waited till they got up before they would fire as a confirmation of their coolness as well as bravery, is very certain; that the French fired in the same manner, I mean like running fires, without waiting for words of command, and that Lord Stair did often say he had seen many a battle and never saw the infantry engage in any other manner is as true.[46]

In addition to describing the process of taking cover, this passage also describes the tendency of soldiers to fire without orders. In the stress of battle, eighteenth century soldiers would frequently eschew the controlled firings by volleys of ranks and platoons that they practiced on the drill square.[47] In another battle connected to the War of the Austrian Succession, Prestonpans during the Jacobite 1745 rebellion, Lord Dunmore observed that, 'the Fire of our Foot was infamous, Puff, Puff, no Platoon that I heard'.[48] Dunmore's use of the sound of firing, 'Puff, Puff', is illustrative that soldiers were firing without orders, using their own judgment.

---

44 Telford, *Wesley's Veterans*, Vol.I, pp.89-90.
45 Philip Doddridge, *Some Remarkable Passages in the Life of the Honourable Col. James Gardiner: Who Was Slain at the Battle of Preston-Pans, September 21, 1745;* (Printed for G. Hamilton and J. Balfour: Edinburgh, 1747), p.253.
46 Rosalind Alicia Frankland-Russell-Astley et al., *Report on the Manuscripts of Mrs. Franklin-Russell-Astley: of Chequers Court, Bucks* (London: Historical Manuscripts Commission, 1900), p.278.
47 J.A. Houlding, *Fit for Service: The Training of the British Army, 1715-1795* (Oxford: Oxford University Press, 1981), p.351.
48 Anon, *The Report of the Proceedings and Opinion of the Board of General Officers, on Their Examination into the Conduct, Behaviour, and Proceedings of, Sir John Cope, Peregrine Lascelles, and Thomas Fowke, from the Time of the Breaking out of the Rebellion in North-*

Having described what the experience of battle looked like for infantrymen in this era, the chapter will now turn to how Methodists used the experience of battle for their own ends. Methodist soldiers saw battle not simply as a time for fatalism, but as an opportunity to display to the world what type of soldiers they were. For these men, battle became a performative experience, through which they could demonstrate the sincerity of their religious convictions through the lack of fear they felt at the prospect of death. By demonstrating not fatalism but a joy in combat, Methodist soldiers performed their faith for all to see, and hoped to win converts to their societies.

Just before the Battle of Fontenoy, Sampson Staniforth indicated that he had, 'stepped out of the line, threw myself on the ground, and prayed that God would deliver me from all fear, and enable me to behave as a Christian and good soldier'.[49] This type of language fills the writings of Methodist veterans. Another was heard shouting in the midst of battle, 'O, how happy I am!'[50] John Evans, a Methodist private soldier in the English artillery, was mortally wounded and yet continued to praise God, attempting to use his religious fervour to convert the soldiers around him.[51] Soldier William Clements reported in a letter describing the Battle of Fontenoy, 'the Lord took away all fear form me, so that I went into the field with joy. The balls flew on either hand, and the men fell in abundance... but I scare knew whether I was on earth or in heaven. It was one of the sweetest days I have ever enjoyed'.[52] Sentiments like this make it clear that Methodist soldiers viewed battle as a type of paranormal experience, where the hand of God could decisively felt, and his judgment could be delivered immediately. During the Battle of Fontenoy, John Haime was confronted by an officer of his regiment, who in response to the carnage around him, literally asked, 'Haime, where is your God now?'[53] Haime then reports that a cannonball came and struck off the doubting officer's head. Such a story may seem to defy reality, but what really matters is that Haime viewed battle as a transcendent experience where such an experience could be possible. Haime continued, 'I have seen many good and glorious days, with much of the power of God; but I never saw more of it than this day'.[54] Considering the incredibly graphic nature of the battlefield as described above, Haime's elevated experience was a natural response to the horror and chaos of combat.[55]

In the British Army, as a result of the relatively small number of Methodists, these displays of religious fervour in order to evangelise to fellow soldiers, and give

---

Britain in the Year 1745, till the Action at Preston-Pans Inclusive (London: Printed for W. Webb, 1749), Appendix, p.38.
49   Telford, *Wesley's Veterans*, Vol.I, p.78.
50   Telford, *Wesley's Veterans*, Vol.I, p.80.
51   Anon., *The Arminian Magazine* (London: J. Fry &, 1778), p.280.
52   Wesley, *The Journal of the Rev. John Wesley*, Vol.I, p.511.
53   Telford, *Wesley's Veterans*, Vol.I, p.34.
54   Telford, *Wesley's Veterans*, Vol.I, p.34.
55   Yuval Noah Harari has addressed the way in which soldiers presented combat as 'the ultimate experience' in the eighteenth century. The descriptions of Methodist veterans fit well into that paradigm. See Yuval Harari, *Ultimate Experience: Battlefield Revelations and the Making of Modern War Culture, 1450-2000* (London: Palgrave Macmillan, 2014).

confidence to the performer. These religious displays went beyond fatalism: they were designed to encourage other soldiers in piety to Christ. As his regiment lay under fire at the outset of the Battle of Lauffeld, Sampson Staniforth recalled, 'while we lay on our arms, I had both time and opportunity to reprove the wicked. And they would bear it now'.[56] Methodists soldiers also boasted regarding their fearlessness under enemy fire, and believed that this was a sign of their righteousness. John Haime recalled meeting a badly wounded Methodist, who he asked, 'Have you got Christ in your heart?' The Methodist soldier replied, 'I have, I have had Him all this day'.[57] Methodist preachers attempted to instil this fearlessness in their soldiers. Before British troops marched off to confront the Jacobites during the '45, Charles Wesley noted that he prayed over soldiers, '…and solemnly commended them to the grace of God, before they set out to meet the rebels. They were without fear or disturbance, knowing the hairs of their head are all numbered, and nothing can happen but by the determinate counsel of God'.[58] Fearlessness in the face of death, these preachers and soldiers believed, demonstrated the validity of their religious beliefs.

This fearlessness in the face of death could even occur off the battlefield. Duncan Wright employed this thinking while comforting a soldier slated for execution in September of 1758. This soldier, Joseph Newton of Derbyshire, was a deserter. Unlike many instances of execution for desertion which were commuted by eighteenth century commanders, the government had decided to make an example of Newton, and other soldiers across Ireland, by not commuting their sentences.[59] Wright began to minister to this man a week before his execution was scheduled to occur, and managed to convert him to Methodism. The Thursday before his execution, Wright notes, 'his soul was set at liberty. From that time he witnessed a good confession to all that spoke to him. Everyone that saw him to the place where he was shot could not but admire the serene joy that appeared on his countenance'.[60] Wright was particularly impressed that, 'his calm, happy death made a deep impression on many of our soldiers; for they could not but discern the difference between him and one they saw die awhile before at Dublin, who showed the greatest reluctance'.[61] Wright attached great importance, not to the fatalistic acceptance of death and hope for spiritual rebirth on the part of Newton, but, rather, the power it had to impress other soldiers. Fatalistic bravado was not merely a tool of battlefield motivation, but one which had the potential to win many converts for Methodist societies.

For the Methodists, being fearless or even joyful in the face of death gave them the opportunity to display their loyalty to their faith, and potentially convert new members for their societies. The Methodist soldiers then faithfully reported their actions to leading Methodists such as Wesley, explaining to him that displays of

---

56 Telford, *Wesley's Veterans*, Vol.I, p.90.
57 Telford, *Wesley's Veterans*, Vol.I, p.34.
58 Jackson, *The Journal of Charles Wesley*, entry for 11 November 1745.
59 For an excellent example of this practice of commuting sentences, see SCL, MSS L2017F30, orderly book of HRH the Duke of Cumberland from April to October of 1745.
60 Telford, *Wesley's Veterans*, Vol.II, p.26.
61 Telford, *Wesley's Veterans*, Vol.II, p.26.

such devotion before the enemy had, 'made the officers, as well as common soldiers, amazed: and they acknowledge it to this day'.[62] British Methodist soldiers combined their religious calling and place within the British military as a means of performing their religious devotion, impressing the world around them, and corresponding with the leading figures of their religious movement.

The tales of battlefield devotion displayed by Methodist soldiers made their way back to John Wesley via letters, as discussed above. At home, Wesley then used those same stories in order to both gain favour with authorities and continue his open-air preaching. In October of 1745, Wesley travelled to Doncaster, in order to preach to a camp of soldiers there. In order to gain permission to preach, he wrote the governor, Matthew Ridley, describing the bravery of Methodist soldiers in Flanders, the wounds they suffered on the battlefield, and their religious devotion. Describing the death of Methodist soldier John Evans, Wesley argues that Evans, for as long as he was able, exhorted his fellow soldiers to, 'Fear God and Honour the King'.[63] Wesley was able to use descriptions of Methodist soldiers' performance in battle to justify his preaching to secular authorities, and continued to particularly prioritise soldiers as a target for his religious instruction.

Army Methodism After 1748

Though the height of Methodist activity in the army was in the 1740s, Methodist soldiers continued to be active in the army after the great Methodist revival. Although fewer diarists in the Seven Years War era show the strong influence of religious sentiments, we should carefully note that this community of deeply religious British soldiers endured into that era. Methodist minister Samuel Walker created a strong Methodist society within the 58th Regiment of Foot at Truro during this period. According to the nineteenth-century editor of Walker's papers:

> A great alteration, however, took place; punishments soon diminished and order prevailed in the regiment, to a degree never before witnessed, and the commander at length discovered the excellent cause of this salutary change. Genuine zeal had now its full triumph and its rich reward—the officers waited on Mr. Walker in a body, to acknowledge the good effects of his wise and sedulous exertions, and to thank him for the reformation he had produced in their ranks.[64]

One of the soldiers wrote a letter to Reverend Walker after the 58th left Truro, confirming this:

---

62 Wesley, *The Journal of the Rev. John Wesley*, Vol II, p.2.
63 Wesley, *The Journal of the Rev. John Wesley*, Vol.I, p.502.
64 Edwin Sidney and Samuel Walker (eds.), *The Life, Ministry, and Selections from the Remains of the Rev. Samuel Walker* (London: Baldwin and Cradock, 1838), p.153.

> I judge no man: many would desire to die the death of the righteous, that would not desire to live their life; and [I] know that has been my case. Serjeant Moore for ever blesses the day that ever he saw Truro, and we both hope in the Almighty God to see it again, and to hear the glad tidings of salvation as formerly.[65]

During the Seven Years War, particularly in Ireland, Methodism continued to spread in the British Army. During a trip to Canterbury in February of 1756, John Wesley noted, 'an abundance of soldiers and many officers', came to hear him preach. The next day, he had a meal with a colonel, who said, 'No men fight like those who fear God: I had rather command five hundred such, than any regiment in his Majesty's army'.[66] Likewise, nearly a year later, in 1757, Wesley noted:

> I went with T. Walsh to Canterbury, where I preached in the evening with great enlargement of spirit; but with greater in the morning, being much refreshed at the sight of so large a number of soldiers. And is not God able to kindle the same fire in the fleet which he has already begun to kindle in the army?[67]

Indeed, Methodism continued to be such a potent force in the British Army that, in 1759, Sir Robert Nugent urged William Pitt to use John Wesley (and George Whitefield) as a recruiting tool for the British Army, since Methodism continued to have influence in the Army.[68] Duncan Wright enlisted in the 10th Regiment of Foot in 1754 in Ireland, at the outset of the Seven Years War. He spent the entirety of the war in Ireland, marching to threatened parts of the country, and putting down riots. In the course of his time in the 10th, he saw John Wesley and Thomas Walsh preach, and eventually resolved to become a Methodist preacher himself.[69]

By the time of the American War of Independence, soldiers' memoirs contain language giving their overt religious affiliation. Don Hagist has uncovered previously unknown and unpublished material on the most famous British common soldier of this era, Roger Lamb. Further examination of this material makes it clear that Lamb was a Methodist. While he did not date his conversion until 16 May 1786, it is clear he had encountered Methodists before that time. Upon returning to his native Ireland, Lamb was confronted by the preaching of Methodists in Dublin: 'it pleased the Lord by the ministry of the Methodist preachers to convince me of sin, righteousness and judgement, the thoughts of death and eternity filled me with fear'. Lamb continued, 'I should have remarked that while in the Army I was a most extraordinary sinner. I had almost filled up the measure of my iniquities'.[70] Despite

---

65 Sidney and Walker (eds.), *Rev. Samuel Walker*, p.157.
66 John Wesley (ed. John Emory), *The Works of the Reverend John Wesley, A.M* (Methodist Book Concern: London, 1839), Vol.III, p.623.
67 Wesley, *Works of the Reverend John Wesley*, Vol.III, p.623.
68 Snape, *Religion and the Redcoat*, p.63.
69 Telford, *Wesley's Veterans*, Vol.II, p.106.
70 NAM, 2010-11-16, Roger Lamb's Scrapbook, p.144.

occurring after his discharge, his conversion was a result of military networks. Lamb recalled, 'Quarter Master Burgess (of the first Regiment of horse) who is now a Methodist preacher, was at that time in Dublin. He was a nursing father to me, he frequently followed advised and instructed me'. It seems this soldier was largely responsible for Lamb's conversion, and he recalled that Burgess' 'temper and upright walk had a good effect on my mind'.[71] The British Army bore a large degree of responsibility for his developing Methodism.

Even after his discharge from the military, Lamb defended his Methodist co-religionists to suspicious military officers. Lamb petitioned Colonel William Henry Clinton, Quartermaster General of Ireland, at the turn of the century. William Henry Clinton was the son of Lieutenant General Henry Clinton, who Lamb had served under in America. Lamb travelled to Clinton's offices on the recommendation of General Calvert and Colonel Mackenzie, and met with the younger Clinton. In a scrapbook, Lamb recorded notes on the conversation. After confirming his recommendation, Clinton asked Lamb about his current employment, as a teacher in a Methodist school on Whit Street in Dublin. At the suggestion that he should be appointed as a schoolmaster for the Hibernian school, Lamb asked, 'But I hope my being a Methodist would not disqualify me for holding a military or civil situation under government[?]' Clinton responded, 'Indeed, Mr. Lamb, I think that every man should choose the best religion he could, nevertheless, I think the Methodists carry religious matters too far'.[72] Lamb, not content to let the slight to his religion rest, replied, '[G]ive me leave to say, sir, that I know the Methodists are very loyal to his Majesty's person and government'.[73] Although his Methodism proved an impediment to being employed by the government, Lamb was able to secure status as an out-pensioner from the Chelsea Hospital as a result of the patronage he enjoyed, and the devotion he displayed as a Methodist loyalist.[74]

Thomas Cranfield, who enlisted in 39th Regiment in August of 1777, also recorded his story of religious conversion. Just before being deployed to Gibraltar, Cranfield entered a church on Sunday morning, being, 'prompted by curiosity… The word, under the guidance of the Holy Spirit was brought powerfully home to his mind, so that he became convinced of sin, and of the necessity of salvation through the Redeemer'. This conversion experience prompted him to learn to read, and he recorded that he had soon met, 'with very good friends, who give me good advice'.[75] During the American War of Independence, once again, there was little interest in the work of chaplains, but a small but significant minority of devout soldiers continued to minister to the spiritual needs of the British Army.

In April of 1775, John Wesley noted that his preaching resonated particularly with the officers of the Royal Highland Regiment. Officers had previously ordered soldiers to attend Wesley's sermons in April of 1778. In August of 1782, while preaching

---

71 NAM, 2010-11-16, Roger Lamb's Scrapbook, p.144.
72 NAM, 2010-11-16, Roger Lamb's Scrapbook, p.114.
73 NAM, 2010-11-16, Roger Lamb's Scrapbook, p.128.
74 NAM, 2010-11-16, Roger Lamb's Scrapbook, p.134.
75 Richard Cranfield, *The Useful Christian; a Memoir of Thomas Cranfield* (Religious Tract Society: London, 1844), p.12.

in Plymouth, John Wesley was surprised when: 'A little before I concluded, the Commanding Officer came into the Square with his regiment; but he immediately stopped the drums, and drew up all his men in order on the high side of the Square. They were all still as night; nor did any of them stir, till I had pronounced the blessing'.[76] This points to the idea that not only did Methodism survive in the ranks, and as the century continued, was increasingly endorsed by officers.

Methodism would stay with the British Army off and on the battlefield into the Napoleonic era.[77] Soldiers continued to benefit from many of the same factors which had facilitated its rise in the first place: the most important being officer's confusion about how to react to the growth of Methodism. The most famous British Army officer from this era, Arthur Wellesley, the Duke of Wellington, originally shared John Wesley's last name, but was no lover of the Methodist movement. In 1811, he wrote to the Adjutant-General, Sir Harry Calvert, 'Methodism is spreading very fast in the army… the meeting of soldiers… to sing psalms or hear a sermon read by one of their comrades is, in the abstract, perfectly innocent'. However, he also hoped that a dedicated chaplain might convince these Methodists to abandon their meetings, or, 'prevent them from becoming mischievous'.[78] Other officers would yell and curse at Methodist soldiers, much as they did in the 1740s.[79] Methodism was neither officially sanctioned or repressed, and as a result continued to play a role in army life.

Commemorations of Methodist Soldiers

One of the Methodist soldiers, Sampson Staniforth, who survived the grim battles of the War of the Austrian Succession, lived a relatively old age. Upon his death, the *Methodist Magazine* published a poem, imaginatively describing Staniforth's experiences in both military and religious worlds:

> Sampson in youth–like the unbroken steed–
> With British soldiers, ranked in flaming red,
> To Flanders marched to meet the Gallic foe:–
> Twas there the youth first learned himself to know.
> Back to his native country he returns;
> A different flame now in his bosom burns.
> Discharged from Royal William's loyal band,
> Enlists in Jeslu's nober ranks to stand.
> No changeling he–firm in his Master's cause;
> A Bible-Christian, subject to its laws;

---

76   John Wesley, *The Works of the Rev. John Wesley in Ten Volumes* (New York: J.J. Harper, 1826), Vol.IV p.98.
77   Snape, *Religion and the Redcoat*, pp.138-150.
78   Antony Brett James, *Wellington at War: a Selection of His Wartime Letters* (Vancouver: Simon Fraser University, 1989), pp.213-214.
79   Snape, *Religion and the Redcoat*, p.150.

A soldier, husband, Christian, man of worth,
Such died the venerable Staniforth.[80]

Published in the last decade eighteenth century, the poem demonstrates a particular type of commemorative culture, one which valued soldiers who were both martial and religious. The list of Staniforth's accomplishments is particularly important. According to the poet, he was a 'soldier, husband, Christian, man of worth'. In addition to providing a convenient rhyme, the list connects many portions of Staniforth's identity: military, local and familial, religious, and social values are all bound up in the description of Staniforth's legacy. The fact that many of the early stories of the Methodist soldier-preachers were published in the 1780s and 1790s gives us a sense that Methodism was growing in strength in Britain as a whole, and that it was becoming easier for soldiers to mesh religious and martial identities. Despite the words of 'Jack Careless', divinity and slaughter were increasingly discussed by the same men in the eighteenth century.

Methodists used a confused official response to their religious message to their advantage in the battle for the soul of the British Army. The lack of official repression (as well as small signs of approval from some officers) allowed Methodism to survive in the army. As Methodist soldiers went to battle, they displayed fearlessness which they believed would win new converts to their faith. For them, battle became an elevated realm where God's judgment could be instantly dispensed, and they could demonstrate their devotion to God. Tales of this battlefield courage were used by Methodist preachers like John Wesley to further the spread of Methodism away from the battlefield. Far from being a phenomenon local to the War of the Austrian Succession, Methodism continued to play a role in army life from the end of the War of the Austrian Succession into the Napoleonic era.

Bibliography

Archival Primary Sources
National Army Museum, London (NAM)
    2010-11-16 Roger Lamb's Scrapbook
Society of the Cincinnati Library, Washington DC (SCL)
    MSS L2017F30, HRH the Duke of Cumberland's Orderly Book for April to October 1745

Published Primary Sources
Ancell, Samuel, *A Circumstantial Journal of the Long and Tedious Blockade and Siege of Gibraltar from the Twelfth of September, 1779, to the Third Day of February, 1783. ... In a Series of Letters from the Author to His Brother* (Liverpool: J. Schofield, 1785).
Anonymous, *The Arminian Magazine* (London: J. Fry & Co, 1778).

---

80 *Methodist Magazine*, 1799, p.608.

Telford, John, *Wesley's Veterans: Lives of Early Methodist Preachers*. Vols. 1-7 (Salem, OH: Schmul Publishers, 1912).

Anonymous, *The Report of the Proceedings and Opinion of the Board of General Officers: on Their Examination into the Conduct, Behaviour and Proceedings of Lieutenant-General Sir John Cope, Knight of the Bath, Colonel Peregine Lascelles, and Brigadier-General Thomas Fowke, from the Time of the Breaking out of the Rebellion in North-Britain in the Year 1745, till the Action at Preston-Pans Inclusive* (London: Printed for W. Webb, 1749).

Cranfield, Richard, *The Useful Christian; a Memoir of Thomas Cranfield* (London: Religious Tract Society, 1844).

Doddridge, Philip, *Some Remarkable Passages: in the Life of the Honourable Col. James Gardiner: WHO Was Slain At the Battle of Preston-Pans, September 21, 1745, With an Appendix Relating to the Ancient Family of the Munro's of Fowlis* (Edinburgh: Printed for G. Hamilton and J. Balfour, 1747).

Frankland-Russell-Astley Rosalind Alicia, John Cutts, Charles Russell, John Croke, and S.C. Lomas, *Report on the Manuscripts of Mrs. Franklin-Russell-Astley, of Chequers Court, Bucks* (London: Historical Manuscripts Commission, 1900).

Mercoyrol, Jacques de, *Campagnes De Jacques De Mercoyrol De Beaulieu*, Edited by Auguste Le Sourd and Vogüe Charles Jean Melchior, (Paris: Renouard, , 1915).

Sidney, Edwin, and Samuel Walker, *The Life, Ministry, and Selections from the Remains of the Rev. Samuel Walker* (London: Bladwin and Cradock, 1838).

Telford, John, *Wesley's Veterans: Lives of Early Methodist Preachers*. Vol. 7. 7 vols (Salem, OH: Schmul Publishers, 1912).

Wesley, Charles, *The Journal of the Rev. Charles Wesley, M.A. ... To Which Are Appended Selections from His Correspondence and Poetry*. Edited by Thomas Jackson (London: Methodist Press, 1849).

Wesley, John, *The Journal of the Rev. John Wesley, A.M.*. Edited by Thomas Jackson (London: Wesleyan Conference Office, 1865).

Wesley, John, *The Works of the Reverend John Wesley, A.M.* Edited by John Emory (London: Methodist Book Concern, 1839).

Published Secondary Sources

Abraham, William J., and James E. Kirby, *The Oxford Handbook of Methodist Studies* (Oxford: Oxford University Press, 2009).

Berkovich, Ilya, *Motivation in War: the Experience of Common Soldiers in Old-Regime Europe* (Cambridge, United Kingdom: Cambridge University Press, 2017).

Bonomi, Patricia U., *Under the Cope of Heaven* (New York: Oxford University Press, 1986).

Browning, Reed, *The War of the Austrian Succession* (New York, NY: St. Martin's Griffin, 1993).

Butler, Jon, *Awash in a Sea of Faith* (London: Harvard University Press, 1990).

Collins, Kenneth J., *A Wesley Bibliography* (Wilmore, KY: First Fruits Press, 2017).

Cormack, Andrew Edward, *'These Meritorious Objects of the Royal Bounty': the Chelsea Out-Pensioners in the Early Eighteenth Century* (Great Britain: Published by the Author, 2017).

Englund, Peter, *The Battle That Shook Europe: Poltava and the Birth of the Russian Empire* (London: I.B. Tauris, 2013).
Harari, Y., *Ultimate Experience: Battlefield Revelations and the Making of Modern War Culture, 1450-2000* (New York: Palgrave Macmillan, 2014).
Hempton, David, *Methodism and Politics in British Society: 1750-1850* (London: Routledge, 1984).
Houlding, J.A., *Fit for Service: the Training of the British Army, 1715-1795* (Oxford: Oxford University Press, 1981).
Landa, Manuel De, *War in the Age of Intelligent Machines* (New York: MIT Press, 1991).
Langford, Paul, *Polite and Commercial People: England,1727-83* (Oxford: Oxford University Press, 1989).
Lynn, John A., *The Bayonets of the Republic: Motivation and Tactics in the Army of Revolutionary France, 1791-94* (Urbana: University of Illinois Press, 1984).
Phillips, Jason, *Diehard Rebels: the Confederate Culture of Invincibility* (Athens: University of Georgia Press, 2010).
Phillips, Jason, "Battling Stereotypes: A Taxonomy of Common Soldiers in Civil War History." *History Compass* 6, no. 6 (2008), pp.1407–25.
Porter, Roy, *English Society in the Eighteenth Century* (London: Allen Lane, 1982).
Snape, Michael F., *The Redcoat and Religion* (London: Routledge, 2008).
Spring, Matthew H., *With Zeal and with Bayonets Only: the British Army on Campaign in North America, 1775-1783* (Norman: University of Oklahoma Press, 2008).
Thompson, Edward P., *The Making of the English Working Class* (London: Victor Gollancz Ltd, 1963).
Wilson, Peter H., *A Companion to Eighteenth-Century Europe* (Chichester, West Sussex, UK: Wiley-Blackwell, 2014).

5

The Role of the Army in Suppressing the Gordon Riots, 2–9 June 1780

Brendan Morrissey[1]

Introduction

In the space of just 24 hours beginning at about 7:00pm on Wednesday 7 June 1780, British troops in London – Regular, Militia and Volunteer – acting on a General Order from the King, issued through the Privy Council, killed more people than in the entire 38 years (August 1969 to July 2007) of Operation Banner during the Troubles in Northern Ireland – and quite possibly more than twice as many.[2] Yet, whilst the Troubles and the relatively low-key Peterloo Massacre of 1819 have attracted plenty of coverage, the anti-Catholic Gordon Riots – undoubtedly the most serious civil disturbance in England in what was a politically turbulent century – are virtually unknown to modern generations of the British public. This chapter will consider the legal position of the Army in dealing with riots, how its command structure – both civilian and military – helped or hindered that role, and the tactics it used to suppress the mobs that operated on the streets of London during that violent week in 1780.

---

1   The author would like to express his thanks to Dr J.A. Houlding and Professor Gregory Urwin for their assistance in tracking down and supplying information from the various Army Lists.
2   The actual number of people shot by the British Army in Northern Ireland between 1969 and 1999 was 307 (see 'Sutton Index of Deaths' at < https://cain.ulster.ac.uk/sutton/>, viewed 18 September 2020). The 'official' number of dead from military action in the Gordon Riots is usually given as 285 (Anthony Babington, *Military intervention in Britain: from the Gordon riots to the Gibraltar Incident* (New York: Routledge, 1990), p.27), however, this takes no account of the large numbers of dead bodies known to have been carried away by the rioters, or observed floating in the Thames and either deposited downriver, or taken out to sea by the currents. Contemporary observers, such as N. W. Wraxall, Historical Memoirs of My Own Time (Philadelphia: Carey, Lea, and Blanchard, 1837), estimated over 700, which would equate to about 0.1% of London's population at that time.

Timeline of the Riots

Other than veterans who have served in Northern Ireland during the heyday of the Troubles, it is extremely difficult for most of us to imagine the full fury of an eighteenth-century mob, and we can only rely on the less lurid or biased contemporary accounts of the Gordon Riots to educate us. At the time, they were described as the worst disaster to befall London since the Great Fire of 1666. Equally, it is hard to understand the impact that the riots had abroad, with many politicians and commentators across Europe predicting the end of Britain's constitutional monarchy and all manner of other dire consequences. Thus, it is not surprising that these riots led – slowly, but inexorably – to greater reform in policing than any other single event in this period. The timeline of the riots can be summarised as follows:

- Friday, 2 June – March from St George's Fields to Parliament to hand in a petition, led to attacks on members of both Houses. Crowds dispersed by the Foot Guards and 16th Light Dragoons, but attacks on Catholic chapels and other property followed.
- Saturday, 3 June – Day of relative calm; Magistrates dispersed mob in Moorfields without a need to call for troops.
- Sunday, 4 June – Further riots in Moorfields; troops arrived, but were not allowed to act.
- Monday, 5 June – More riots across London.
- Tuesday, 6 June – Rioting increased still further; troops were deployed to protect Parliament and the homes of the wealthiest citizens; Newgate Prison was 'liberated' and burned.
- Wednesday, 7 June ('Black Wednesday') – Widespread rioting and arson; all other prisons in London were 'opened' and destroyed; bridge tollgates and watch-houses were attacked. Attempts to storm the Bank of England and the Navy Pay Office, and rumours of other intended targets (including the release of the inmates of Bedlam and the lions from The Tower of London menagerie), led to the Proclamation by the King and the General Order for troops to act without the presence or orders of Magistrates.
- Thursday, 8 June – Rioting subsided, with troops regaining control everywhere.
- Friday, 9 June – Start of complaints that there were too many troops on the streets.

In just five days, the situation had deteriorated from one in which detachments of the Foot Guards and 16th (Queen's) Light Dragoons had, without any resort to violence, managed to eject a boisterous mob from the Houses of Parliament after they began attacking members of both Houses, to wholesale bloodshed.

Civil Disturbance in Eighteenth-Century England

Going into the final quarter of the eighteenth century, the politicians and public of Great Britain and Ireland were still decades away from accepting the idea of the type of non-military police force that we take for granted today. Whilst it was true that there were parish constables and urban night watchmen who performed some policing duties, their powers were limited and – broadly speaking – not much greater than those of the ordinary citizen under the Common Law. As a consequence, the more robust forms of law enforcement still fell to the Army; unfortunately, such enforcement was entirely reliant on the political will (and, more often, the personal courage) of a magistrate to not only request the presence of soldiers, but also, when necessary, to command them to act.

The severity of the Gordon Riots, and their violent outcome, resulted in politicians becoming more amenable to creating a permanent police force, and also to reviewing the law regarding riot and the response of the authorities. In particular, there was a move to clarify the legal misconceptions held by many elements of society, as to when, and how, lethal force could be used, and who could order it.

A series of public disorders throughout the eighteenth century – but particularly in the middle third of the period – saw the Army repeatedly called in to quell civil unrest, despite all the legal and social inhibitions mitigating against such interventions. One very conservative estimate has over 160 major riots occurring between 1740 and 1780 in England alone; indeed, it was said that 'no nation rioted more easily or more savagely than England'.[3] Riot was seen as part and parcel of the fabric of English society, and such behaviour was regarded by many, across all social classes, as an Englishman's right, and even – in extreme cases – a legal duty. The concept of inalienable rights – which had spearheaded the initial claims of the American Colonists and their supporters in Great Britain and Ireland – had, throughout the eighteenth century, seen 'mob rule' acquire a tacit acceptance as a legitimate tactic of the dispossessed, or the wronged. During the Gordon Riots, Charles James Fox declared he would 'much rather be governed by a mob than a standing army'[4] – a staggering piece of hypocrisy for a man whose party later accused the government of being unprepared to deal with the riots.

The recent film about the Peterloo Massacre has suggested that the approach of both State and Army were invariably heavy handed and brutal in suppressing even the mildest of public protests. However, close examination of even the extreme example of the Gordon Riots and how they were dealt with, suggests that this was far from the case. Not only was the killing of so many rioters very much the exception rather than the rule, but the leniency shown to the mob in the early days of the riots was largely responsible for forcing the Government into such a response. Nor should it be forgotten that the Gordon Riots were exceptional in that they arose, not from a reduction in the quality of life of the masses, but from an attempt by the Government to right an injustice against a minority; the only other example of such

---

3   J.H. Plumb, *The First Four Georges* (London: B T Batsford, 1956) – quoted by J. Sharp, *A Fiery & Furious People: A History of Violence in England* (London: Random House Books, 2016), p.345.
4   E.P. Thompson, *The Making of the English Working Class* (London: Pelican Books, 1968), p.72.

a response from the public was the London riots of 1753 against the naturalisation of Jews.

The Law of Riot

In 1714, Parliament had passed the Riot Act, which included the following proclamation that was supposed to be read aloud by a Magistrate (also known as a Justice of the Peace) to any assembly threatening a breach of the peace:

> Our sovereign lord the King chargeth and commandeth all persons, being assembled, immediately to disperse themselves, and peaceably to depart to their habitations, or to their lawful business, upon the pains contained in the act made in the first year of King George, for preventing tumults and riotous assemblies. God save the King.[5]

This law made it a felony for 12 or more persons to remain in the area of a disturbance after one hour from the reading of the proclamation. Unfortunately, the poor drafting of the law led to various misinterpretations. One was that the proclamation had to be clearly heard by everyone present and, moreover, heard in its entirety. Neither act was easy to achieve in the midst of a riot, whilst the latter had also led to all sorts of legal debates – for example, as to whether a failure to include the phrase 'God save the King' negated the reading.

However, there were two much more important misconceptions, both of which gave rise to serious concerns in respect of the response of the authorities to the Gordon Riots. The first was the near-universal belief amongst Magistrates (and rioters) that once the proclamation had been read, the authorities were then obliged to wait one hour before they could take any further action, and that – in the minds of the rioters at least – during that hour, the mob had *carte blanche* to act at will. The other was that the troops were not allowed to open fire, or take any other potentially lethal action against a mob, until after the Riot Act had been read *and* the Magistrate himself had ordered them to so act. The former misconception was specifically addressed by the Lord Chief Justice, Lord Mansfield, in subsequent debates in Parliament, in which he stated that the Act merely created a new crime of being part of a group of 12 or more persons associating, in public, in the vicinity of a disturbance after the proclamation had been read. What it did not do, he asserted clearly, was to vary the existing Common Law that acts of felonious violence within that time, allowed the Magistrate to act against those responsible.[6] In any case, with respect to the events of June 1780, these circumstances had been specifically circumvented by the General Order issued by the Privy Council and signed by the King, as will be discussed below.

---

5   1 Geo I, Stat.2, Ch.5 – the act is often cited as 'The Riot Act, 1715' as it came into effect from August of that year; however, it was enacted in 1714.
6   W. Cobbett (ed.) *Cobbett's Parliamentary History of England* (London: Private, later Hansard, 1803), Vol. XXI, pp.694-698.

The Response of Government to Civil Disturbance

In the vast majority of cases, the strategy in dealing with any civil disturbance was straightforward. Complaints from householders to the local magistrate were passed on to the relevant secretary of state in London. The secretary of state would then forward this intelligence to the War Office (Horse Guards), with his own recommendations and approvals. From there, the Secretary at War would send an urgent letter to the commander of the nearest military unit, ordering him to march to the locality of the disturbances and assist the civil power. Unfortunately, even in peacetime, the over-all response time of this process was far from rapid, given the speed of eighteenth century communication, the paucity of troops in England and Wales (Scotland and Ireland were well garrisoned), the state of the roads, and – a factor commonly overlooked by social historians – the availability of appropriate quarters *en route* in which to house the troops, if the march was to take more than a single day. A response could be delayed even further, if not prevented entirely, by the weather, the size and duration of the disturbances, and by the personality (or lack thereof) of the relevant public officials at either end of the response system.

One plus, however, was that the eighteenth century had seen the creation of turnpike trusts, which had gradually taken over the upkeep of major roads into the main cities and towns. For good or evil, all 13 major roads into London were controlled by them and by 1780 the Bath-London stagecoach took less than 24 hours to travel in either direction. However, most of these roads were still un-metalled outside urban areas, and a factor beyond the control of any official was that the same rains that might destroy harvests and cause unrest in rural areas, would also wash away roads, delaying any initial communication and the arrival of any official authorisation to act, further adding to the time it would take troops to respond. Depending on the exact location of a disturbance, it could take up to 10 days for complaints to reach London, be dealt with by the appropriate figures, and an order to move be in the hands of the commanding officer of the designated contingent.

The Legal Position of the Army

A magistrate, faced with civil disturbance, had the right to call upon any citizen to assist him in quelling disorder, often referred to as the *Posse Comitatus* – literally the power of the county – which had existed in the Common Law since the 9th century. This permitted the sheriff of a county to call every citizen to his assistance to catch a person who had committed a serious crime (felony), and fine and/or imprison anyone who did not comply. The provisions for *Posse Comitatus* were repealed by the Criminal Law Act 1967,[7] but a second subsection allowing a sheriff to take 'the power of the county' if he faced resistance while executing a writ and providing for the arrest of resisters, is still in force. In previous centuries, this had usually proved adequate in dealing with most forms of civil unrest and had evolved

---

7   UK Public General Acts, 1967, Ch.58.

into the 'hue and cry' which remained a Common Law procedure until the 1820s.[8] It is tempting to think that, as they were merely 'citizens in uniform', soldiers could also be co-opted into this process. However, popular (albeit erroneous) understanding of the law, and the political and social dislike of civilians for the Army, made this difficult, if not impossible, for purely practical reasons. Unlike in US law, there was never any written prohibition on using the regular armed forces in this way. Indeed, the development of the law had preceded the establishment of standing armed forces within the British Isles and Ireland, although militias had been used to enforce the *Posse* law during the English Civil War. On rare occasions earlier in the eighteenth century, individual Magistrates had appealed directly to a nearby Army unit for support, but, as the century wore on, this came to be regarded increasingly as a breach of protocol, and therefore unconstitutional – as were any movements of troops without orders from London.

The unpopularity of the Army amongst civilians during this period, though surprisingly often ameliorated by good relations between an individual unit and the local population of the area in which it was quartered, is so well known as to have become a cliché. Whilst only a few of the most extreme Whigs, on either side of the Atlantic, still seriously entertained the idea of disbanding the Army entirely at every outbreak of peace, it was still easy to find a sympathetic ear for any complaint centred on the necessity of billeting troops entirely on the public, especially outside of London. More worryingly, and in spite of the obvious distaste shown frequently by public officials for using the Army to control the mob, politicians such as Edmund Burke would typically portray both magistrates and soldiers as stern oppressors of public liberty. The City of London, in particular, was highly politicised and the reluctance (or even downright refusal) of City magistrates to employ the Army in crowd control was frequently remarked upon during public disturbances in previous decades, and not just during the Gordon Riots. Even under Tory governments and/or during a threat of invasion, any programme of barrack-building outside of Ireland and Scotland would have been strangled at birth inside Parliament. Thus, the only viable strategy for any Government was to attempt to predict civil disturbances and try to be as efficient as possible in quartering troops in and around areas likely to be the scene of such mass misbehaviour. Inevitably, however, the military training, discipline and cohesion of individual regiments suffered, as they spent so much of their time marching from one location to another (frequently arriving only after the disturbances had abated).

Innkeepers bore the brunt of quartering – in fact, the origin of the term 'public house' comes from the definition of which buildings could house troops, either in garrison or whilst on the march. The poor subsistence money they were paid (made worse by rampant inflation from the 1750s onwards), together with poor discipline and dubious recruitment practices, made any attempt to quarter troops in the same area for very long extremely unpopular with virtually all sections of the local

---

8   Enacted officially by the Statute of Westminster (1285) 13 Edw. I, Ch. 1 & 4, and repealed by (1827) 7 & 8 Geo. IV, Ch.27.

community.[9] As the eighteenth century wore on, it became quite common to see innkeepers haul down their signs whenever the prospect of quartering reared its ugly head. As mentioned above, the Army did not help its own cause: more serious issues of indiscipline, often involving the connivance of officers – occasionally up to and including general rank – led to fulsome and grovelling apologies being delivered to civilian authorities. Examples included an unapproved march through the City of London led by the Lord Mayor in person, through the rescue of a general from sheriffs, to the suppression of the 1768 St George's Fields riots in which an innocent man, uninvolved in the disturbances, was shot dead by troops. It is worth noting that all three incidents involved detachments of the King's own bodyguards, either the Foot Guards or the Household Cavalry. Worse still, such events attracted the interest of a burgeoning Fourth Estate, which discussed them in extensive and embarrassing detail – guaranteed to be lurid, if not always accurate.

The Secretary at War

Since 1768, there had been four Secretaries of State, whose portfolios included responsibility for the deployment and political direction of troops in wartime, although it is worth noting that such matters were not a primary task for any one of them. The four posts were the Secretary of State for the Northern Department (Scotland, Northern England and relations with the Protestant states of Europe), the Secretary of State for the Southern Department (the rest of England, Wales, Ireland, and relations with all the Catholic and Muslim states of Europe); the Secretary of State for North America (the 13 Colonies, Canada and the Caribbean); and the First Lord of the Treasury – a post invariably held by the Prime Minister, who could, on financial grounds alone, overrule the other three. From 1782, and in some part due to the crises generated by the American War and the Gordon Riots, the three regional Secretaries were reorganised to cover Home, Foreign, and Colonial affairs, respectively.

However, the most important civilian in the context of the day-to-day running of the Army was the Secretary at War. Originally the military secretary to the commander-in-chief in the field, by the mid-1700s the post had become the embodiment of Parliamentary control over the Army, especially in periods where there was no commander-in-chief in Great Britain. Responsible for routine administration, discipline and finance, the Secretary at War sat in the House of Commons and introduced the annual Army estimates. Since 1735, it had also been his duty – on pain of dismissal from office – to remove troops from places where elections were to be held. Whilst none of the relevant legislation specifically required this, a similar procedure was invariably undertaken when judges arrived to sit in Assizes. Again,

---

9   A prohibition against a standing Army in peacetime without the consent of Parliament, meant that all military law was codified and controlled by the annual Mutiny Acts, passed first in 1688, 1 Will. & Mar. Ch.5, and each year thereafter until 1879; the provisions included a ban on quartering troops in private residences, and payment for the quartering of troops was first included in the 1692 Act – 4 Will. & Mar. Ch.13.

although not required by law, for disciplinary reasons troops were invariably also removed from towns where fairs, circuses and horse-races were to take place.

Until 1778, the worst of these obstacles had been offset by the prescience and efficiency of the then Secretary at War, William Wildman Shute Barrington, 2nd Viscount Barrington.[10] As an Irish peer, Barrington did not sit in the British House of Lords and hence was available to become an MP, in which role he served for 38 years (1740-1778), during which time he was also Secretary at War for two periods, 1755-1761, and 1765-1778. Although nominally a Whig, he served in Tory governments and took a hard line against the rebelling American colonists; this and his links to the ill-fated John Burgoyne saw the eclipse of his political star. Understanding the nature of this part of his role almost perfectly, Barrington had kept his finger on the pulse of the nation when it came to civil disorder, and although even his system had encountered a major flaw (see below), he could always be relied upon to have regular troops close to problem areas at the right time. His successor was Charles Jenkinson (1729-1808), later Lord Hawkesbury and eventually 1st Earl of Liverpool.[11] A close confidant of the King and Secretary at War from 1778 to 1782, Jenkinson was far from incompetent, but did not have Barrington's sense of impending trouble: in May and June of 1780, the Gordon Riots caught the Government on the hop, the War Office having made no preparations or issued any movement orders prior to the riots, and Jenkinson away at his country retreat until 4 June.

The cumbersome process of magistrates applying to the Secretary of State for military aid, and then relying on that request to be passed to the Secretary at War, rather than personally asking for assistance from the nearest troops, meant that many riots simply went unpoliced. However, by the mid-1750s, applications straight to the Secretary at War – whilst ostensibly beyond protocol – became more common and the previous incumbent, Barrington, had used such applications as an opportunity to develop a more streamlined process. Officers were also given more flexible orders, in order to overcome any reluctance to respond to riots in a nearby area not specifically mentioned, despite obvious links between the different disturbances. They were also required to report on the nature of the disturbances and what actions they had taken, as a form of intelligence gathering and to promote best practice.

However, Barrington was also keen to keep military involvement in civil disorder to a minimum. In January 1766, he sent out secret orders to several regiments in well-known trouble spots to respond instantly to appeals from magistrates if rioting broke out. If the riots did not occur, these orders were to remain secret and they were not entered into letter books, preventing any scrutiny by Parliament. Unfortunately, the system did not work because he omitted to inform the magistrates, who were by now well-schooled in not applying directly to military officers.

---

10   History of Parliament Online: *BARRINGTON, William Wildman, 2nd Viscount Barrington (1717-1793) of Beckett, Berkshire,* at < https://www.historyofparliamentonline.org/volume/1754-1790/member/barrington-william-wildman-1717-93>, viewed 18 September 2020.
11   JENKINSON, Charles, first Earl of Liverpool, in S. Lee (ed.) *Dictionary of National Biography* (London: Smith, Elder & Co, 1892), Vol.29, pp.309-310.

As it was, the two principal Secretaries of State for the Northern (Viscount Stormont)[12] and Southern (the Earl of Hillsborough)[13] Departments, attempted – in Jenkinson's absence – to handle the matter in the traditional way. They passed information and encouragement to magistrates and left it up to them to request troops if they felt that the situation required it; at the same time, both secretaries told the War Office to have troops ready and directed the senior officer of the 3rd Foot Guards to prepare fast-response detachments from the force at Somerset House, the troops stationed at the Tiltyard and the Savoy being too far away to protect the Catholic chapels of foreign embassies if they were attacked. However, after 5 June, the two Secretaries ceased directing operations, and became, in effect, a glorified post box, passing intelligence to the Secretary at War (and later also the commander-in-chief) about the mobs and the future location of planned riots. When the commander-in-chief, Lord Amherst, was given unfettered control the following day, they joined the rest of the Cabinet in begging the King to step in and authorise a more robust process for dealing with those situations where magistrates could not, or would not, act.

In fairness to Jenkinson, there was no apprehension of danger (and certainly not of the potential disaster about to evolve) prior to 2 June, or for 2-3 days thereafter, and he only returned to London on the evening of 4 June. Whilst it is tempting to compare this with the far better state of readiness usually found under his predecessor, it is perhaps unfair to see this disturbance – and certainly the eventual extent of it – as being as predictable as food/tax riots, or trade/labour disputes. On the morning of 5 June, Jenkinson met with Lieutenant General Craig, the senior officer of the Foot Guards,[14] Major General the Marquis of Lothian, the senior officer of the Horse Guards and Gold Stick,[15] and Lieutenant General William Amherst, the Adjutant-General and younger brother of the commander-in-chief. They agreed to deploy four troops of the 16th Light Dragoons to Southwark and Lambeth, but as matters became more serious, the commander-in-chief himself took personal control of the military response at midnight on 5/6 June.

---

12 David Murray, Viscount Stormont and later 2nd Earl of Mansfield (1727-1796) was the last Secretary of State for the Northern Department, serving as such from 1779 to 1782; he inherited his earldom from his paternal uncle, William Murray (1705-1793), who was Lord Chief Justice from 1756 to 1788.
13 Wills Hill, Earl of Hillsborough (1718-1793) was the last Secretary of State for the Southern Department, serving from 1779 to 1782; he had previously been Secretary of State for the Colonies from 1768 to 1772 and had opposed any concessions to the American Colonists.
14 Francis Craig (DoB unknown-1811), joined the Coldstream Guards in 1742, and by 1773 was 1st Major, before transferring to the 1st Guards in 1775 as lieutenant colonel and deputy to HRH William, Duke of Gloucester, the regiment's colonel. He became a major general in 1775, a lieutenant general in 1777, and a general in 1793.
15 William John Kerr (1737-1815) joined the 11th Dragoons in 1754 and served in various cavalry regiments in England and Ireland before being made lieutenant & lieutenant colonel in the 2nd Troop, Horse Grenadiers, in 1771, and then Captain and Colonel of the 1st Troop of Horse Guards in 1777; as such, he was automatically appointed Gold Stick, or personal bodyguard to the Monarch, although he was later removed by the King for supporting the Prince of Wales in a dispute between the two. He became a major general in 1777, a lieutenant general in 1782, and a general in 1796.

It is also worth mentioning at this point that the role of the War Office itself, in responding to civil unrest, had also atrophied over this period, although neither magistrates nor public were aware of this. Much time was wasted in following the time-honoured process of applications to the civil authorities for military aid, which could then be passed on to the Secretary at War. However, Jenkinson's absence meant that there were no out-letters relating to the riots before 5 June, and from the next day, matters passed to the commander-in-chief, rendering the secretary at war no more than his military secretary. Other than sending a detachment of Chelsea Pensioners to defend Drummond's Bank, Jenkinson did nothing to counter the riots beyond arranging the march of regulars and Militia into the London area – most of whom only arrived once the riots had been contained. Nevertheless, Stormont wrote three letters to him on 4 June, ordering him to augment the detachments at the Tilt Yard and the Savoy (both used to store military supplies) from 5 June; to instruct the commander of the detachment at the Tower to be prepared to support magistrates; and to ensure that all of the Foot Guards were ready to march.[16]

The Commander-in-Chief and Adjutant-General

An important distinction between the Gordon Riots and other civil disturbances of the era preceding the introduction of a civilian police force was the unique personal involvement of the commander-in-chief. Legally, of course, the commander-in-chief was ultimately the King, but usually (and despite the exceptional personal interest of the early Hanoverian monarchs in improving the Army) there was a general in charge of overall administration. At the time of the Gordon Riots, the Commander-in-Chief was General Lord Amherst, and at his right hand was his younger brother, Lieutenant General William Amherst, the Adjutant-General. The duties of the latter role involved issuing orders to the Army, receiving monthly returns from the regiments, regulating officers' appointments and leave, overseeing military reviews and manoeuvres, and all disciplinary matters. Jeffrey Amherst (1717-1797) had joined the 1st Foot Guards in 1735 and saw action in Europe in both the War of the Austrian Succession and the Seven Years War, before taking command in North America in 1759. In 1772 he became Lieutenant-General of the Ordnance, was ennobled as Baron Amherst in 1776, and became General and Commander-in-Chief in the expectation of a French invasion in 1778. He had previously declined command in North America when the government rejected his plans to send 75,000 troops there. William Amherst (1732-1781) was commissioned into the 1st Foot Guards in 1755 and served in America during the Seven Years War in which he led the recapture of St John's in the final action of the war. He was appointed Adjutant-General in 1778, but died in office three years later.

Almost at once, Amherst senior received letters from Stormont and Hillsborough saying that magistrates needed a large body of cavalry to keep order, and detailing attacks on Catholic houses and chapels. At this stage, it seems to have dawned on

---

16 The National Archives (TNA), SP37/20, f.29, f.31 and f.33.

those in charge that the riots had moved on from the merely sectarian, to a plundering host on a larger scale than in human memory. Amherst immediately re-deployed the single troop of the 16th Light Dragoons stationed at Lambeth to north of the river, ordering them to call in at Whitehall for an update *en route*. Three other cavalry regiments – the 3rd Dragoon Guards at Colchester, the 3rd Dragoons at Petworth, and the 4th Dragoons at Canterbury – were ordered to march to London with all speed, whilst ensuring that they were capable of service once they arrived. However, despite all of these arrangements, rioting was even worse on 6 June, with attacks on Newgate Prison, the homes of Sir George Savile (who had introduced the Catholic Relief Bill), Sir John Fielding (a leading magistrate and founder of the Bow Street Runners in 1750), Lord Mansfield (the Lord Chief Justice), and the few magistrates who had made themselves conspicuous by doing their duty. Savile's house was saved by the arrival of a 150-strong detachment of the 3/1st Foot Guards, and Mansfield's by the 16th Light Dragoons and the Northumberland Militia, who formed a defensive ring around it. This last incident was one of the few actions leading to bloodshed prior to 7 June: initially, the 16th had charged the crowd and cut down three rioters, without fatalities, but had then been surrounded before being rescued by some Horse Grenadiers and a detachment of the 1st Foot Guards. The latter fired on the mob (killing seven and wounding several others) under orders from a magistrate who had first read the Riot Act.[17]

The Privy Council meeting of 6 June saw the King request a clarification of the law, which was duly given by the Attorney-General, overturning years of clouded and misguided interpretation, and led to the General Order. On the same day, the King had written:

> I highly approve of having ordered the 3d. Regt. Dragoon Guards, the 4 Troops of the 3d. Dragoons, and the 4th. Dragoons to come to the Capital for I am convinced till the Magistrates have ordered some Military Execution on the Rioters this Town will not be restored to Order…[18]

With more troops on the move, Amherst now had the numbers and from the evening of 7 June the power to use them. However, for much of 7 June troops still marched aimlessly around London, as there was no strategy for defeating the rioters, beyond opposing them wherever and whenever they appeared. The initiative still lay with the mob, which could choose its points of attack: these had now clearly expanded to include almost any foreign embassy or wealthy residence, not just Catholic ones. Commercial concerns (most especially distilleries), financial institutions, or anywhere where it was thought that large sums of money would be stored, and public utilities were also considered to be targets. Before the General Order took

---

17 TNA, WO34/103, f.311 – Lieutenant Howell, 16th Light Dragoons, WO34/103, f.270 – Cornet Hinde, and WO34/103, f.103 – Lieutenant Colonel Woodford, 1st Foot Guards. Note that certain Foot Guards officers had dual rank – for example, a captain would also rank as a lieutenant colonel in the Army; in such reports, the Army rank is generally used.

18 Kent Records Office, Amherst MSS (U.1360), 074/64; the author is obliged to Dr J.A. Houlding for alerting him to this document.

effect, the rioters managed to cause considerable amounts of damage, with critics of Amherst noting that he was concentrating troops in a few locations and leaving large areas unprotected – one fellow officer wrote that he thought it strange that Amherst had only 300 of his 12,000 men actually stationed in the City (in fact, the over all total was nearer 9,500 at that time, at least some of whom were recovering from forced marches, but the point is still a valid one).[19]

Unfortunately, the only reliable detailed numbers and dispositions we have date from 8 June, and there are many gaps in the reports from detachment commanders as to where they were, and in what strength, before that date. Amherst's plan appears to have been to station large numbers of troops in a few chosen locations where there was a particular threat, and, from those forces, to detach smaller groups to answer specific requests for help elsewhere. Yet, having created his reserve, Amherst appears to have been reluctant to actually use it, and the criticism of leaving the most vulnerable target, the City, unguarded is a well-founded one. Perhaps he thought that Lieutenant Colonel Thomas Twistleton at the Bank would be able to assist, but the latter felt his post was already under-manned and refused all requests for detachments. As a consequence, once the attacks on the Bank ceased, the mob turned its attentions to private houses in the Square Mile, where they were relatively unhindered. Only in and around Broad Street, where the Middlesex Militia drove the mob away, were they opposed. Throughout the day – and in subsequent days when called on to explain – both Amherst and Jenkinson, and the Government as a whole, pleaded that there had been too many requests and from such a large area that it had been impossible to respond to all of them in a timely fashion. However, the numbers of troops uncommitted throughout the day suggests that this was far from the case, given that the Northumberland Militia was successfully despatched to protect Mansfield's house at Kenwood,[20] and an MP recounted how, at noon, he had requested troops to protect the King's Bench Prison and the nearby brewery, but the troops did not arrive until 9:00 p.m. (in time to save the brewery!); in fact, local legend has it that a nearby publican actually sent for troops whilst delaying the rioters with free beer.

On the evening of 8 June, Twistleton reported to Amherst that the arrival of the various detachments at their appointed stations had established 'the utmost tranquility' across London.[21] The following morning, a threatening mob appeared, but the arrival of a body of troops soon dispersed them. Twistleton's daily reports made constant reference to regular patrols impressing the local citizenry, and also aided constables in rounding up suspected rioters and escaped prisoners: one group of Foot Guards captured 80 suspects, although only 59 appear to have been brought in, the rest being released. However, this last task was one that did not endear troops to the public, and there were newspaper reports of them 'chasing the populace'.[22]

---

19   Colonel (later Lieutenant General) the Hon. Charles Stuart to Lord Bute, quoted in E. Stuart Wortley, *A Prime Minister and His Son* (London: Murray, 1925), p.182. For troop movements and dispositions, see Appendix I.
20   *The Public Advertiser*, 7 June.
21   TNA, WO34/103, f.258 – Lieutenant Colonel Twistleton, 3rd Foot Guards.
22   *London Evening Post*, 8 June.

Whilst it is obvious that the homes of peers and MPs, and places of public importance, were priorities for defence; humbler premises received no help, and in most cases not even a reply. The failure seems to have been the result of a combination of factors – principally the lack of manpower within Amherst's own office to deal with all of the requests, and the inability of Amherst to deal with a problem that, to be fair, was of a size and nature of which neither he, nor anyone else around at the time, had any experience. One newspaper described Amherst as 'running about and wringing his hands with fear, not knowing what orders to give':[23] it is difficult to know how accurate this is, but it is perhaps unfair to be too critical of him given the unique nature of the situation. Suffice to say that, as in previous London riots in the 1760s, the system appeared to really start working only once the need for it had ceased.

The General Order

On the afternoon of Tuesday 6 June, the Privy Council met to discuss the seriousness of the situation on the streets of the capital. Well aware of the impossible situation that the troops were being placed in, the King, on receiving confirmation from the Attorney-General that troops could fire on a mob at their own discretion, and despite opposition from several Council members, agreed to release the following proclamation:

> By the KING.
> A PROCLAMATION.
> George R.
>
> WHEREAS a great Number of Disorderly Persons have assembled themselves together in a Riotous and Tumultuous Manner, and have been guilty of many Acts of Treason and Rebellion, having made an Assault on the Gaol of Newgate, set loose the Prisoners confined therein, and set fire to and destroyed the said Prison: And whereas Houses are now pulling down in several Parts of Our Cities of London and Westminster, and Liberties thereof, and Fires kindled for consuming the Materials and Furniture of the same, whereby it is become absolutely necessary to use the most effectual Means to quiet such Disturbances, to preserve the Lives and Properties of Individuals, and to restore the Peace of the Country: We therefore, taking the same into Our most serious Consideration, have thought fit, by and with the Advice of Our Privy Council, to issue this Our Royal Proclamation, hereby strictly charging and exhorting all Our loving Subjects to preserve the Peace, and to keep themselves, their Servants and Apprentices, quietly within their respective Dwellings, to the End that all well-disposed Persons may avoid those Mischiefs which the Continuance of such riotous

---

23 *The London Courant & Westminster Chronicle*, 10 June.

Proceedings may bring upon the Guilty: And as it is necessary, from the circumstances before-mentioned, to employ the Military Force, with which We are by Law entrusted for the immediate Suppression of such Rebellious and Traiterous [sic] Attempts, now making against the Peace and Dignity of Our Crown, and the Safety of the Lives and Properties of Our Subjects, We have therefore issued the most direct and effectual orders to all Our Officers, by an immediate Exertion of their utmost Force, to repress the same, of which all Persons are to take Notice.

Given at Our Court at St. James's, the Seventh Day of June, One thousand seven hundred and eighty, in the Twentieth Year of Our Reign.

God save the King.[24]

The Order was supported by the following instruction from the office of the Adjutant-General the following morning:

In obedience to an order from the King in Council the military to act without waiting for direction from the Civil Magistrates and to use force for dispersing the illegal and tumultuous assemblies of the people.[25]

It is worth noting that the tone of War Office communications changed noticeably from this point on, from one of maintaining the status quo of supporting the civil power and nothing more, to instructions to attack and disperse mobs. For the first time in the eighteenth century, troops had been given authorisation to act independently of a magistrate in suppression of civil disorder.

The Attitudes of the Rank-and-File

One problem that caused considerable concern at the time was how the rank-and-file viewed the riots and their perpetrators. Most troops – including the Foot Guards – were quartered on the public when not on guard duty, and thus lived alongside the mob and associated with them on a daily basis. However, the Gordon Riots brought an extra dimension, given that every soldier's enlistment oath required him to uphold and preserve the Protestant Succession. Only one diary of an ordinary soldier survives from the time, that of Sergeant (then Corporal) William Pell of the 1st Foot Guards, which exists only in manuscript form in the Grenadier Guards' archives. Sadly, it does not cast much light on the views of the men in the ranks, nor indeed on how the riots were handled. For example, Pell is not very informative in terms of how the General Order was discharged, as his detachment was charged with guarding what was quite possibly the only alcohol-producing establishment in the whole of London that was not attacked on the night of Black Wednesday – he even remarks on being able to catch up on some sleep! Nevertheless, the relevant section of the diary has been quoted in Appendix II, below.

---

24 TNA, WO34/103, f.100.
25 TNA, WO4/110, f.287.

However, it is interesting to note that, when push came to shove, the men gave their officers little or nothing to be concerned about in terms of doing their duty when ordered. One Guards officer, who was part of the garrison of the Bank, wrote:

> The dash with which the men went out last night, to rescue an house that the mob had attacked, was as apparent as the sulkiness they before went out with, knowing they were to be ill-used, and not to defend themselves; and after the first fire, they were all very cool; so cool as to fire single shots.[26]

This comment suggests that, by this stage at least, the men in the ranks had had enough of magistrates who were at best ineffectual, or at worst in collusion with the people trying to injure the soldiers.

The only exception the author has found to this is a report that on 23 June, three sergeants of the 3rd Foot Guards attended the rooms of a magistrate to hear him examine Private Thomas Hiddie (or Kiddie) of Lieutenant Colonel Stephens' company, accused that on 6 June he 'beat down the door and walls of Newgate Prison' and later did 'encourage others to go to the King's House and burn him in the middle of his furniture'. Sadly, there is no further documentary evidence of what happened to Hiddie/Kiddie, as there are no further notes in the letters file and the two Muster Rolls for the 3rd Foot Guards for 1780 are both missing. However, he was still serving in the same company in 1781, so quite possibly the charge was dismissed, but we shall never know for sure.[27]

For their part, the events of the evening of 7 June gave the rioters a nasty shock: having become used to the soldiers doing nothing, the response to the King's order was all the more devastating. On 9 June, Barrington wrote to Jenkinson, praising the conduct of the troops.[28]

Numbers & Dispositions

Even by the standards of the typical professional forces that abounded across Europe in the late eighteenth century, the British Army was tiny, as well as unpopular. This problem was exacerbated by the predilection to disband almost all units raised for a war once a peace had been achieved, thus losing large numbers of experienced men. The American War saw a massive increase in both manpower and numbers of units by 1780: three regiments of Foot Guards (seven battalions), 104 marching regiments of foot (110 battalions), four strong troops of Household Cavalry; and 30 regiments of line cavalry (more regiments of all types were formed in 1781-83). In March 1780, 'South Britain' (England and Wales) was garrisoned by 5,866 cavalry, 19,249 infantry, and 36,287 militia, distributed around the country.[29] Of these, 1,700 horse, 5,700 infantry and almost 6,000 militia were deployed in London during the

---

26 TNA, WO34/125 f.115 – Lieutenant Wilmot, 3rd Foot Guards.
27 TNA, WO34/103, f.162 and WO12/1784 (1779), 1785 (1781) and 1786 (1782).
28 British Museum, Liverpool MSS, Add. MSS 38214, 9 June 1780.
29 P. Mackesy *War for America* (London: Bison Books, 1993) – Appendices.

Gordon Riots, although about one third of the foot units did not arrive until after 'Black Wednesday'.[30]

Whilst the Duke of Cumberland had introduced a rotation policy of sorts for overseas garrisons in the 1750s, its benefits were reduced in wartime as units recently serving abroad would have been drafted before returning to Europe, further weakening them. Three units that were brought into London to quell the riots – the 16th Light Dragoons and the 18th and 52nd Foot – had all been drafted and sent home from North America. Two of those regiments had been sent home at the end of 1778, the third (18th Foot) at the end of 1775; consequently, the ranks of the 16th Light Dragoons and 52nd Foot would have been full of men with one year's service or less.

The Gordon Riots saw detachments from all seven battalions of the Foot Guards and all four troops of Horse Guards and Horse Grenadier Guards, deployed onto the streets of London. The seven battalions of Foot Guards at this time numbered just over 3,700, even allowing for the large detachment in America and 150 or so guarding the King and Queen. However, only just over 1,500 were committed to posts in affected areas, and it is frequently overlooked that many of the Household troops were quartered 'off base' in various establishments in and around London.[31]

Yet even this number still required the further presence of nine more regular regiments of horse and foot. These comprised the 3rd Dragoon Guards, 3rd, 4th and 11th Dragoons, 16th Light Dragoons, and the 2/1st, 2nd, 18th and 52nd Foot: however, the 18th only entered the capital the day after the rioting had subsided, and needed a few days to recover from its forced march from Woburn, whilst only half of the 52nd was present. Also employed were 10 Militia regiments, all single-battalion units like most of the line infantry of that time. The Buckinghamshire, North Hampshire, South Hampshire, Northamptonshire, Northumberland, and 2nd West Yorkshire Militia were present throughout the Riots; the Cambridgeshire, Hertfordshire, and Westminster (Middlesex) Militia were only ordered into London on or after 8 June; the Staffordshire Militia some time thereafter.

A large number of troops were stationed at the Bank (this had grown to 534 men by 8 June), a similar number at the Tower, and a further 100 in St Paul's churchyard. Outside the City, there were detachments at Burlington Gardens (150 men), the Tiltyard (61) and the Savoy (52), whilst security details at the homes of several prominent politicians, important mills at Bromley, the Sardinian Embassy and The Admiralty accounted for another 226. The bulk of the remainder was established in the camp set up in St James' Park, along with the 550 men of the four cavalry troops of the Horse Guards and Horse Grenadier Guards.[32]

---

30 TNA, WO34/103, f.203 for the units and WO34/189, f.80 for approximate strengths as at 1 July.
31 See Appendix II for Corporal Pell's 'walking tour' of London carrying orders to the 'outliers' to report for duty at Horse Guards.
32 A full list of detachments and locations, as at 8 June, is given in Appendix I.

Tactics

Apart from an embryonic reporting process started by Barrington for his own education back in 1757, the Gordon Riots were unique in that Amherst – probably aware of the attacks of Burke and other politicians after the Wilkes Riots of 1768-1769 – had deliberately ordered, from the start, that any officer answering a call for troops or otherwise acting against the mobs, submit a report of what had been done and what had happened. Interestingly, there is no written record of that order to file a report, but many of the reports themselves refer to it. Given the nature of eighteenth century politics and the unpopularity of the Army, one can hardly blame Amherst for not wishing to be surprised by a politician second-guessing him. It was perhaps ironic that the subsequent criticisms by politicians, when they eventually did come, were related not to the severity of the military response to the riots, but to the infringing of the 'ancient rights' of the inhabitants of the City (particularly by rejecting their offers to assist in their own defence), and in the troops subsequently disarming many quasi-military groups after the riots.

Tactically, it is difficult to know exactly how troops dealt with rioters, as it is rare for such matters to be discussed in reports of these actions – whether by participants or observers. Certainly, none of the letters in the WO34 cartons at The National Archives give much, or indeed any, indication of how troops formed up preparatory to confronting rioters. Nor do they detail any special tactics that might have been employed, and it is tempting to merely assume that the Army used the same formations and manoeuvres as it did on conventional battlefields. However, for obvious reasons, such an approach could not always be applied and did not always work, even when it was. Training was outside the brief of the Secretary at War, who was neither a lawyer, nor a soldier; unfortunately, nor does it appear to have been considered by those politicians or soldiers whose job it properly was.

The most common – and reasonably effective – 'tactic' used throughout the eighteenth century was simple intimidation. While it was equally possible that the appearance of red coats might provoke the mob, there were also innumerable occasions when the presence of troops in formed bodies was enough to persuade a crowd to behave itself. Sometimes, even a weak force could act as a steadying influence, or at least deter worse excesses than a mob was already committing. However, this tactic could very quickly be undermined – as indeed it was during the Gordon Riots – by the simple refusal of the magistrate(s) on the spot to read the Riot Act, thus rendering the troops impotent, given that a mob could be reasonably certain that the troops would not act of their own volition. In such circumstances, the presence of the troops became a danger primarily to themselves as rioters became more daring in their behaviour.

A key factor in these situations was the personality of the commanding officer of the troops on the spot, who had to demonstrate appropriate measures of forcefulness, understanding, calm or resolution to proceed with his duty – however unpleasant the outcome might be. Equally, numerous incidents disproved the idea that the troops were there simply to crush the populace on behalf of a repressive

Establishment.³³ In 1780, 150 men of the 3/1st Foot Guards frightened away a destructive mob from Sir George Savile's house,³⁴ whilst light dragoons and Militia surrounded Lord Mansfield's house at Kenwood.³⁵ In a subsequent incident in Norwich, later that month, an anti-Catholic mob was deterred from rioting by the presence of dragoons in the city.

Another tactic, relating to the protection of premises, was to form a purely defensive ring around them. Ideally, this would (and the War Office went to great lengths to ensure that it did as often as possible) involve the presence of a magistrate; however, it could also require the troops to be unattended, which could obviously leave them in a vulnerable position and exposed to the mob's fury. This could make the soldiers themselves exceedingly sulky as the crowd took liberties with them and the premises they were supposed to be protecting. A detachment of the Coldstream Guards, forming a ring around a bonfire in Moorfields on 4 June, had to stand and watch (the magistrate remaining inactive) as rioters tossed furniture and other items over the soldiers' heads onto the blaze, although the subsequent arrival of more troops permitted the formation of a larger cordon, which ended this behaviour so that a fire engine was later able to douse the fire.³⁶ However, another detachment was unable to protect a Catholic chapel, as the attending magistrate did not (or would not) read the Riot Act until after it had been set on fire; the mob dispersed after the reading, but most likely this was in response to the arrival of cavalry.³⁷ Other officers reported a failure to curb the mob's predilection for cutting the hoses of fire engines.³⁸ Ultimately, the deterrent value of any defensive force invariably departed the moment it was withdrawn, resulting in the need to establish permanent guards on vulnerable edifices, such as the Savoy, the Haymarket Theatre, or regular detachments to protect mobile assets, such as the monthly guard assigned to the Royal Navy Pay Office in Broad Street, to guard the transport of money to Portsmouth. However, the most important of these was the Bank of England Piquet, first posted on 6 June, following the burning of Newgate Prison; by 8 June, it had grown to 534 men.

The final option was offensive deployment of troops, in which any action could be either limited (the vast majority of cases), or all-out up to and including firing on the crowd. The former ranged from pushing and shoving, in which one might imagine that the superior discipline and formational solidarity of the soldiers might be considered to give them some little advantage over the mob, through various levels of fisticuffs, to the more determined use of clubbed muskets and flats of swords. As matters became more violent, whilst still falling short of lethal force, a lack of military discipline, greater anonymity, and access to throwable objects would tend to favour the rioters. In 1780, prior to the issuing of the General Order, a few

---

33 TNA, WO34/104 f.8 – Captain Gardner, 16th Light Dragoons.
34 TNA, WO34/103, f.345 – Lieutenant Colonel Lake, 1st Foot Guards.
35 TNA, WO34/103, f.85 – Lieutenant Bygrave, 16th Light Dragoons.
36 TNA, WO34/103, f.14 – Ensign Gascoyne and WO34/103, f.20 – Lieutenant Thornton, both Coldstream Guards.
37 TNA, WO34/103, f.24 – Lieutenant Calvert, Coldstream Guards.
38 TNA, WO34/103, f.18 – Lieutenant Fanshawe, 1st Foot Guards.

minor successes were achieved with this level of violence. One enterprising officer surrounded and detained a small mob in a market by blocking all the exit routes, dividing his force in half, and approaching them from two directions.[39] Another chased a similar group from Leicester Fields to Golden Square, caught them and confiscated their iron bars, cudgels and flags, at which they dispersed.[40] A party of light dragoons, sent to defend Lord Mansfield's house in Bloomsbury Square and acting without orders, charged three times through the mob trying to attack the building: however, the mob appears to have just parted on each occasion and the only casualty was a trooper whose horse fell and broke his arm.[41]

Ultimate force was generally seen by all concerned – and certainly by officers on the spot – as the last resort and only to be contemplated when all other forms of restraint had been tried and had clearly failed. That said, it is surprising how often during the eighteenth century that lethal force was employed by troops, whether in suppressing riots or countering smuggling gangs. Unsurprisingly there were rare instances where individual soldiers, sorely tried by missiles from the crowd (and even bullets on a few occasions), fired without orders, but, equally, it was not unknown for soldiers to be the first fatalities in such clashes. However, in such circumstances, political posturing by MPs eager to score a cheap point, and weak magistrates, could be as much to blame as the actions of the rioters themselves, as proved to be the case in the early days of the Gordon Riots. This was recognised quickly by the Government and the Secretaries of State wrote to magistrates, both individually and collectively, emphasising the importance of calling for troops, and using them, when public order and their own authority was being insulted.

The Bloomsbury Square mob outside Lord Mansfield's house, having withstood the charges of the light dragoons, were subsequently confronted by a detachment of the 3rd Foot Guards, who were pelted with stones and other rubbish, before another Foot Guards contingent and some men of the Horse Grenadier Guards arrived, accompanied by a magistrate, who read the Riot Act. The crowd continued to hurl missiles, until eventually they provoked a response by rescuing some men held by constables in a nearby house. At the first order to the troops to open fire, only a few men obeyed, and the crowd maintained its posture for a few minutes before withdrawing, the few casualties suggesting that the troops had, with or without orders, deliberately fired high (that this was a common occurrence can be deduced from the number of innocent bystanders and spectators killed whilst on the periphery of eighteenth-century riots).[42] The incident illustrates that the troops, including their officers, displayed extreme levels of humanity in dealing with rioters; officers commanding detachments would frequently put themselves at risk by advancing alone to address the mob and persuade them to disperse, whilst others ordered their men to fire high.

It is tempting to assume – as many magistrates and other civilian dignitaries did at the time – that mounted troops were the best antidote to rioting civilians.

---

39   TNA, WO34/103, f.18 - Lieutenant Fanshawe, 1st Foot Guards.
40   TNA, WO34/103, f.360 – Captain Bertie, 1st Foot Guards.
41   TNA, WO34/103, f.270 – Cornet Hinde, 16th Light Dragoons.
42   TNA, WO34/103, f.103 – Lieutenant Colonel Woodford, 1st Foot Guards.

However, there were several reasons why this was not always the case. On a number of occasions during the Gordon Riots, cavalry pursuing crowds of rioters could end up like a dog chasing cars, unsure what to do when it actually caught one.

It is certainly true that cavalry could arrive more quickly than infantry, and this in itself could be a massive deterrence to disorder; as a consequence, cavalry detachments were frequently used to patrol the streets of London during the 1780 disturbances, particularly during daylight. Equally, a mob in a rural location, or a large open area of ground in a town or city, could be surrounded and broken up, then dispersed. However, if a mob was densely packed, armed, and determined (not least by their previous experiences of troops refusing to act), it could present a similar obstacle to formed cavalry as an infantry square. Most London streets were not wide, side-streets still less so, and sections of the mob could withdraw into the latter, making it look as though they had dispersed, thus drawing the cavalry onto the main body. Throwing firebrands at the horses was a popular tactic, which could panic the animals, causing the riders to lose control. There were occasions when horse alone could achieve a result – in one of the few incidents to occur after the night of 'Black Wednesday' a half-troop of Horse Guards was trotting down Fleet Street to relieve a similar detachment that had helped defend the Bank the previous night, when it was attacked by a mob. Unable to load the muskets that had only just been issued to them, they defended themselves with fixed bayonets, and whilst the officer in charge and three men were injured, around 20 rioters were killed outright and another 35 carted off to hospital, many of whom later succumbed to their injuries.[43]

The end result, as several commanders on the ground quickly worked out on 7 June, was that the most effective method of dealing with mobs was, as with a conventional enemy, to combine cavalry with infantry. For example, Lieutenant General Charles Rainsford, commander of the camp in Hyde Park, sent out cavalry escorts with all detachments deployed to counter mobs. Rainsford had started his career in the cavalry before transferring to the Foot Guards and had commanded troops at the King's Bench prison in Southwark during the 1768 riots. In his defence of The Bank, Twistleton employed not only infantry inside the building, but a troop of Horse Guards and, apparently, also a platoon of light infantry, in neighbouring side streets in order to complete the rout of any assaults by the mob.

The Use of Artillery

The Gordon Riots appears to have excited a discussion that had not occurred previously in the eighteenth century, with regard to crowd control in Great Britain and Ireland – namely, the employment of artillery against mobs. The suppression of civilian uprisings in other nations during the 18th and 19th centuries suggests that the use of this level of force was counter-productive to a much greater extent than the use of other forms of lethal force, and aside from a plan put forward in 1756, by Lord Tyrawley, commander of the Coldstream Guards, which suggested the

---

43   C. Hibbert, *King Mob* (Stroud: Sutton, 2004), p.128.

sighting of artillery purely to defend London's bridges,[44] had never been considered previously. A great deal of Amherst's correspondence in the early days of June 1780, was with General William Belford of the Royal Artillery, concerning the security of Woolwich and other sites that held large quantities of powder and arms. Belford indicated that, on 6 June, he had emplaced a dozen light 6-pounders, typically used as battalion guns, each equipped with 10 rounds of ball and 50 of case shot – the type of ammunition most useful against crowds. Belford was also keen to move the guns to wherever else they might be useful, asking that 36 horses be provided if this proved to be the case, and also insisting that he be put in overall command of such a mobile force, irrespective of the rank of other officers assigned to it.[45] After the Riots, Belford was awarded £330 for his 'good service', but died just three weeks later, following a short illness.

Elsewhere, some light guns were moved from the Tower to the South Hampshire Militia at Lambeth; these were sent clandestinely by river, so as not to alert or excite the mob.[46] There was also a proposal by Lord Hillsborough to place small howitzers on Blackfriars Bridge (again, in a purely defensive role); the riots subsided too quickly for this to be acted on, but the consideration being given in various quarters to the use of artillery, albeit defensively, shows how serious the situation had become.[47] On 7 June, Amherst sent to Woolwich for gunners to man the cannon in Hyde Park: this followed a concerned note from Rainsford stating that, after sending out all the requested detachments, he had only 150 men left to protect the camp and its six guns. When the powder magazines at Purfleet were threatened, a detachment of two light cannon and 50 gunners under Captain William Congreve, was quietly rowed across the river from Woolwich and positioned to defend the place.[48] However, a request for four guns made by the Lord Mayor, Brackley Kennett, was refused. Kennett was Master of the Worshipful Company of Vintners, and Lord Mayor from 1779-1780. His performance during the Gordon Riots was such that, in 1781, he was convicted of criminal negligence during the disturbances, and fined £1,000.

Conclusions

The nature and excesses of the Gordon Riots caused many in the Government to consider how best to respond to such civil disorder in the future. The trials held in the wake of the riots allowed Lord Mansfield to clarify previously murky, or misinterpreted law. Whilst Amherst had shown, perhaps understandably, the indecision of a man thrust into a situation with no manual to follow (and to which he could not simply respond as if confronted with a military enemy), in all other respects,

---

44 British Museum, Holderness MSS, Eggerton 3444, f.64-69 – 2nd Baron Tyrawley to Cumberland.
45 TNA, WO34/103, f.30 – Lieutenant Colonel Belford RA.
46 TNA, WO34/234, f.8 – General Amherst.
47 TNA, WO34/103, f.69 – Hillsborough.
48 TNA, WO34/103, f.282 – Disposition of Posts.

the Army had – as always – done the job it had been asked to do. Furthermore, a Royal Engineer officer named Debbieg had proposed improved defences for both the Bank[49] and the New River Board, London's main source of drinking water.[50] Yet clearly, the declaration of Martial Law weighed heavily on the minds of some who wished to avoid putting troops in such a position again – whether out of sympathy for the Army, or detestation of it.

Unfortunately, two factors prevented progress – first, the corruption and venality of the constabulary system was widely (in fact, almost everywhere outside of the capital) seen to be a 'London problem' and hence any solution to such problems was deemed irrelevant in the shires; second, the highly politicised nature of Continental police forces, particularly that of France, convinced many that any Government-run force would be incompatible with the political freedoms enjoyed in Great Britain. However, a significant experiment was the creation in 1798 of the Thames River Police, the first regular professional police force in London. Set up to reduce the thefts that plagued the world's largest port and financed by merchants, the force was directed by Patrick Colquhoun, whose work *A Treatise on the Police of the Metropolis* (1796) set the tone for police reform, and consisted of a permanent staff of 80 men and an on-call staff of more than 1,000. Two features of this new force were innovative: first, it used visible, preventive patrols; and second, officers were salaried rather than stipendiary, and were prohibited from taking fees. The venture was a complete success, and reports of crimes dropped appreciably, despite fears that it had been modelled on the far more politicised *Gendarmerie Nationale* in France (which in fact it had, but only in terms of its structure). Notwithstanding the counter-arguments, the Government had passed an act to extend the system of Bow Street Runners, set up by the Fielding brothers in 1750, and in 1786 a police force of 40 mounted and 400 dismounted constables was set up in Dublin, then the second largest city in the Empire; this force was improved in 1795 and 1808 and Dublin was reputedly almost crime-free when Sir Robert Peel became Chief Secretary for Ireland in 1812. Nevertheless, it would take the Peterloo Massacre and considerable further civil unrest in the hard years following the Napoleonic Wars, before a full-time force was policing the streets of London.

---

49 TNA, Maps & Plans: MP/H/13 – Lieutenant Colonel Debbieg to Governors of the Bank of England, which led to the historic Guards picket, but his other proposals – including two towers and a connecting walkway covering the roof, and the purchase and demolition of surrounding properties, were quietly shelved.

50 TNA, WO34/103, f.245, f.246 and 34/104 f.92 – Lieutenant Colonel Debbieg, who was shocked at the vulnerability of London's main water supply, and assigned an initial guard of 40 men, later increased to 160 by day and 195 at night; again, more elaborate proposals – including American-style blockhouses and a garrison of 700 men – were rejected as too expensive.

Appendix I
Numbers and Movement of Troops into London during the Riots, and their locations and dispositions on and around 8 June, 1780

Table 1: Strengths of the Various Corps based in, or Ordered to, London

Cavalry		Regular Infantry		Militia Infantry	
Horse Guards	292	1st Foot Guards (3 bns)		Hertfordshire Militia	560
Horse Grenadier Guards	244	Coldstream Guards (2 bns)	3,724	North Hampshire Militia	538
3rd Dragoon Guards	212	3rd Foot Guards (2 bns)		South Hampshire Militia	461
3rd Dragoons	215	1st Foot (2nd Battalion)	646	Northumberland Militia (estimated)	600
4th Dragoons	216	2nd Foot	591	2nd West Yorkshire Militia	578
11th Dragoons	221	18th Foot (estimated)	500	Northamptonshire Militia (estimated)	500
16th Light Dragoons	323	52nd Foot (5 coys; estimated)	250	Buckinghamshire Militia (estimated)	550
				Middlesex Militia (estimated)	550
				Cambridgeshire Militia (estimated)	550
				Stafford Militia (estimated)	550
Total Cavalry	1,723	Total Regular Infantry	5,700+	Total Militia Infantry	5,500+

Table 2: Movements and Locations of the Various Corps

Corps	Date orders sent	Original Location	Destination
3rd Dragoon Guards	4/5 June	Colchester, Essex	London
3rd Dragoons	4/5 June	Petworth, Sussex	Croydon
4th Dragoons	4/5 June	Canterbury, Kent	Greenwich & Deptford
N. Hampshire Militia*	5 June	Staines, Middlesex	Hammersmith & Fulham
3rd Dragoons	7 June	Croydon, Surrey	Kensington, Chelsea & Knightsbridge
11th Dragoons	7 June	Newbury, Berkshire	Hammersmith, Fulham, Kensington, Turnham Green, & Knightsbridge
2/1st Foot	7 June	Hertford, Hertfordshire	Hyde Park encampment
18th Foot	7 June	Woburn, Bedfordshire	Hyde Park encampment
Hertfordshire Militia	7 June	Barnet, Hertfordshire	Hyde Park encampment
Northumberland Militia	7 June	Islington	Hampstead & Highgate
Northamptonshire Militia (2nd division)**	7 June	Uxbridge, Middlesex	Hammersmith, Fulham & Putney
52nd Foot (5 Coys)	8 June	Dartford, Kent	Greenwich & Deptford
Buckinghamshire Militia (5 coys)	8 June	Bromley, Kent	Woolwich Docks
Buckinghamshire Militia (5 coys)	8 June	Kingston-on-Thames, Surrey	Deptford
Middlesex Militia (1st division)	8 June	Staines, Middlesex	Brentford & Kew
Cambridge Militia (100-man detachment)	8 June	Barnet, Hertfordshire	Kenwood
Cambridge Militia (remainder)	8 June	Barnet, Hertfordshire	Hampstead, Highgate & Kentish Town
Northamptonshire Militia (2nd division)	8 June	Fulham, London	Lambeth, Vauxhall & Wandsworth
2nd W. Yorkshire Militia	9 June		
Stafford Militia	Unknown	Unknown	Unknown

* On 6 June, the South Hampshire Militia was ordered to remain in its quarters in Lambeth.

** On 7 June, the 1st division of the Northamptonshire Militia was ordered to remain in quarters in Lambeth.

Table 3: Dispositions and Locations – TNA, WO34/103, f.208

The Bank 534	Queen's Guard 32
The Museum 454	Ormond Street 31
The Exchequer 205	Count Hasley 25
The Asylum 180	Mr Thrales (Brewery) 25
The Artillery Grounds 150 (dragoons)	Admiralty 24
The Excise Office 150	St Paul's (annexe) 20 (dragoons)
Borough 150	Lord Rockingham 20
The King's Guard 104	Kensington 13
London Bridge 104	Lord North 12
St Paul's 100	Lord Stormont 12
Bridewell Hospital 100	Sir George Savile 12
Clerkenwell, Newham & Hick's Hale 95	Lord George Germaine 12
New River head & Boarded River 95	Bromley (Metcalfe Mills) 12
Camp duties 76	Clare Market 12
Tilt Yard 61	Warwick Street Chapel 12
Savoy 52 (addition, small det. there already)	Magazine, Hyde Park Camp 10
Sardinian Ministry 42	**GRAND TOTAL: 1,517**

Appendix II
Extract from *A Narrative of the life of Sergeant Willm. Pell First Foot Guards (written by himself) from his first Inlisting, Jany. 18th, 1779.*

Pell's original spelling has been used throughout; some words in the original manuscript are completely illegible and where these occur, a _____ has been inserted; any insertions by the author, for the sake of clarity, are contained within square brackets.

> About the first of June 1780, a vast concourse of people assembled in St George's Fields, at the instance of Lord Ge[orge] Gordon to go to the Parliament House to petition against something that had, or was about to take place in favour of the Papists. They proceeded over London Bridge, by St Paul's to the Strand, I saw them march past the Horse Guards, ten or twelve abreast, with colours and flags with "No Popery" wrote on them.
>
> In the evening, some depredations were committed, Justice Hyde's house was pulled down; and whoever they might be, or whatever their pretence, it was the foundation of great riots.
>
> This caused great alarms, the Guards were called out, and all outliers were ordered to repair to Head-quarters. On this account, I had a very fatigueing [sic.] march one night to warn them, they lodged so wide one from another. I shall just mention my round but none but those that know London can form any idea of it. I set off from the Horse Guards at about five o'clock in the evening, went over Westminster bridge to Lambeth, then to the Mint in the Borough – Tower Street – Wapping Wall – Webb Square – Bishopsgate Street – Islington Turnpike – Grays Inn Lane – Swallow Street Longacre, Grosvenor's Square – Knights-Bridge – Westminster. I arrived at my lodgings about 5 o'clock in the morning. I had not been in bed above an hour, when I was called up, & had almost the same route to go over again. This was owing to my having an order to warn part of the outliers only, or, (I could have warned them all at once.) however, I was to go & warn the remainder, that walk brought blood thro' my stockings.
>
> Things at that time were a serious aspect, London was all in a bustle, people began to be afraid not only for their property, but for their lives; the different Guards were augmented, & picquets were added. Detachments were sent to Noblemen's houses and Public Buildings for their protection, particularly to the Bank. Regiments of Horse & Foot were daily pouring into London, so that it seemed like a seat of war; all the avenues to the Metropolis were guarded, & troops patrolled the streets night & day.
>
> But notwithstanding the vigilance of the military, many depredations were committed; several buildings were burnt down, or destroyed otherwise. Many people had threatening messages signifying their houses would be destroyed next; the Kings, & Queen's palace was threatened.
>
> Soldiers were always sent on information, but the mob payed no attention to them; otherwise than to use them ill, with iron bars & pelting with brick-batts etc.

Thus things passed on for four or five days, the civil power lost their authority, or could not act; no remonstrations would do, therefore the Martial Law was first in force.

On the Wednesday evening, previous to out being encamped, a detachment, consisting of two hundred & fifty men; was ordered from the Guards, & commanded by Sir Jno. Wrotlesly [Wrottesley]. It fell to my lot to go with that detachment, but previous to our marching from the Parade; a circle was formed, & the orders were that wherever we saw a mob, if they would not disperse by fair means, to fire on them.

Each man was furnished with thirty rounds of ball cartridges.

After that, we marched over Westminster Bridge when I counted eight fires. The King's Bench prison was all in ablaze from one end to the other, the Fleet prison, & a distiller's house in Holbourn. Newgate had been burnt before, & all the prisoners let out. We marched across St George's Fields to the Haymarket in the Borough, there we halted, formed a square and faced outwards. All the windows as we passed were illuminated, & ribbons & flags were blowing about in numbers; and No Popery wrote on all doors and shutters.

Durying [sic.] our halt at that market, several bands of people came down High St from London Bridge; crying No Popery & with poles & flags etc. Sir Jno. Wrottesley told them he did not want Popery no more than they did but, they must not go about in bands that way; he had them disperse and ordered their poles to be taken from them, told them whatever they might think of the soldiers, they certainly would fire upon them if they did not disperse.

After waiting there sometime, the detachment marched to Esquire Thrales whose house was threatened that night; there the men had plenty of bread, cheese & porter. All the avenues leading to the house were examined, & not a person suffered to stand about.

Sometime after, the commanding officer ordered a detachment from the number he commanded to stay at that brewery all night; consisting of one officer, two sergeants, two corporals, & fifty private men. I very much wished to go forward, but I was one of the corporals that was ordered to remain there. The other men marched to Black Friars Bridge, the toll-house at the foot of which was on fire; and a chest of half-pence throwed about the road (that I was informed of after). Soon after they were gone, I heard much firing in different parts of London, but we were reasonable enough where I was, I got two or three hours good sleep upon the _____ in the yard, & in the morning we returned to the Parade.

_____? That part of the detachment before _____ of marched over Black Friars Bridge, up Fleet-market, to the Distillery in Holbourn; but on marching up Fleet Market, Sir John was shot at off the top of an house (but missed him) when one of the Grenadiers shot at the man & brought him down upon the pavement. There was some bustle and Sir John broke his sword, but the soldiers subdued & got _____? When he came to the

Distillery, some more were found dead through drunkenness & suffocation etc.

Gentlemen were very loath to fire upon the people, but all they could do or say otherwise was of no avail, the devastations became more flagrant, and the conflagration increased. But there were no more riot after that night, therefore the remedy had the desired effect; it was said one hundred, or more might be killed in different parts of the town, but the exact number, & who they were, was never known.

Perhaps on this account, some suffered innocently, buy however that might be there was every caution given in the newspapers & by hand bills desiring every one to keep within that night for the soldiers would certainly fire upon the mob wherever one might be found.

That bustle occasioned the Brigade of Guards to be encamped in St James Park opposite the Mall & several regiments of infantry were encamped in Hyde Park. The camp of the Guards where [sic] pitched on the seventh and eighth of June, 1780.

All the time I was in camp, I did my duty with the greatest pleasure & (never?) had any _____ better, the Guards did duty there by Brigade, & what was very singular, I was mounted the King's Guard, when there was not a [?] of the regt to which I belonged, but _____.

We remained in camp until the fifteenth of August 1780, that morning the camp broke up, & the usual change of quarters took place, throughout the Brigade, instead of the twenty-fifth. And on the twenty-eighth of August, I was appointed Quarter Master Corporal. That promotion was altogether unexpected, for I had had not the least information whatsoever of any such coming, neither did such a thing enter my thoughts.

By that promotion, I had new employ altogether, had nothing to do with the company to which I belonged, ____ the duty of the Regiment, as it respected [?] no more doing guards & field days.

My business related to the stores giving out & taking in ammunition & watch coats etc, to attend the marching of companies at certain times (for then _____ all poor ball as well as blank cartridges) & taking care of the _____ equipage.

Bibliography

Archival Sources
British Museum
    Liverpool MSS.
    Holderness MSS.
Grenadier Guards Regimental Archives
    Sergeant W. Pell, *A Narrative of the life of Sergeant Willm. Pell First Foot Guards (written by himself) from his first Inlisting, Jany. 18th, 1779.*
Kent Records Office
    Amherst MSS (U.1360), 074/64.
The National Archives, Kew
    MPH/13, Plan of the Bank of England, City of London, showing proposed alterations for its better security; adjacent properties to be purchased (owners named). Descriptive key to adjacent properties. Originally filed with report of 15 Sept 1780 by Lt Col Hugh Debbieg.
    SP37/20, Papers concerning the Gordon riots in London in 1780.
    WO4/110, Secretary-at-War, Out Letters. General Letters.
    WO34/103, 104, Commander-in-Chief's Letter Books.

Published Sources
Anon., *A List of the Officers of the Army* (from 1754: *and of the Corps of Royal Marines*) (London: Various Years).

Babington, Anthony, *Military intervention in Britain: from the Gordon riots to the Gibraltar Incident* (New York: Routledge, 1990).

Cobbett, W. (ed.), *Cobbett's Parliamentary History of England* (London: Private, later Hansard, 1803).

Hayter, A.J., *The Army & The Crowd in Mid-Georgian England* (London: Macmillan, 1978).

Hayter, A.J. (ed.), *An Eighteenth Century Secretary At War: The Papers of William, Viscount Barrington* (London: Bodley Head, 1988).

Hibbert, C., *King Mob* (Stroud, Gloucestershire: Sutton Publishing, 2004).

Houlding, J.A., *Fit for Service: The Training of the British Army 1715-1795* (Oxford: Clarendon, 1981).

Mackesy, P., *War for America* (London: Bison Books, 1993).

Rogers, Colonel H.C.B., *The British Army of the Eighteenth Century* (London: Allen & Unwin, 1977).

Sharp, J., *A Fiery & Furious People: A History of Violence in England* (London: Random House Books, 2016).

Shoemaker, R.B., *The London Mob: Violence and Disorder in Eighteenth Century England* (London: Hambledon & London, 2004).

Stuart Wortley, E., *A Prime Minister and His Son* (London: Murray, 1925).

Thompson, E.P., *The Making of the English Working Class* (London: Pelican Books, 1968).

Wraxall, N.W., *Historical Memoirs of My Own Time* (Philadelphia: Carey, Lea, and Blanchard, 1837).

6

'No British Ship Sighted': The British Garrison on Minorca and the Siege of St Philip's Castle, 1756

Robert Tildesley

The island of Minorca was one of the more unusual British territories of the eighteenth century. It had a sizeable European population, with varied cultural backgrounds and associated traditionally-held rights. They did not speak the same language as the rulers and predominantly practised a different faith, and, importantly, had also previously been subject to a still-extant and powerful European state. It was a territory where troops were often left without assistance and officers sent to finish out their careers. The lieutenant governor at the time of the siege in 1756 was 86 and certainly had been put out to pasture. During the period of study, furthermore, Minorca was not properly represented by a form of civil government. In normal circumstances, an appointed governor was tasked with administering the island for civil matters however, there was constant absenteeism of the governors after Richard Kane (1733–36). This resulted in all those duties passing to the lieutenant governor, who during the 1750s was Lieutenant General Sir William Blakeney.[1] The lieutenant governor was always a military officer who also held the role of supreme commander of the garrison. Thus, civil government in Minorca was handled by military officials.

It is important to understand the island in its wider geographical context. William Cunninghame in his journal evocatively describes Mahon harbour as, 'the appearance of a river always smooth water generally good anchoring ground everywhere … It is the finest and safest harbour ever I saw.'[2] This excellent harbour was positioned just two days sailing from the French and Spanish coastlines including the French naval base at Toulon, making it a vital point for control of the Western Mediterranean. Despite that, the island did also have some significant drawbacks. First, it was sparsely populated; coupled with the rocky terrain, this meant that it

---
1 During most of this period the governor was Lord Tyrawley.
2 National Army Museum (NAM) 1968-07-225, William Cunninghame, *Journal of a Journey to Minorca*.

was not self-sufficient for foodstuffs which in turn made it a difficult position in which to station large bodies of troops. It also suffered from its own strategic position, being two days sailing from hostile coastlines but as much as two weeks distant from ships leaving Portsmouth. This made Minorca one of the most isolated British possessions in Europe.

It was this island that became the focal point in 1756 of French and British interests as the Seven Years War began. British control threatened French naval operations and there was a hope amongst the French court that taking the island and offering it back to Spain could procure a critical ally in the coming conflict. French forces invaded, and, despite a relief fleet, the garrison was unable to hold out and was forced to capitulate, leaving the island in French control for the remainder of the war. This event caused a great deal of uproar in Britain, not only because it was a major defeat for both land and naval forces, but it also marked one of the first losses of British territory during the war. The public outcry was extensive and even the king became involved in looking for what went wrong. The fall of the island brought about the collapse of the government and led to the rare execution of an admiral. However, the purpose of this chapter is to address the measures that most significantly impacted upon the garrison and the extent to which they can and can be drawn together as factors leading to the eventual capitulation of Minorca in 1756.

First, however, there is a need to address the elephant in the room for every study regarding Minorca, that of Admiral Byng. The Byng controversy has dominated much of naval and Mediterranean Seven Years War historiography and dominates almost all attempts to look at the events that transpired on the island in 1756. Byng's failure to either land reinforcements on the island, including many of the garrison's officers who had been on leave, or drive away the French fleet from their blockade, essentially doomed the garrison, leading to the eventual capitulation. Indeed, even some of those who would criticise the garrison understood that naval failings were the single greatest factor leading to the capitulation. Cunninghame wrote in his explanation of events leading to the end of the siege that 'had there been any British fleet in those seas the French fleet never would have ventured out of Toulon'.[3] However, despite the strong inter-relationship between the island and the navy, the fleet and Byng will not be the focus of this study, nor will their actions in relation to the naval engagements and tactics. Instead, only the navy's actions as they directly relate to the garrison and island will be discussed. If Byng had been able to successfully defeat the French fleet under La Galissonière, then the events on Minorca would likely have been very different. However rather than attempt to analyse all the occasions where events could have taken a different path, for the purposes of this chapter it will be treated as a fixed constant that the British fleet failed. There are detailed studies available in both English and French that look at the naval battle,[4] but little work has been done on the garrison or on the siege itself. By focusing on the

---

3   NAM 1968-07-227-1, William Cunninghame, *Journal of the Siege of St Philip's Castle in the Island of Minorca* (Unpublished).
4   See N.A.M., Rodger, *The Command of the Ocean, A Naval History of Britain, 1649-1815* (London: Allen Lane, 2004) pp. 690-692.

garrison and only the direct assistance from local naval forces, the factors directly relating to the army's role in the defence of Minorca can be identified.

This, therefore, leads onto questions of wider strategic policy. This is not an attempt to analyse and explain British foreign policy in general, or the British government's prosecution of the war. Rather, it will focus on British policy that was directly related to Minorca. Any wider discussion is beyond the means of this study, and therefore it is instead prudent to focus on the details of how these principles worked in practice in the case study of Minorca. This will involve looking at officials lower down the chain of command than the Duke of Newcastle or Admiral Anson, instead looking at the institutions which had a regular and direct influence on affairs in Minorca. By investigating affairs in this manner, it will be possible to determine how systems were implemented and organised regarding Minorca.

The main offices which formed the crux of Minorca's military organisation were the Treasury and Ordnance Office, and the agents of the Commissary General. The Treasury had a clear impact on how the island was run: the allocation or withholding of funds directly impacted not only its ability to operate effectively, but also shaped practises and strategies in order to align with Treasury budgetary requirements. The Ordnance Office, further down the chain of command than the Treasury, dealt with the specifics relating to many of the affairs that were directly within the remit of the garrison and their daily expenditures. The supply of food and ammunition was handled by the Ordnance Office and the Commissary General, while the repayments for additional costs were managed by the Ordnance Office singularly. In addition to this, the fortifications that formed one of the primary costs of the garrison were the joint responsibility of the Treasury and Ordnance Office. These institutions demonstrate the levels of agency government present on Minorca and how decisions from the centre filtered down to impact small garrisons on the fringes of British interests.

To understand how the British army on Minorca and how it operated, both administratively and militarily, it is necessary to identify and explain some of the terms and theories that are going to form the framework of this chapter. The army's activities need to be separated from those that were carried out as part of the civil governance of the island. Despite often also forming part of the duties of the lieutenant governor, due to the absence of the governor, it was a very different set of duties to that required as commander-in-chief of the garrison. Although these two elements of the role cannot be entirely separated, by taking this approach the military duties of the garrison can be addressed. Additionally, the garrison's supply situation directly related to both combat and administrative effectiveness. Without adequate supplies not only do the issues of hunger and disease appear within bodies of troops, but also it is necessary to add the complexity of relations with local civilian populations, with whom soldiers would often clash when an inadequate supply of food was being received. It is also important to highlight the other supply issues, aside from food, that impacted the garrison, such as ammunition and, crucially, information. By investigating these supply systems, a better understanding of the strength of the garrison can be established, as can its effectiveness as a strategic force. Finally, it is important to address the events of the siege in 1756 and the resulting criticism of the garrison. By looking at these longer-term factors as well as the siege itself, then effective conclusions can be drawn as to factors impacting the garrison's ability to successfully defend Minorca.

Although the civil administration of the island will not be covered, some words do need to be said regarding relations between the British and the Spanish inhabitants (Hereafter referred to as Minorcans). This is necessary in order to understand some of the issues from which the garrison suffered with respect to civil relations, and their resulting consequences during the siege. Protestant British rule brought with it many issues for the Catholic Minorcans who inhabited the island. They were now ruled by a different religious group who also opened up the island to groups that had been previously prohibited and controlled, such as Jewish and other international merchants. Indeed, one of the first requests that Richelieu, commander of the French forces, received after being presented with the keys of the old capital upon landing was that the French would drive out the heretics and 'Jews'.[5] Relations were constantly frayed, with many examples of British forces acting in a heavy-handed manner towards Minorcans with little attempt to understand their historical privileges. Complaints were often laid against British forces for intervening in the election of magistrates for the various parts of the island.[6] At times, armed groups of Minorcans even threatened the garrison at St Philip's Castle, the main fortress on the island.[7] The garrison's position on the island needs to be understood in this context. Faced with a hostile populace, it had to make decisions regarding the defence of the island in the knowledge that they would be opposed, whether covertly or overtly, by the majority of Minorcans.

The British presence on Minorca, and especially the siege, has seen very few historical works. Even amongst more general histories it has remained something of a side note. This has been of course partially due to Byng. The Byng affair been the dominant focal point for historians whose attention has turned in the direction of Minorca. This focus has left the garrison itself woefully understudied. Those studies that have used some of the sources from the garrison have focused on the way it relates to the statements made about Byng and the testimonies that came out over the course of his subsequent trial and execution. The study most referred to by scholars, is Brian Tunstall's *Admiral Byng*.[8] Tunstall makes an excellent attempt at providing a summary of events occurring on the island taken from some of the published sources that were available, while mostly focusing on the events of Byng's life. Tunstall's work has become the main reference point for other historians and the sources he used became the first point of call for subsequent works. The issue with the attention paid to Byng, when attempting to understand Minorca, can be seen most clearly in texts such as *At 12 Mr Byng was Shot* by Dudley Pope.[9] This book sets out with the clear objective of exonerating Byng from what the author

---

5   NAM 1968-07-226, William Cunninghame, *Journal of the Siege of St Philip's Castle in the Island of Minorca* (Published).
6   The National Archives (TNA) PC 1/60/8, Privy Council Report on the Arrest of Magistrates. 1750.
7   TNA PC 1/6/41, Privy Council Report requiring response from General Blakeney, August 1755.
8   Brian Tunstall, *Admiral Byng* (London: P. Allen, 1928).
9   Dudley Pope, *At 12 Mr Byng was Shot* (London: Phoenix, 1962).

viewed as the cruel and malicious attacks on him by the government and admiralty.[10] These texts only use the easily-available sources and do not seek to delve into the full documents produced by the garrison, preferring to rely on those which came out after the siege. Because of the focus on Byng and the fallout from his actions, very little attention has been paid to the sources relating to the garrison.

Janet Sloss' study of the French occupation of the island also has some brief mentions of the garrison.[11] Sloss logically starts at the French invasion of Minorca and thus discusses the forces arrayed against the French. However, because the main focus of the work is not on the British troops but rather the French, very few sources have been used to support her arguments of a weak and inefficient garrison. Her main sources for most of the discussion are the journals of William Cunninghame, the validity of which will be discussed later. Wider works on the Seven Years War, due to their scope, only use the sources that have been used for some of the smaller studies, such as those of Sloss or Tunstall, and no attempt has been made to look at the other direct sources from the garrison. The most recent of these, Baugh's history of the war, spends only a few pages discussing events on Minorca and that is in relation to what would later happen to Byng.[12] Only one dedicated study has been published on the British in Minorca over the entire period, that being Desmond Gregory's *Minorca, The Illusory Prize*.[13] This work covers the entire period of the British occupation of the island from 1708 to 1802, and has used the most original sources of any work in order to achieve this. However, with regards to the garrison during the middle of the century, especially into the Seven Years War, there are some flaws in his work. Gregory's main sources for the 1750s are the Cunninghame journals and testimonies used by other historians. His other original sources include some diaries, but are mostly restricted to letters between members of the government. These sources are mostly those which discuss events on the island rather than looking at material from the garrison itself.[14] In addition to this, Gregory only dedicates one chapter to the defence of Minorca for the entire period of 1708 to 1756 while the rest of the text focuses on civil administration and the rule of law on the island.[15] This lack of historical attention to the military garrison and the strategic situation on the island is the reason why many of the attempts to understand the fall of the island have been lacking in detail.

The sources available for studies into Minorca are certainly varied, and in some cases very detailed. However, very few of them have been thoroughly researched. Much of the primary source focus in studies on Minorca has been on the earlier period under Governor Kane and the documents from the Stanhope collections, or the later period under Lieutenant General Murray (1778–1782). There are three main journals that comprise one of the major bodies of material. The first is *A*

---

10   Pope, *Mr Byng*, p.ix.
11   Janet Sloss, *A Small Affair, The French Occupation of Menorca During the Seven Years' War* (Tetbury: Bonaventura Press, 2000).
12   Daniel Baugh, *The Global Seven Years' War 1754-1763* (London: Routledge, 2011).
13   Desmond Gregory, *Minorca, The Illusory Prize* (Rutherford: Farleigh Dickinson University Press: 1990).
14   Gregory, *The Illusory Prize*, pp.251-254.
15   Gregory, *The Illusory Prize*, p.5.

Full Account of the Siege of Minorca by the French published circa 1756/57.[16] This source highlights public views on the siege and the material that was in circulation immediately after it. Though it is unclear if the author was present at the siege, there are certain elements within the journal which correlate to details that were only brought up in sources regarding the trial of Byng, such as details regarding French ship movements on the north side of the island.[17] Despite this, the source is a window into how the narrative of the siege was playing out in the public eye. It also includes numerous details of events from the French side that are not present in other sources, such as the names of ships and commanders, along with some of the events that transpired after Richelieu returned to France.

The other major published journal is entitled *A Faithful and authentic account of the siege and surrender of St. Philip's Fort, in the Island of Minorca*.[18] It too recounts the events of the siege but the details are more accurate on the British side of affairs, having been taken from the minutes of the siege drawn up by one of the officers. While it has no information regarding the French forces other than what the garrison knew at the time, it is one of the few published sources that appears to draw upon documents produced by the garrison rather than just recollections. These journals together help inform our understanding of both events that transpired and the information circulating after the siege.

There are also the collected papers that were drawn together during the trial of Byng. These are the *Papers Relating to the Loss of Minorca*,[19] and *The Trial of Admiral Byng*.[20] *The Trial* is the full transcript of the court-martial of Byng, including his own testimony regarding Minorca and that of Lieutenant General Blakeney. These testimonies formed the basis for much of the future discussion on the siege and the garrison. In addition to this, the testimonies of these high-ranking individuals, when placed against their agendas and the evidence from other sources, produce an important framework for assessing the details of the siege and attempting to understand the narrative of events. The *Papers* are a collection of intelligence reports, naval orders, and other letters, all of which lead up to the French invasion and the dispatch of Byng's squadron. They demonstrate the availability of information of French movements to the garrison but not the government's responses to these details. There are, however, letters missing from the papers and therefore, though this is likely simply an omission, there is the possibility of collusion directly relating to political interests involved in Byng's trial. For example, some of the letters from the envoys in Lisbon and Barcelona are missing yet relate details of the siege as it

---

16 Anon., *A Full Account of The Siege of Minorca: By The French, In 1756. With All The Circumstances Relating Thereto* (London: A and C Corbett, N.D.).
17 Anon., *Full Account*, p.23.
18 Anon., *A Faithful and authentic account of the siege and surrender of St. Philip's Fort, in the Island of Minorca. Containing, every particular occurrence and remarkable incident. An account of the strength of the garrison. The Second edition. Officer on the Spot.* (London: H.B Russia, 1757).
19 Captain H.W. Richmond (ed.), *Papers Relating to the Loss of Minorca in 1756* (London: Publications for Naval Record Society: 1913).
20 Anon., *The Trial of the Honourable Admiral John Byng* (London: R Manby, 1757).

was going on.[21] Certainly some historians have argued that there were deliberate attempts by the government to shape the evidence involved at the trial.[22]

Another source directly relating to the events of the trial is *Answer to an Infamous Libel*.[23] This document was produced regarding Blakeney, most likely drawn from Byng's statements in the proceedings. It takes the form of an open letter directed to Byng from the anonymous author. As a result, the document lists and attempts to counter each of the criticisms laid against Blakeney by Byng. These sources provide useful comparisons between the different facts and beliefs that were present in England after the siege, but their accuracy comes into question when compared with sources clearly produced by the garrison at the time.

The most commonly drawn upon sources directly relating to the events of the siege are the journals of William Cunninghame, deputy/chief engineer at St Philip's (there is some dispute in the sources as to which title he formally held by the end of the siege). Cunninghame produced three journals during the 1750s. One, *Journal of a Journey to Minorca*,[24] details his travels through France to the island to commence his duties as deputy engineer at St Philip's. Cunninghame also produced a second journal, which was most likely written at some point during the siege.[25] The journal starts abruptly with Cunninghame in Nice, from where he was ordered to return to assist St Philip's. This section was clearly written after he arrived in Minorca and from that point the journal continues with a day-to-day account up until just after the surrender. The final journal is an edited version of the siege journal clearly intended for publication.[26] There are significant differences between the siege journal and this edited version. This version seeks to explain, in a teleological manner, the fall of Minorca to the reader.[27] Due to both the volume of text and the level of detail that Cunninghame has included in parts, historians have treated these journals as invaluable sources when researching Minorca. However, their author had disputes with members of the garrison and had an agenda relating to his own reputation which he felt was jeopardised by the siege. He was not appointed chief engineer following the death of the previous incumbent in 1754. As a result, Cunninghame quit his post and was returning home to Britain to take up a lieutenant colonelcy in another regiment when the news of the invasion and orders to return reached him. With his future military reputation on the line, his journals show him as an eager officer who was always proposing schemes of varying complexity to commanders who decided against implementing the vast majority of them. Cunninghame certainly appears to have felt underappreciated. His second siege journal demonstrates that he sought to appropriate blame against those higher up the command chain than himself, especially Lieutenant General Blakeney. Cunninghame's journals provide excellent sources of evidence in some respects, such as his view on engineering matters

---

21 TNA SP 89/50/241, Letter from Castres in Lisbon, 20 April 1756.
22 Pope, *Mr Byng*, p. 240.
23 Anon., *A Full Answer to an Infamous Libel, etc.* (London: W. Reive, 1757).
24 NAM 1968-07-225, *Journal of a Journey*.
25 NAM 1968-07-227-1, *Journal of the Siege* (Unpublished).
26 While a copy of the manuscript exists, it is unclear if it was successfully published.
27 NAM 1968-07-226, *Journal of the Siege* (Published).

and on the activities of the French, as he often conversed with the chief engineer of the French forces given his fluency in that language. However, when it comes to matters such as problems within the garrison, tactical decisions, and reasons for the surrender, his views must be balanced against the other available sources. This is especially the case with his published journal which contradicts information he placed in his siege journal. Cunninghame, furthermore, was not at the highest levels of decision-making within the garrison and had an axe to grind on some issues, especially as he felt his future career might be threatened by the older officers. His journals must be understood in that context.

There are a large number of sources which do not appear to have been used by many of the historians looking at Minorca, especially in relation to the long-term operation of the garrison. Captain D'arvey's *Journal of the Siege* is one of these sources.[28] This journal clearly recounts the events of the siege as they happened each day, the writer understanding the significance of the siege and wishing to record the events. His entries run from just before the French landing until the eventual capitulation, with very few days missed. This source is especially useful when used in comparison to Cunninghame, but also with the later published journals. In addition, D'arvey was the highest-ranking combat officer to have written a journal regarding events. Although Cunninghame was a major, his role as an engineer did not place any troops under his command.

Another of the main untapped sets of records are the accounts kept by the garrison and other financial documents produced throughout the various stages of Minorca's supply chain. The largest of these are the Ordnance Office Bill Books.[29] Produced every six months for the entire period of study by both head storekeepers on the island, Robert Boyd and Edward Blakeney,[30] they provide the most detailed picture of how the garrison operated on a daily basis. In addition to this, they can be used to illuminate larger trends within the supply system of the garrison by tracing the costs of these through the receipts and accounts. The Bill Books cover costs of two distinct parts of the garrison's finances: fortifications and incidents. These are calculated separately then added together to provide a three-month total in each six-month account. The fortifications budget is fairly self-explanatory, covering repairs to parts of the defences and also covering the increased construction costs of adding additional defences to the various forts present on Minorca. The incidents budget is a rather more ambiguous one, as there are examples of it being used to fill gaps in other parts of the finances. Its main purpose was for sudden costs such as collapsed walls, or paying for local aid such as unloading supply shipments. However, it was also the budget used to meet the costs of visiting dignitaries, ambassadors, and envoys from other countries. The Bill Books were diligently kept and allow for close study of the garrison as an operative unit.

There is also a large body of unused sources which comes from a range of documents showing different parts of the complicated machinery around the handling of a garrison like Minorca. There are the papers from the commissary general which

---

28   TNA WO 55/556/2, Captain D'arvey, *Journal of the Military Proceedings at Minorca, 1756*.
29   TNA WO 53/490-507, Ordnance Office Bill Books 1746-1756.
30   The latter seemingly no relation to the Lieutenant Governor.

relate to food supply and costs of supplying the island as well as the intricacies of creating a stable supply network in the Mediterranean.[31] There are also War Office papers, which show the costs of paying the garrison by the government, and also the formal on-paper size of the garrison.[32] Furthermore, they show the salaries and ranks of the various officers on the island. From this, not only can one establish the organisation of the garrison but also see how it was understood by officials in London. Finally, there is also a large catalogue of various letters, reports, and files from spies, envoys, the Privy Council, and the Treasury which can serve to clarify elements of the operation of the garrison. When used in tandem, they can improve our understanding of the connectivity between the various jurisdictions and responsibilities of the organisations which together ran Minorca. When used in conjuncture with some of the more popular sources they can provide a rounder picture of the garrison on Minorca. By combining all the documents on the garrison, it is possible to understand multiple layers of the military on Minorca, how it operated, was supplied, and defended. By drawing all these strands together, it is possible to explain many of the factors behind the fall of Minorca in 1756 and the overall strength and organisation of the garrison leading up to this point.

There were three fortified locations on Minorca. The small outpost at Fornelles on the northern coast, which required a garrison of 50 men; the inherited Spanish fort at the old capital of Ciutadella, which usually had around 200 men; and, finally, the main fortifications centred on St Philip's Castle on the cliffs above Mahon. By the 1750s, St Philip's had been greatly expanded from its original size and there had been changes in the defences from the original plans drawn up by General Stanhope in the 1710s.

The single greatest shift in Minorcan fortifications prior to 1756 was the abandonment of Queen Anne's Fort. This fortress, designed to defend Mahon harbour, was situated on a nearby promontory known as Cape Mola. The strategic advantages of such a fort had been clear to British engineers since the acquisition of the island. Cunninghame noted that because of the lay of the land, Cape Mola was a strategic wonder, being only able to be assaulted along a single thin stretch of rocky ground.[33] Cape Mola, indeed, reached a higher point of elevation than St Philip's Castle, and its views had strong lines of fire across the entrance to the harbour. The construction of Queen Anne's Fort had begun in 1720, but no more than a watchtower and some groundwork had been laid by the 1750s.[34] The garrison had even stopped accounting for Queen Anne's Fort as a separate fort with its own troops by 1747.[35] Given the small size of the garrison, it is perhaps unsurprising that they were unable to create and man an additional fort.

The cancellation of Queen Anne's was also blamed on the added cost it would have incurred, which was one of the perennial issues with fortifications on Minorca.

---

31 West Yorkshire Archivse (WYA), WYL 100/PO/5, Papers Relating to Lord Irvin, Commissary General.
32 TNA WO 24/235, War Office Papers Relating to Minorca and Gibraltar.
33 NAM 1968-07-225, *Journal of a Journey*.
34 NAM 1968-07-225, *Journal of a Journey*.
35 TNA, WO 24/262, War Office Returns, Minorca and Gibraltar, 1747.

The problem was that the solid rock layers which comprise the island made the construction of forts, especially those containing subterranean sections, increasingly difficult. Indeed, Cunninghame identifies Queen Anne's strategic importance but also the issues and costs that would be incurred in constructing such a fort.[36] In the end, the decision not to build Queen Anne's Fort rested with the government, rather than the garrison. The lack of additional central funds directed towards its construction meant that there were not the available resources to construct additional forts alongside the upkeep of the current defences. As a result, there were only a few ruins on Cape Mola when the French arrived. This decision would cause issues for the survival of St Philip's. The higher elevation of Cape Mola and its position, where it faced the narrowest part of the defences at St Philip's, made it a prime candidate for an artillery battery. During the siege, French batteries were positioned there in order to attack the fort and cover vessels entering Mahon harbour.

The main fortress on Minorca was St Philip's itself. The fort had been manned and expanded since the British move to Mahon following the occupation of the island.[37] By the 1750s, the fort was extensive, and was best described by Cunninghame in his journal:

> The castle of St Phillips is a small square of 4 bastions. The line of defence 140ft. The capital wall is above 90ft high. The ditches cut out of the rock proportionately large and deep and the outworks and ditches are also. The whole works consist of the above square,
> 4 Gunner Ravelins
> 4 Counterguards
> 4 Puller Ravelins
> 1 Capeniere with a palisaded covered way and glacis.
> To cover these are:
> 4 lunettes
> 2 redoubts
> 2 standing cavaliers at the side.
> Charles Fort which is a small sided square with short flanks and fort Marlbourogh ane insignifigant redoubt on the high ground on the south side of St Stephens Cove over which it has a pontoon communication covered from in salt. All these are full of subterranean of all sorts.[38]

The main approach to St Philip's was a road which ran into Mahon and on to Ciutadella on the other side of the island. It was this road which would be vital to the French advance in 1756, as it represented one of the critical weaknesses in the defences of St Philip's. What was more, this was through the fault of the garrison and commanders, not the government. Rather than increase the contact between the garrison and the local population, which was a frayed relationship at the best of times, the decision was made to allow construction of a town right at the base

---

36 NAM 1968-07-225, *Journal of a Journey.*
37 Gregory, *Minorca*, p.158.
38 NAM 1968-07-225, *Journal of a Journey.*

of the walls. The had additional housing for officers such as the chief engineer,[39] as well as taverns and brothels for the garrison itself. This cluster of buildings, known as St Philip's Town, was a major weak point in the overall defences. Straddling the approach road, St Philip's Town provided cover to advancing enemies and blocked certain firing arcs from the walls. This flaw had been identified by commanders, and part of the town was scheduled to be demolished in the 1740s. However, to avoid having to interact more closely with Mahon's population, only that part which joined directly onto the curtain wall and the outworks was demolished, leaving a narrow channel between them and the rest of the town. It still proved serious impediment for the defence of the fortress. Despite discussions between the officers about demolishing the whole of St Philip's Town in the event of an invasion, French maps of the siege show much of the town was still standing, and indeed parts of it appear to have been used to cover the construction of gun emplacements. The presence of St Philip's Town greatly assisted the French by undermining British fortifications: its retention, simply to allow for the continued convenience of the town's services that otherwise would require travel to Mahon, was an undoubted error.

One of the most vital elements of defences at St Philip's were the subterraneans.[40] Due to its position on the cliffs above Mahon, the fortress had, as part of its construction, extensive passages dug into the rock below the fort. These tunnels reached from the top of the cliffs all the way to St Philip's Cove below the fort, where a jetty had been constructed. This allowed for the ingress and egress of supplies and men directly from the sea without having to use Mahon harbour itself. Indeed, some of these tunnels also served as storage facilities for men and material. One tunnel contained 16 waggons with room to walk beside.[41] These tunnels were vital for any attempted defence of the fortress. Not only did the tunnels allow for the safe storage of supplies if the enemy were able to direct fire over the walls, but they also allowed safe transit of troops to parts of the outworks without having to risk them being placed under fire. These passages, vital though they were, were not a guarded secret. Given their role as part of the storage solutions for the garrison, they were often frequented by labourers performing tasks such as powder storage and decanting, as well as moving materials to different parts of the fortress.[42] As a result, any force that attacked St Philip's would understand that gaining a foothold in the subterraneans would be one of the pivotal factors in bringing about the successful capitulation of the garrison.

The nature of the subterraneans, being set into solid rock, meant that they required little maintenance. Only a few references have been located within the budget for the garrison regarding repairs to one of the tunnels.[43] These tunnels were the lynchpin of the defences at St Philip's, they were recognised and rightly maintained and defended by the garrison as one of the key strategic positions within the

---

39 TNA WO 53/492, Ordnance Office Bill Book 1748.
40 Note: This was a common term used in the sources of the time in reference to any underground parts of a fortress. NAM 1968-07-227-1, *Journal of the Siege*. (Unpublished).
41 NAM 1968-07-225, *Journal of a Journey*.
42 TNA WO 53/507, Ordnance Office Bill Book 1755.
43 TNA WO 53/502, Ordnance Office Bill Book 1753.

fortress: the entry of French troops into them in 1756 would mark one of the final stages prior to capitulation.

The last major part of the defences of St Philip's, and one of the greatest difficulties for any garrison, was their scale. As already shown, the number of component parts of the fortress was extensive, with additional redoubts and forts that were designed to cover key locations around St Philip's but were not connected to the fortress directly, such as Phillipet and Fort Marlborough. Such an extensive fortress would require a large garrison in order to effectively defend all parts of the works. The fort, therefore, was fit for purpose in terms of the strategic significance of the island, but the garrison was not increased to the level required to defend it. For example, Cunninghame in one of his many defence plans drew up the number of men he felt would be required in order to mount an effective night perimeter guard of the outer walls. Once he had included all the outer forts his total came to 2,700 men.[44] However, in 1754 the total number of men taking rations was 2,102. This was for the number of men in Mahon and St Philip's and does not include the troops at Ciutadella and Fornelles but was still the greatest proportion of the garrison.[45] According to Cunninghame's calculations, in order to maintain an effective night patrol more men would be required than were present in the entire garrison. Simply put, by 1756 the garrison was too small for the task. It had been increased by one battalion during the War of the Austrian Succession but that was withdrawn as soon as the peace treaty came into effect.[46] Even had this additional battalion been retained, it would only have placed the full strength of the garrison just below 3,000 men. The large lines of St Philip's were therefore impossible to defend effectively with the men available, and yet no attempts were made from London nor requests from Minorca for additional men even as the conflict with France scaled up in the 1750s.

One of main factors behind this failure to reinforce the garrison appears to be disinterest, rather than an active attempt to keep the garrison small. There are no letters concerned with the size of the garrison on the island; indeed, one of the few papers from government archives simply states that each of the battalions present on Minorca was exactly 815 men strong, regardless of the actual situation on the island.[47] Even when troops were allocated to the garrison, after the French had landed, this still amounted to only 500 men. Had the garrison been of an adequate size, given the fortifications it was expected to defend, then Minorca could have been in reality the significant strategic location its fortifications would indicate.

The siege of Minorca in 1756 lasted 76 days, or 79 if one counts the time for the formal terms of surrender to be arranged, and is one of the defining events during the British presence on the island. Indeed, Gregory uses it as break point between his two phases of occupation.[48] The siege marked the first interruption in British control of the island since 1709 and ushered in a six-year period of French rule. It

---

44   NAM 1968-07-227-1, *Journal of the Siege* (Unpublished).
45   WYA WYL 100/PO/5/II/20, Bread Ration 1754.
46   WYA WYL 100/PO/5/II/13, Bread Ration 1748.
47   TNA T 1/368/82, Estimate Charges of His Majesty's Forces in the Plantations, 1756.
48   Gregory, *Minorca*, p.6.

also represented one of the most important defeats for the British during the early stages of the Seven Years War and resulted in significant public backlash at home, most aptly demonstrated, as discussed earlier, with the attitudes and accusations that surrounded the trial of Admiral Byng. The Byng trial also brought into the public domain a great deal of opinions and arguments regarding the garrison's handling of the siege. Many of these criticisms, that they did not do their duty sufficiently, were levelled against Blakeney and the other officers of the garrison. With the background and organisation of the garrison taken into account, and the various problems that arose from this, it is necessary to discuss the particular criticisms they faced after the siege. By analysing the garrison's ability to hold the island and the actions that they took on this account, these criticisms can be properly addressed and their validity stated. In addition, this will demonstrate how effective a garrison like Minorca was in operating, given the support structure that had been established.

The first aspect can be simply phrased, how effectively did the garrison defend Minorca? In terms of the entire island, the garrison certainly failed to defend it, with the orders from Blakeney being for the smaller detachments of the garrison at Ciutadella, Fornelles and Mahon to retreat to St Philip's in the event of an enemy landing.[49] Had French forces successfully landed at the intended location, just to the west of Mahon, then this plan would have resulted in the loss of nearly a third of the garrison, which would have been cut off from St Philip's by the French.[50] However, this strategy was the only effective one available given the state of fortifications in the other harbours which were small and had not been updated since before the British had occupied the island. Had the troops been permanently stationed at St Philip's then they would not have been able to effectively administer the island, nor defend it against small incursions such as Barbary raids. The overall defensive strategy was to defend St Philip's and trust in relief or reinforcement by sea that would force the French to retire. This was a sound plan, given the supply situation on Minorca which could, as discussed, barely sustain the garrison, let alone the almost 16,000 men brought over by Richelieu.[51] The extensive nature of the fortifications of St Philip's and its outworks required every man available to man the defences, and even then the available numbers were considered insufficient to effectively hold all the length of the works. While the overall strategy was certainly one which sought to maximise the strengths of the garrison, significant criticism was made against Blakeney, mostly by Cunninghame and Byng's supporters.

This criticism was centred on two major events prior to the commencement of the siege. These were on the state of the defences at St Philip's and on the damaging of roads and buildings in order to hamper the French. Cunninghame was recalled by Blakeney before the French forces had finished embarking and had left Toulon, requesting that he return to aid in the defence, writing that the council of war 'join'd me in opinion that your appearance here is highly necessary.'[52] Blakeney was

---

49   TNA WO 55/556/2, Captain D'arvey Journal.
50   Gregory, *Minorca*, p.172.
51   Baugh, *Seven Years' War*, p.182.
52   NAM 1968-07-227-1, *Journal of the Siege* (Unpublished).

a constant supporter of Cunninghame and had argued in favour of his promotion to chief engineer but was overruled by the Duke of Bedford, who preferred the more senior figure of Major Bastide. Regardless of that support, Cunninghame clearly blamed Blakeney for the inadequacies that he noted in the garrison. Cunninghame mentioned issues with the palisading and support works and felt the need to purchase £1,300 of timber in Nice to send to Mahon out of his own pocket – a not inconsiderable sum, when one considers that the lieutenant governor's yearly income at this time was only £730. He also noted that the ideas he had been suggesting about defences before his departure, 'will now be found necessary'.[53] The Ordnance Office Bill Books do, however, show increases in the spending on the fortifications over 1754–55. The Bill Books show that the total spent by the Ordnance Office rose from £1,300 to £1,700, including activities such as repairs to the drawbridge and repair of the artillery steps.[54] While not a vast increase in the total amount spent on defences, it does indicate that steps were being taken to improve the quality of the works at St Philip's.

However, Cunninghame viewed certain elements of the timber support frames and palisades, to be badly in need of repair and hence his purchase of additional timber before the French landed. This raises a debate regarding the condition of the defences and the extent to which they had been allowed to fall into disrepair. The increased cost shown in the Bill Books does indicate an identification of problems within the defences and endeavours to fix them. However, it is evident that not enough money was available in the short space of time between the French intentions being recognised and the invasion itself, as the defences were left in a poor condition for lack of maintenance and the sums required to fully repair them would have been high. While men like Cunninghame tried to supplement the defences, it was only attempted once the direction of French troops was understood and therefore much of the work could not be completed before landings began. This is one of the permanent issues that faced the garrison with respect to maintaining their fortifications. While Blakeney appears to have been attempting to improve the situation, the lack of adequate funds from the government prevented any definitive progress and as such it fell to individuals such as Cunninghame to have to spend their own money trying to help defend St Philip's.

Cunninghame's blame of Blakeney for the condition of the defences appears unfounded, although he could be criticised for attempting to improve things too late. However, Cunninghame's position as deputy chief engineer meant that he was not always privy to the full details of how the capital was allocated. Indeed, his diary shows that he was often not invited to the war councils where these issues would be discussed. His blame was directed at the highest authority he could observe, but the evidence shows that this problem was caused higher up the chain of command and lay with the Treasury and Ordnance Office rather than the lieutenant governor.

The other major criticism that Cunninghame lay, one with which Sloss fully agrees, was that no troops were sent out to skirmish with the French and slow their advance. This would have involved either attacking small bodies of French troops

---

53 NAM 1968-07-227-1, *Journal of the Siege* (Unpublished).
54 TNA WO 53/504-507, Ordnance Office Bill Books 1754-55.

or destroying the roads in advance of the French. On this point the sources appear to contradict one another. Cunninghame's published version of his journal sets out his case stating that 'Frequent proposals were made to the Commander in Chief to send out reconnoitres, several offered themselves volunteers to observe when the enemy began to move and work, but except three times I don't remember that any was allowed to go out.'[55] In addition to this, he added a lengthy section on how he felt a successful defence should be carried out. He noted several parts of the high road that should be broken up, but he also noted that 'many things in the above scheme were found wanting'.[56] However, there is evidence that while skirmishing parties were not sent out, rightly, given the size of the French forces and the hostile nature of the population, parties of engineers — including Cunninghame himself — were sent out by Blakeney to carry out actions included in the proposed defence scheme. In his intelligence report, one of the men, Soloman Arrovas, who was sent out to reconnoitre the French force provided information relating to other British troops on missions on the island.

> I was order'd ... to go as far as Ciutadella in the Island of Minorca, to see after Capt Robert Preston Major Cunninghame and his party. It was reported that they were taken by the French ... I met with another party of Lieut Wicket of Colonel Dunofs Regiment; destroying the bridge and the roads ... I went as far as the bridge to observe the motions of the enemy where I found the bridge broken down that I could go no further.[57]

Arrovas' report clearly shows not only that troops were ordered to observe the enemy movements, and in reasonable numbers, but that Cunninghame was amongst one of the parties of troops ordered to do this. Arrovas' report is further verified by the journal by Captain D'arvey which states that 'Major Cunninghame was sent with a force to pull down the bridges and break up the road, he was covered by a Captain's party'.[58] These sources corroborate the argument that troops were sent out by the garrison in order to observe and slow down the French advance without engaging them. The only source that supports Cunninghame's view of minimal input from the garrison is the later-published *Answer to an Infamous Libel*. It states that the roads being on solid rock prevented them from being easily demolished by troops.[59] The author of the response has not been verified, and it would therefore seem that their presence was not at a high enough level within the chain of command to have known about the troop movements. Alternatively, and a more likely conclusion, the author had not been present at the siege and only had available the printed material that was in circulation during and after the trial of Byng. This would explain the connection between the response and Byng's statements during the trial in favour of the letters and papers from officers and men during the siege which had not been

---

55   NAM 1968-07-226, *Journal of the Siege* (Published).
56   NAM 1968-07-226, *Journal of the Siege* (Published).
57   TNA T 1/371/39, Report by Soloman Arrovas.
58   TNA WO 55/556/2, D'arvey Journal.
59   Anon., *Answer to Infamous Libel*, p.17.

published. Therefore, the garrison did attempt to slow the French advance and remain informed of their movements until they were forced into St Philip's.

Regarding the presence of skirmishers, Arrovas' worry at the beginning of his report that Cunninghame and his men had been captured indicates one of the main reasons why Blakeney appears to have avoided actively attacking the French as they advanced towards Mahon. With so few troops available in order to man the significant defences of St Philip's, Blakeney intended to use every man at his disposal in order to strengthen his position and hold out longer. It is also for this reason, it appears, that the request was made to the British naval forces that operated out of Minorca, Commodore Edgecumbe's squadron, to remain in Mahon harbour, protected by a boom, and to transfer all fighting seamen and marines to the fort. This request was rejected by the captains of the squadron, but a small force from HMS *Dolphin,* the smallest vessel in the squadron, was left behind under Captain Scroop, the vessel's commander.[60] These men were left under Scroop's command were placed inside St Philip's with the other troops from across the island. By attempting to avoid any unnecessary casualties and bolster the garrison with the naval squadron it is clear that, given the size of the garrison, the strategy that had been developed was to slow the French without risking losses, and then to focus on the main defences at St Philip's, with all men at Blakeney's disposal.

Over all, the criticisms which have been levelled against the garrison in general, and Blakeney in particular, regarding the opening phases of the siege appear to be unfounded. Reconnaissance and road destruction certainly appear to have occurred. The defences were neglected and suffering for want of much needed repairs but, as has been shown, this was a perennial problem for the garrison based upon the lack of resources from the government, especially money, and not wholly because of the mismanagement of the garrison. This meant that they required more men to defend them than if they had been in good condition. Also, tactically, Blakeney made the right call in refusing to have his men engage in any skirmishing with the advancing French force, as the loss of men would have done far greater damage to the ability of the garrison to hold St Philip's than the short amount of time that would have been gained by rear-guard actions. The garrison understood the advantages it possessed and correctly attempted to use them. They understood their role in the defence of the island as one of delay.

Cunninghame also levels another criticism against the garrison, relating to the civil governance and the relations between the garrison and the local population. Cunninghame believed that the latter, especially those that had been involved in the maintenance and supply of the garrison over the preceding period, should be compelled by force, if necessary, into St Philip's at the commencement of the siege in order to prevent any key information reaching the French forces. The French certainly were handicapped by a lack of reliable information; Sloss has demonstrated that their primary source regarding the island and St Philip's was the history of the island written by Lieutenant John Armstrong several years earlier.[61] This text was not only out of date but, according to Cunninghame, contained numerous

---

60   TNA WO 55/556/2, Captain D'arvey Journal.
61   Sloss, *A Small Affair*, p.13.

inaccuracies even at the time of its publication.[62] There was certainly an argument to be made in favour of collecting those that might have key information and placing them safely within the garrison to secure this information from the French. We know that some of the Spanish did end up in St Philip's during the siege. Sources vary, but a number of roughly between 40 and 60 appear in the various charts drawn up by those recording the siege. However, given the evidence from the Ordnance Office, this would still leave a sizeable number of men who had laboured on one project or another over the previous few years at large on the island.

Despite these issues with information, the rounding up of citizens on the island would not only have been unfeasible but also likely counterproductive. Once the Minorcans learnt of the French invasion, they rapidly dropped any pretence of remaining loyal to the British. Not only was Richelieu presented with the keys to Ciutadella when he landed, but Arrovas also notes in his reports that 'I heard the enemy marching and saw some Spaniards breaking open the fields which I supposed to be for the French to pass'.[63] This not only demonstrates the level of opposition that was present on the island against the British but also lessened the impact of their attempts to damage the roads and slow the French advance as the Spanish allowed them to move around those obstacles. Furthermore, there is evidence that shows that the population was, in some cases, actively hostile to British troops. There were cases of attacks on British soldiers throughout the period, and one journal notes that some following the French invasion took place on some of the outlying sentry posts by the Minorcans even as the French were leaving Ciutadella.[64] This hostile population would have significantly hampered any efforts to skirmish effectively with the French forces as they advanced. It also can be argued to be one of the main reasons why Blakeney did not attempt to bring into St Philip's those Minorcans who had knowledge of parts of the interior. Not only would troops have had to go in large numbers to bring them, as they would have certainly resisted such attempts, but it also would have been required to set guards upon them in case they attempted to escape from the fortress, where they would now be in possession of even greater information regarding the strength of the garrison. Indeed, the *Response to Libel* argues this exact point: the hostile population prevented any meaningful attempts at control. Although French intelligence was certainly assisted by the British reluctance to bring Minorcan workers into the garrison, the possible costs of such actions would also have been high, as the population was actively hostile and assisted the French in their efforts. The garrison was isolated and forced to focus all resources on the defence of St Philip's rather than on controlling the populace.

Possibly the largest complaint laid against the garrison and Blakeney, by his critics, was that they capitulated too early and without putting up enough of a fight. By the time of the main assault of St Philip's, the siege had been going on for three months with almost daily bombardment, threat of assault by sea, especially after the failure of the relief fleet, and constant vigilance was required to maintain the defences over the extensive works. The main assault by the French on 27 June attacked all major

---

62   NAM 1968-07-225, *Journal of a Journey*.
63   TNA T 1/371/39, Arrovas Report.
64   TNA WO 55/556/2, Captain D'arvey Journal.

areas of the fortress. Captain D'arvey even noted that French troops in boats were scaling the cliffs whilst attacks on all parts of the walls were being carried out.[65] This highly coordinated assault allowed them to carry some of the outer defences and redoubts and even make their way into parts of the subterraneans which, as shown earlier, were critical for the defence of St Philip's. Furthermore, the attack succeeded in wounding Cunninghame and capturing the second-in-command of the garrison, Colonel Jeffries, who had been instrumental in the defence as the highest-ranking officer able to traverse the defences (Blakeney by this point was suffering from gout and was unable to walk unaided). Although the troops that had gained the Marlborough Fort were driven out with a mine, D'arvey states that the defences were badly damaged. This contrasts with Cunninghame's account, which argues that the fortress was still very much defensible and that the capitulation occurred too soon.[66]

It is therefore necessary to look at the impact of the siege on the defences, supplies, and men of the garrison to understand whether or not the capitulation occurred too early. It should be stated that even if Cunninghame was correct in his assumptions it is likely that the fortress would still have capitulated before Admiral Hawke, who was on route with a second relief fleet, arrived from Gibraltar given his position at the time of the actual capitulation.[67] The first point is, of course, the foothold in the subterraneans. As these stretched to almost all major parts of the fortress and contained many of the remaining stores, they would have to be defended constantly from the French, who could push further in at any time. Therefore, this increased the total area which required defending by a garrison which, as has already been shown, was too small for effective defence even before casualties. One of the concerns on the minds of the garrison commanders would have been their inability to spread their limited resources around to the defences in the event of another full-scale assault. Even if Cunninghame's opinion that the defences were in good order was correct, it seems doubtful that the already-depleted garrison could have held off another assault when there were even more areas to defend.

In addition to this, there is some disparity amongst the sources as to the quality of the defences. Cunninghame claims that they were in good order and that the breaches that had been made in the walls were 'as such as when they mounted by scaling ladders the shortnes of them obliged the soldiers to scramble singly over each other'.[68] There is little mention of the quality of the entire fortifications within the other sources, either strength or weaknesses. Instead, the other sources appear to show a resignation towards the idea of capitulation. In his journal, D'arvey does not express surprise about the capitulation after listing the places that the French had taken in the first assault. Rather, he seems to have been resigned to the situation: many of his entries towards the end, much like Cunninghame's, conclude with statements that no British fleet had been sighted.[69] This shows how low morale was

---

65 TNA WO 55/556/2, Captain D'arvey Journal.
66 N.A.M 1968-07-226, *Journal of the Siege* (Published).
67 Gregory, *Minorca*, p.170.
68 NAM 1968-07-226, *Journal of the Siege* (Published).
69 TNA WO 55/556/2, Captain D'arvey Journal; NAM 1968-07-227-1, *Journal of the Siege* (Unpublished).

becoming towards the end of the siege, and that the officers understood that they could not hold for much longer, even if the actual length of time was a disputed issue. This is mirrored in the *Faithful and authentic account of the siege and surrender* journal: rather than discuss the ability of the fortress to hold out, the author uses his last remarks to highlight how difficult holding parts of the fortress had become. 'The Marlborough fort was attacked by seven hundred men, led by a prince of the blood … it is needless to say more to the honour of this fort, than that it was defended by a captain and 50 men.'[70] In addition to this, the *Response to Libel* adds that many of the fort's guns were now out of order, having been destroyed over the course of the siege.[71]

A fort's ability to hold against aggression is predicated upon both the number of men able to defend it, but also the morale of those men. Cunninghame's account, though not without its issues, is the perception of an engineer who understood the nature of fortifications. However, as this chapter has sought to demonstrate, he did not necessarily have sound military judgement or understand the garrison he was assisting. The other journals show, if not defeatism, then a resignation that they could not hold against another assault. This, combined with the losses that they had suffered and the lack of a British fleet arriving, meant that morale was low and it would have been extremely difficult to energise the men to further defence. The capitulation terms offered were very favourable to the British: they were to be taken on French ships to Gibraltar, having marched out of the fort in good order, and were allowed to continue fighting the French.[72] Had the deal been harsher it is possible that the surrender might not have occurred at that point, but by capitulating when he did, Blakeney preserved his four battalions for future fighting in the war.

The tactical decisions made by the garrison were therefore mixed in their effectiveness. By not attempting to slow down the French advance, especially given the hostile population, it proved possible to save men for defending the fortifications. However, they had failed to adequately prepare, by leaving much of St Philip's Town standing which provided cover for the enemy. As the siege continued, it seems to have become clear that they could not rely upon relief and Blakeney therefore sought the best terms possible for their surrender. The final assault had certainly carried parts of the defences, and, while French casualties might have mounted in further assaults, they would also have resulted in the loss of the entire garrison to imprisonment. Cunninghame and Byng's supporters, who levelled this criticism upon the garrison, did so to improve their own positions, and while some of the arguments appear justified, the garrison was still able to hold the fort for a length of time, inflict significant casualties,[73] and honourably surrender. Indeed, the garrison had achieved their main objective, to defend Minorca for as long as possible and await relief, and it is when that relief failed that the idea of capitulation became inevitable. Given the vast array of issues that the garrison faced, they were still remarkably

---

70 Anon., *Faithful and authentic account of the siege and surrender*, p.47.
71 Anon., *Answer to Infamous Libel*, p.13.
72 NAM 1968-07-227-1, *Journal of the Siege* (Unpublished).
73 Gregory, *Minorca*, p.176.

able to conduct an effective defence of St Philip's and last almost long enough for a second relief fleet to make it to the island.

Minorca was an afterthought garrison, with little information reaching the central government of how processes had been established there in order to cope with the unique peculiarities that were faced by successive lieutenant governors. Without an active governor, the island's population had to be controlled by military officials, and tension was the inevitable result. Yet no attempts were made to improve the situation other than slight reprimands for the more extreme cases of military intervention in civil affairs. This left the garrison isolated within a hostile populace, with blame in this case equally upon the garrison itself for failing to meld policy around the needs and expectations of the locals; but also the lack of assistance, with no civil administrators sent to assist what were, in most cases, elderly military officers with no experience of civil governance. Despite holding a key strategic position in the Mediterranean and a substantial modern fort to defend it, there was little in the way of effective administration of the defences in Minorca.

With the expensive but badly needed Queen Anne's Fort scrapped, no additional funds were sent to allow for the upkeep of St Philip's and, as such, much of the fort was badly in need of repair by the time of the invasion. Although the garrison did their best in keeping the fort active and in good condition, the budget did not allow for this to be kept to a high standard. The garrison officers were clearly worried about parts of the fortifications, but the slow movement of affairs in London, especially in regard to the allocation of funding, prevented anything more than jury-rigging parts of the defences. Had the fort been in good condition then it is likely that it could have been held for longer, but, even then, the issue of manpower was never addressed. St Philip's, in poor condition, required a number of men that the government was clearly unwilling to provide. Thus, the ability of the garrison to hold for any length of time was drastically reduced. This was a governmental decision, and the end result of failure to act can be clearly seen. Had the garrison been bolstered, then Minorca would have been a place of significant strategic threat with the ability to defend itself even if the fleet was unable to prevent troops landing.

While Minorca had been able to develop a reliable supply system over the years of occupation, it was meddled with and starved of funds in ways which hurt not only the garrison but also relations with the Minorcans. Despite mismanagement by those appointed to control the supplies, the system still functioned until meddling from London occurred. Then the system broke down, supplies suffered, and the quality of the garrison was reduced. Had more attention been paid to the practices that had been developed to supply the garrison, and greater credence given to issues of funding when they were raised, then the supply system for Minorca would not only have been more robust but also would have been able to supply more troops and render the island a stronger military base.

The siege itself is where most criticism has been laid. The evidence has shown, however, that the garrison's position was one of significant weakness. Undermanned, with an ageing and dilapidated fortress, a hostile local population, and a large proportion of officers absent, the situation was dire. That being said, with all those factors taken into account, the garrison officers clearly made some sound tactical decisions, correctly conserving the few men they had to give time for relief forces to arrive and making best use of the resources and defences at their disposal. They had, however, also made some errors, in not fully preparing for a long siege, most likely because of the belief in relief by sea. The capitulation was not directly after the failure of the fleet: the garrison fought on until they were finally put under too much pressure. With the loss of parts of the fortress, mounting casualties, no sign of relief and the capture of the second-in-command, Lieutenant General Blakeney took the best capitulation agreement possible, with his men to be returned to British territory at French expense and at liberty to continue fighting.

The loss for Britain was a strategically significant island, but not one that they appeared to have any intention of making use of. Nor did the Spanish join the war as the French had hoped. Over all, the garrison's capitulation, given the failure of the fleet, was inevitable, but was accelerated more by longer-term factors rather than by any errors in military decision-making during the siege. These issues had been caused by a negligent management of the island, which would have likely collapsed sooner had not there been effective agents making the system work. The few attempts at intervention caused more problems than they solved and required additional work from the garrison to rectify.

Minorca was a forgotten island, a staging ground for a small Mediterranean fleet, a place ageing or ineffective officers were sent to see out their careers. Little attention was paid to how the island was administered and few resources were ever diverted in its favour. Minorca's garrison was left to its own devices, not by choice but by apathy, and it was this apathy that was to blame for many of the issues which beset the garrison and led to the eventual fall of the island, and one of the biggest losses for Britain during the Seven Years War.

Bibliography

Manuscript Sources
National Army Museum (NAM)
    1968-07-225, Journal of a Journey to Minorca.
    1968-07-226, Journal of the Siege of St Philip's Castle, (Published).
    1968-02-226-1, *Plan du Fort Phillipe, Avec les Attaques, Leve par les Ingenieurs depuis le Siege*.
    1968-07-227-1, Journal of the Siege of St Philip's Castle, (Unpublished).
The National Archives (TNA)
    PC 1/60/8, Report on the Arrest of Magistrates, 1750.
    PC 1/6/41, Report Requiring Response from General Blakeney, 1755.
    SP 89/50/241, Letter from Castres in Lisbon, 20 April 1756.
    SP 89/50/245, Letter from Castres in Lisbon to H. Fox, 10 May 1756.
    SP 89/50/251, Letter from Castres in Lisbon, 25 May 1756.
    T 1/368/82, Estimate of the Charge of His Majesty's Forces in the Plantations, Minorca and Gibraltar, 1756.
    T1/368/77, Petition on Gunpowder Landing, 1757.
    T 1/368/85, One Years Contingency of Minorca from the Separate Accounts of Following Lieutenant Governors, 1743-1750.

T 1/371/39, Report by Soloman Arrovas on Intelligence Reports.
T 1/382/114, Petition of Greek Volunteers, 1757.
WO 24/248, Establishment of His Majesty's Forces in Minorca and Gibraltar, 1745.
WO 24/262, Establishment of His Majesty's Forces in Minorca and Gibraltar, 1747.
WO 24/273, Establishment of His Majesty's Forces in Minorca and Gibraltar, 1748.
WO 24/281, Establishment of His Majesty's Forces in Minorca and Gibraltar, 1749.
WO 24/288, Establishment of His Majesty's Forces in Minorca and Gibraltar, 1750.
WO 24/292, Establishment of His Majesty's Forces in Minorca and Gibraltar, 1751.
WO 24/296, Establishment of His Majesty's Forces in Minorca and Gibraltar, 1752.
WO 24/300, Establishment of His Majesty's Forces in Minorca and Gibraltar, 1753.
WO 24/304, Establishment of His Majesty's Forces in Minorca and Gibraltar, 1754.
WO 24/310, Establishment of His Majesty's Forces in Minorca and Gibraltar, 1755.
WO 53/488-507, Ordnance Office Bill Books, 1746-1756,
WO 55/1556/2, A Journal of Military Proceedings at Minorca, 1756.

West Yorkshire Archives (WAY)
WYL100/PO/5/I, Appointment of Henry Pelham as Commissary General.
WYL 100/PO/5/II/11-20, Bill Books for Ammunition Bread, 1746-1754.
WYL 100/PO/5/III/57-77, Correspondence from Minorca to Lord Irvin.
WYL 100/PO/5/IV/10-67, Correspondence from Humpfrey Portman to Lord Irvin.
WYL 100/PO/5/V/1-9, Miscellaneous Correspondence to Lord Irvin.

Published Primary Sources

Anon., *A Faithful and authentic account of the siege and surrender of St. Philip's Fort, in the Island of Minorca. Containing, every particular occurrence and remarkable incident. An account of the strength of the garrison. The Second edition. Officer on the Spot* (London: H.B. Russia 1757).

Anon., *A Full Account of The Siege of Minorca: By The French, In 1756. With All The Circumstances Relating Thereto* (London, A and C Corbett, N.D.).

Anon., *A Full Answer to an Infamous Libel, etc.* (London: W Reive, 1757).

Anon., *The Trial of the Honourable Admiral John Byng* (London: R. Mansby 1757).

Richmond, Captain H.W. (ed.) *Papers Relating to the Loss Of Minorca in 1756* (London: Publications for Naval Record Society: 1913).

Secondary Sources

Baugh, Daniel, *The Global Seven Years' War 1754-1763* (London: Routledge, 2011).

Gregory, Desmond, *Minorca, The Illusory Prize* (Rutherford: Farleigh Dickinson University Press: 1990).

Pope, Dudley, *At 12 Mr Byng was Shot* (London: Phoenix 1962).

Rodger, N.A.M., *The Command of the Ocean, A Naval History of Britain, 1649-1815* (London: Allen Lane, 2004).

Sloss, Janet, *A Small Affair, The French Occupation of Menorca During the Seven Years' War* (Tetbury: Fuerteventura Press 2000).

Sloss, Janet, *Richard Kane, Governor of Minorca* (Tetbury: Fuerteventura Press 1995).

Tunstall, Brian. *Admiral Byng* (London: P. Allen, 1928).

7

'Another Tarnish for British Valour': Responses to Success and Failure in Wellington's Peninsular Army

Zack White

In late September 1808, George Cruikshank's caricature 'Whitlock the Second, or Another Tarnish for British Valour' appeared in London's caricature shops for the first time.[1] Created in response to the recently signed Convention of Cintra, it reflected the public's distaste for this latest development in what would become known as the Peninsular War.[2] Under the terms of the convention, Lisbon was liberated from the occupying French forces in return for the commander of the British forces in Portugal, Sir Hew Dalrymple, consenting to repatriate the French troops and their baggage (a condition which the French exploited to include everything they had plundered from the Portuguese).[3]

Cruikshank's caricature is striking in the way that its primary focus was not on the impact of the Convention on the Portuguese nation, or on the strategic situation in the Iberian Peninsula. Instead, as the print's title implies, he was concerned about the failure to uphold Britain's reputation. This tone was symptomatic of the wider public mood, which exhibited a despondency over Cintra that dampened the initial excitement that news of the Dos de Mayo uprising in Madrid had elicited from the British public.

However, this reaction was by no means limited to civilians, as it was equally apparent amongst the British troops. Captain William Warre remarked in a letter home to his father that 'the indignation expressed in all the English papers at the capitulation [...] is scarce equal to what has been felt by every individual of the

---

[1] George Cruikshank, *Whitlock the second or Another Tarnish for British Valour*, 29 September 1808, British Museum, Museum Number 18521217390.
[2] For a more detailed analysis of how public opinion of the Peninsular War was reflected in caricatures and newspapers, see Zack White, 'From Cintra to Salamanca': Shifting Popular Perceptions of the War in the Iberian Peninsula, 1808-1812', *British Journal for Military History*, 1:3 (June 2015), pp.60-79.
[3] Ian Fletcher, 'The Peninsular War', in I. Fletcher (ed.) *The Peninsular War: Aspects of the Struggle for the Iberian Peninsula* (Staplehurst: Spellmount, 1998), p.5.

army'.[4] Warre's opinion was by no means an isolated one, as Robert Porter expressed the same sentiment in his own letters.[5] Interestingly, both men attributed this discontent amongst the troops to a commonly held perception amongst all ranks that Cintra had caused the army to lose the British public's gratitude for their efforts at Rolica and Vimeiro, where they had defeated the French just a few weeks before.

Whilst not a strategic setback, the Convention of Cintra marked one of a series of episodes in which the morale of the troops appeared to drop. As Charles Esdaile commented at the 5th Wellington Congress, it is too easy to see the Peninsular War as a constant march to victory, and it is impossible to imagine that the morale of the army did not fluctuate in line with its fortunes as the victorious Anglo-Portuguese force was repeatedly obliged to conduct prudent withdrawals in the face of the overwhelming numerical advantage of their French opponents. The Peninsular War was littered with instances where morale collapsed, and where discipline swiftly followed suit, most notably during the retreats to Corunna in 1808-1809, and from Burgos to Ciudad Rodrigo in late 1812. Equally, there were moments where the strategic situation was just as serious as in those instances, yet the troops succeeded in maintaining their cohesion, such as in the wake of their victory at the Battle of Talavera, in 1809, when Wellington was forced to withdraw to the Portuguese border. It is therefore clear that even a brief survey of morale in the British army over the course of the Peninsular War has the potential to answer important questions about the success and cohesion of the British Army on campaign. What circumstances, for example, were required to precipitate a catastrophic collapse of discipline, such as that seen in late 1808-1809? How did the British soldier come to terms with such setbacks, and, in times of success, what did the troops attribute those successes to? More fundamentally, how did British soldiers perceive themselves, and their role in the wider Napoleonic Wars?

Answering these questions is by no means a simple process. As morale is in large part dependent on the mood and perceptions of an individual, it is an extremely challenging concept to identify with total certainty across a large body of troops. In order to ensure that the attitudes and coping mechanisms identified in this chapter are as representative as possible of the British troops who fought in the Iberian Peninsula, a wide range of sources have been consulted. Foremost among these are the memoirs, letters and diaries of British non-commissioned officers and privates. There are, however, limitations to these sources, which must be acknowledged. Firstly, whilst scholars of the Peninsular War are fortunate to be able to access far more first-hand testimony from the rank and file of Wellington's army than for any other conflict in the preceding century, the available material only represents a small proportion of the troops who served.[6] Furthermore, those who did write down their thoughts were obviously the literate within a sub-section of society where literacy rates were low. In order to better determine a representative view across the lower ranks of Wellington's force, the testimony of officers has also been consulted.

---

4 William Warre (ed. E. Warre), *Letters from the Peninsula 1808-1812* (Staplehurst: Spellmount, 1999), p.23. William Warre to his father, 29 September 1808.
5 Robert Porter, *Letters from Portugal and Spain* (London: Longman, 1809), pp.2-3.
6 Charles Oman, *Wellington's Army* (London: Edward Arnold, 1912), p.375.

Whilst potentially influenced by the perceptions of their class, these nonetheless provide valuable insight into the wider perceptions and mood of the army, as the extracts from Warre and Porter have demonstrated above. Where possible, greater emphasis has been given to letters and diaries written during the conflict, as these are less likely to be influenced by hindsight, and are more likely to reflect the raw emotions exhibited during the conflict. Where appropriate, desertion rates, identifiable through analysis of the monthly returns for regiments serving in Spain and Portugal, have also been consulted. These have been supplemented by Wellington's own letters, and the General Orders for the forces under his command, all of which are available at the University of Southampton's Hartley Library.

Through close comparison of this diverse range of sources, it has been possible to identify a number of key themes which interacted to underpin troops' morale throughout the conflict. Firstly, troops generally drew on a basic confidence in their commander, developing a respect for Wellington's talents as a general. More fundamental though, was an intrinsic self-confidence which men exhibited in their own abilities as soldiers, which eclipsed all other considerations, and was based on a quasi-nationalistic belief in their prowess. Closely related to this was an underlying xenophobia which was drawn upon in times of setback in order to shield the men from self-criticism by making their Portuguese and, in particular, Spanish allies scapegoats for the issues that the army was facing. Finally, the shortage of supplies, which was a significant problem for the British throughout the conflict, had the potential to sow discord amongst the troops, and precipitate a collapse in troops' morale.

It is important to appreciate that this chapter forms part of a wider discussion on the motivation of troops in war. Much of this debate has related to combat effectiveness and cohesion. Stephen Westbrook has advocated the importance of 'primary group theory' arguing that 'the moral involvement of the soldier with a larger collectivity is dependent on the formation of psychological bonds between the soldier and the collectivity such that the soldier believes, more or less consciously, that his own welfare and that of the group are related.'[7] He goes on to identify three fundamental components to an army's cohesion: ties to fellow soldiers, *esprit de corps* or ties to the unit, and involvement in the nation's socio-political system.[8] This analysis is an extension of the work of Morris Janowitz, who argued that morale was too simplistic a term to be used by itself, and that a more sophisticated social model was required in order to analyse combat performance.[9]

However, both Janowitz and Westbrook were primarily concerned with troops in combat. More recent work has taken these theoretical principles and examined the extent to which they can be applied to soldiers serving in the long eighteenth

---

7 Stephen D. Westbrook, 'The Potential for Military Disintegration', in Sam Sarkesian (ed.), *Combat Effectiveness: Cohesion, Stress, and the Volunteer Military*, Sage Research Progress Series on War, Revolution and Peacekeeping, Volume 9 (Beverly Hills, Sage Publications, 1980) pp.244-278 (p.251).
8 Westbrook, 'The Potential for Military Disintegration', p.251.
9 Morris Janowitz, *Sociology and the Military Establishment*, 3rd edn (London: Sage Publications, 1974), p.26.

century and their wider experiences as soldiers. Ilya Berkovich's *Motivation in War* draws heavily on Westbrook's models of motivation to conclude that coercion played far less of a role in troop behaviour during the eighteenth century than has generally been recognised, suggesting instead that primary group cohesion was far more important as a motivator for the troops.[10] Similarly, Edward Coss's *All for the King's Shilling* closely examines the applicability of primary group theory to soldiers in Wellington's army, concluding that 'group allegiance, not sociopathic tendencies, the allure of money, or fear of punishment, allowed the British redcoat to become one of the most reliable combat soldiers of the period', whilst also shedding new light on the issue of supplies, by demonstrating that the rations which troops received were nutritionally completely inadequate for the tasks that they had to complete.[11]

By contrast, Andrew Bamford's *Sickness, Suffering and the Sword* places greater emphasis on the value of the regimental system when explaining the success of the British army on campaign during the Napoleonic Wars, in line with the second of the three fundamental components of Westbrook's theory.[12] Other works, such as Michael Hughes's *Forging Napoleon's Grande Armee* or John Lynn's *Bayonets of the Republic* have similarly confirmed the applicability of much of Janowitz's and Westbrooks' theories to the French army during the Napoleonic era.[13]

Nonetheless, whilst these works are able to persuasively outline how units maintained their cohesion both on and off the battlefield, there has been little work studying the factors that cause the disintegration of units, and how soldiers themselves sought to manage and cope with that process. Whilst primary group or regimental ties may have been able to help prevent disintegration, the fact that, within a relatively short space of time, cohesion could collapse before re-forming again demonstrates that other factors must also affect the outlook of troops. These factors are the focus on this chapter, showing that whilst Westbrook's theory is a sound one, there were factors at play in times of setback which could override ties to the primary group, unit, or nation.

Private William Wheeler provided a useful indicator of what mattered to British troops when, in 1816, he wrote:

> If England should require the service of her army again, and I should be with it, let me have 'Old Nosey' to command. Our interests would be sure to be looked into, we should never have occasion to fear an enemy. There are two things we should be certain of. First, we should always be as well supplied with rations as the nature of the service would admit. The second

---

[10] Ilya Berkovich, *Motivation in War: The Experience of Common Soldiers in Old-Regime Europe* (Cambridge: Cambridge University Press, 2017), p.228.

[11] Edward Coss, *All for the King's Shilling: The British Soldier Under Wellington, 1808-1814* (Norman: University of Oklahoma Press, 2010), p.237.

[12] A. Bamford, *Sickness, Suffering and the Sword: The British Regiment on Campaign, 1808-1815* (Norman: University of Oklahoma Press, 2013), p.73.

[13] Michael J. Hughes, *Forging Napoleon's Grande Armee: Motivation, Military Culture, and Masculinity in the French Army, 1800-1808* (New York: New York University Press, 2012); John Lynn, *The Bayonets of the Republic: Motivation and Tactics in the Army of Revolutionary France, 1791-94* (Chicago: University of Illinois, 1984).

is we should be sure to give the enemy a damned good thrashing. What can a soldier desire more?[14]

Wheeler's comment clearly points to two important factors: the ability of the soldier to trust his commander, and supply. Whilst Wellington was never loved by his men in the way that Napoleon was, there was nonetheless a widespread recognition amongst British troops, and respect for the fact, that Wellington was both frugal with his men's lives and did his best to keep them supplied.[15] It should be acknowledged that, since it was written in 1816, Wheeler's comment is undoubtedly affected by the rose-tinted perspective of hindsight. However, whilst Wellington was not guaranteed the approval of his men upon being appointed commander of the expedition which was despatched to Portugal in 1808, he was regarded favourably. Captain Warre commented that 'Sir A. W. [Arthur Wellesley] is a very good officer and much esteemed, and I trust we have neither a Whitelock or Gower among us'.[16] Similarly, when Wellington was sent out to take command of the army for a second time in the spring of 1809, having gone home to give evidence and defend his reputation at the enquiry into the Convention of Cintra, Captain the Hon. Edward Cocks remarked 'Sir Arthur Wellesley has taken the command of the army and inspired fresh spirit into every breast.'[17] Implicit in Cocks' remark is that Wellington's deployment to Portugal in 1809 served as a morale boost in the wake of the disastrous Corunna campaign, something which would in large part have been due to the victories that he had led his army to at Rolica and Vimeiro the previous year. Wellington had a proven record of success, and it is only natural that this bolstered the men's confidence, whilst also implying that the government was committed to continuing the war in the Peninsula, thereby giving the troops another chance to prove themselves in battle. This latter sentiment, as we shall see below, was often at the forefront of the soldier's psyche.

Whilst it is difficult to determine how strong or widespread the support for Wellington was across all ranks of the army early in the conflict, what cannot be disputed is that by 1811 Wellington's unbroken string of victories was recognised and admired by his men. Private John Cooper recalled a conversation with his colleague whilst advancing in the midst of the Battle of Albuera, in which Marshal Beresford, and not Wellington, was in command. As the troops observed the bloodshed around them, one asked Cooper: '"Whore's [sic] ar *Arthur*?' meaning Wellington.

---

14 William Wheeler (ed. B.H. Lidell Hart), *The Letters of Private William Wheeler 1809-1828* (London: Michael Joseph, 1951), p.196.
15 R. Muir, *Wellington: The Path to Victory 1769-1814* (New Haven: Yale University Press, 2013), p.588; Andrew Roberts, *Napoleon the Great* (London: Penguin, 2014), p.510; Zack White, "Old Nosey' and 'The Scum of the Earth': Assessing the relationship between Arthur Wellesley and his troops in the Iberian Peninsula' *Mars & Clio*, 38 (Winter 2013), pp.79-96.
16 Warre, *Letters from the Peninsula*, p.8. Warre to his mother, 27 June 1808. Sir Arthur Wellesley was only made Viscount Wellington following his victory at the Battle of Talavera in July 1809.
17 Edward Cocks (ed. Julia V. Page), *Intelligence Officer in the Peninsula: Letters and Diaries of Major the Hon Edward Charles Cocks, 1786-1812* (Tunbridge Wells: Spellmount, 1986), p.25. 6 May 1809, Coimbra, to his father.

I said, "I don't know, I don't see him." He rejoined, "Aw wish he wor here." So did I.'[18] Albuera was seemingly a moment during which the troops' appreciation of the value of being commanded by Wellington became more readily apparent and was expressed vocally. When he visited the wounded of the 29th Foot following Albuera, Charlie Leslie recalled how Wellington remarked 'Old Twenty-Ninth! I am sorry to see so many of you here!' According to Leslie, the men replied: 'My Lord, if you had been with us, there would not have been so many of us here.'[19] Equally, although written many years later, John Kincaid commented that by 1811 there was a consensus within the army that 'we would rather see his long nose in a fight than a reinforcement of ten thousand men any day'.[20]

Wellington was certainly aware of the morale boosting effect of his presence, commenting that, 'when I come myself, the soldiers think that what they have to do is the most important, since I am there [...] they will do for me what, perhaps, no one else can make them do'.[21] This was not vanity talking, as a number of individuals drew unfavourable comparisons between other commanders and Wellington, based on their experiences under the latter. Thomas Blomfield wrote to his father with concern about how Wellington exposed himself too much during battle: 'God knows what would become of our army if anything befell him, there not being another general in my opinion equal to the task'.[22] George Bell confirmed Wellington's impression in his own memoir, remarking that:

> Every General, as well as regiment, had a nickname. But there was a mutual confidence that could not be shaken between the parties, and they one and all, had the firmest reliance on Wellington. He never came near us without a cheer from the men that made the woods ring. When he appeared, the men would say, 'There he comes with his long nose, boys; you may fix your flints'.[23]

John Cooper recalled his experiences under the command of Edward Pakenham in the War of 1812, commenting that 'had Wellington been there, the Americans would have had less to boast of'.[24] Similarly, Wheeler wrote home to his family in 1815, commenting on the unadulterated joy with which the troops had greeted the

---

18 John Cooper, *Rough Notes of Seven Campaigns 1809-1815* (Staplehurst: Spellmount, 1996), p.63.
19 Charles Esdaile, *Peninsular Eyewitnesses: The Experience of War in Spain and Portugal 1808-1813* (Barnsley: Pen and Sword, 2008), p.167.
20 John Kincaid, *Adventures in the Rifle Brigade and Random Shots from a Rifleman* (Glasgow: Richard Drew, 1909), pp.36-37.
21 Quoted in Michael Glover, *Wellington's Army in the Peninsula, 1808-1814* (London: David & Charles, 1977), p.183.
22 Thomas Blomfield (ed. Jason Blomfield), *Observations of Peninsular War Sieges and Battles* (Adelaide: NP, 2017), p.26.
23 George Bell (ed. Brian Stuart), *Soldier's Glory being 'Rough Notes of an Old Soldier'* (London: G. Bell & Sons Ltd, 1956), p.63.
24 Cooper, *Rough Notes of Seven Campaigns*, p.134.

news that Wellington was to take over command of British forces in Flanders ahead of what would become the Waterloo campaign.[25]

These extracts provide clear support for the argument that Westbrook's theory is largely applicable to the context of the British Army in the Peninsular War. As long as the troops had a commander that they could trust, they could justifiably believe that it was in their interests to remain committed to the army and to fight well.

However, attitudes to Wellington, and other commanders of the period, are more complex than these quotes seem to imply. Despite the esteem which Wellington was held in by all ranks by the middle of the Peninsular War, this confidence in their commander did not always result in unadulterated support and commitment to the cause. Orders or comments by Wellington could cause resentment and even reduce the morale of the troops. A circular letter issued by Wellington following the retreat from Burgos to Ciudad Rodrigo in late 1812 was deeply resented by the troops. In a comment that shows a rare lack of appreciation of the realities on the ground, Wellington wrote to his divisional commanders condemning the fact that despite the army having:

> [S]uffered no privations, which but trifling attention on the part of the officers could not have prevented, and for which there existed no reason whatever in the nature of the service; nor has it suffered any hardships excepting those resulting from the necessity of being exposed to the inclemencies of the weather at a moment when they were most severe […] outrages of all descriptions were committed with impunity, and losses have been sustained which ought never to have occurred.[26]

In truth, the last few days of the retreat had seen the troops receive virtually no rations, as poor staff work by the commissariat department meant that supplies were sent on a different route to the army's line of march. As a result, there was considerable discontent amongst the troops. Whilst some, such as Wheeler, considered the criticism to be justified, Bragge at least initially thought that the damage had the potential to be lasting: 'I thought he [Wellington] would find himself not so popular in the Army. He has now given the infantry tents […] therefore he is again a fine fellow'.[27]

Equally, William Brown reacted with fury when, in accordance with a General Order, all British troops were searched for the plunder that they had acquired after the Battle of Vittoria, and had their new-found wealth summarily removed.[28] Brown

---

25 Wheeler, *The Letters of Private William Wheeler*, p.161. 29 May 1815, Grammont.
26 J. Gurwood (ed.), *The Despatches of Field Marshal the Duke of Wellington* (London: John Murray, 1834-1838), Vol.VI, pp.180-2, Circular Letter from the Duke of Wellington, 30 November 1812.
27 W. Bragge (ed. S. A. C. Cassels), *Peninsular Portrait, 1811-1814: The Letters of Captain William Bragge, Third (King's Own) Dragoons* (London: Oxford University Press, 1963), pp.99-100, 23 May 1813.
28 William Brown, *The Autobiography or Narrative of a Soldier: The Peninsular War Memoirs of William Brown of the 45th Foot* (Solihull: Helion & Co., 2017), p.128; John Green, *The Vicissitudes of a Soldier's Life* (Louth: J & J. Jackson, 1827), pp.169-170.

responded by completely changing his character, and from that moment onwards, his memoir candidly confesses that he took part in a number of thefts and other forms of 'mischief', as he described it.[29] In Brown's opinion, he had been robbed of the spoils of victory which he considered himself to be entitled to, and whilst he did not blame Wellington directly, this example provides interesting evidence of how commitment to the army's cause was something of a transaction. In the eyes of the men, success in battle should carry with it the benefits of plundering the defeated enemy as a reward, and the removal of that privilege was more than Brown was prepared to tolerate, a type of behaviour which further coincides with Westbrook's argument that troop compliance rested on a mixture of coercion and reward.[30] This removal of a key source of reward (the huge quantities of plunder taken in the aftermath of the Battle of Vittoria) may, in part, explain why August 1813 saw desertion rates within Wellington's army that were proportionately as high as they had been during the retreat from Madrid to Ciudad Rodrigo in late 1812.

Desertion rates must be treated with caution when being used as an indicator of morale within Wellington's army. Even high rates such as those seen during the periods mentioned above amounted to around 0.5 percent of troops deployed in the region in any given month, and at their lowest, in March 1811 were a mere 0.02 percent of troops in Wellington's army. Clearly then desertion was by no means an endemic issue within Wellington's force, but this only serves to highlight how episodes such as those seen in November 1812 and August 1813 were anomalies which merit careful scrutiny.

It must be acknowledged that, at least in August 1813, desertion was also affected by the arrival of news that soldiers who had enlisted for a set period would have their service extended by a further three years under a proclamation issued by the Prince Regent.[31] Nonetheless, the peaks in desertions show the importance of re-appraising the applicability of Westbrook's theory. Desertion was the ultimate demonstration of indifference by a soldier to the fate of his colleagues, fundamentally damaging the primary group system of mutual support by indicating that the deserter was prepared to abandon his peers in favour of prioritising his own concerns. Given that the Articles of War stipulated that deserters could be sentenced to death, the risks were certainly high for those who abandoned their unit, both in terms of punishment by the military courts, and ostracization from the peer group which provided vital support on campaign.[32] Furthermore, the willingness to desert rather than extend service demonstrates a lack of commitment to the nation's socio-political aims, identified by Westbrook as a key facet of his model of motivation. The extent of these limitations is exemplified by the efforts that Cooper went to in order to escape the service on the evening before the Battle of New Orleans, as he tried to persuade his colonel to release him, given that his period of service had expired,

---

29   Brown, *The Autobiography or Narrative of a Soldier*, p.132.
30   Westbrook, 'The Potential for Military Disintegration', p.247.
31   WP9/1/2/7, General Orders, Lezaca, 13 August 1813.
32   *Rules and Articles for the better Government of All His Majesty's Forces* (London: George Eyre & Andrew Strahan, 1798), Section 6, Article 4, pp.18-19.

'ANOTHER TARNISH FOR BRITISH VALOUR' 161

before travelling to headquarters to speak directly to Sir Edward Pakenham.[33] Ultimately, even an experienced soldier such as Cooper was not sufficiently invested in the success of the expedition after seven years of service to risk his life any longer than he was contractually obliged. Instead of being motivated by patriotic fervour to continue to fight for his country, Cooper tried, but ultimately failed, to avoid a further battle.

It is clear from the available data that the desertions were markedly skewed by foreign (non-British) units.[34] Units such as the 5/60th, and Chasseurs Britanniques had issues with desertion which have been well documented elsewhere, and which reflect a lack of zeal for the army's cause which further demonstrates the limited applicability of the socio-political facet of Westbrook's thesis to this context.[35] Proportionately, desertion was much lower amongst British units. Regular British regiments made up a much larger part of the army numerically, yet experienced fewer desertions than the smaller 'foreign' contingent. When considered in isolation from their 'foreign' colleagues, British units demonstrated exceptionally low rates of desertion, when calculated as a proportion of British soldiers deployed in each month of the Peninsular War.

A close examination of the data is nonetheless interesting and revealing, as the moments when desertion levels noticeably peaked usually coincided with times of retreat or strategic setback. October and November 1810, for example, saw a spike as the Anglo-Portuguese army withdrew to the Line of Torres Vedras, north of Lisbon, in the face of a renewed French invasion of Portugal under Massena.[36] The figures for January to February 1809 correspond with the aftermath of the Corunna retreat, and the data for November 1812 is clearly a reflection of the retreat to Ciudad Rodrigo.[37]

There is, however, a noticeable exception to this tendency of desertion rates to spike during withdrawals. November 1808 saw, comparatively, one of the worst desertion rates of the period, which can be matched with this despondent extract from the usually optimistic Porter: 'Although Sir John Moore will exert his talents and military powers to the utmost [...] Thirty thousand men, [...] cannot for any

---

33 Cooper, *Rough Notes of Seven Campaigns*, p.129.
34 Statistics for the numbers of troops deployed, the number of British troops deployed and the total number of desertions each month come from Andrew Bamford's online transcription of WO17/2464-2465 and WO17/2467-2476. The number of desertions from British regiments has been calculated by subtracting the desertions from the Chasseurs Britanniques, the Brunswick Regiment, and the units of the King's German Legion from the total number of desertions.
35 See Robert Griffith, *Riflemen: The History of the 5th Battalion, 60th (Royal American) Regiment 1797-1818* (Warwick: Helion and Company, 2019); Alistair Nichols, *Wellington's Mongrel Regiment: A History of the Chasseurs Britanniques* (Staplehurst: Spellmount, 2005). See also Robert Griffith's chapter in this volume.
36 0.1% and 0.15% of British troops deserted in October and November respectively.
37 0.1% and 0.2% of British troops deserted in January and February 1809 respectively. In November 1812 desertions comparatively soared to 0.3% of British troops, up from a figure of 0.1% the previous month.

length of time, perhaps not in the contest of one battle, oppose, without instant annihilation, the accumulating hosts of France.'[38]

This increase in desertions was not the result of the retreat to Corunna, which only began in the last week of 1808. The troops were clearly struggling for motivation during this period, something which may partly have been due to the British disappointment with the Spaniards. Reports back in Britain during the summer of 1808 had been grossly inflated, implying that the Spanish nation had risen as one in arms against the occupying French forces. The reality that the troops were presented with in the Iberian Peninsula failed to live up to the reports which had been so prevalent in Britain, and the confidence of the British army was therefore severely shaken.[39]

This in turn sheds light on a further factor which most commonly manifested itself during retreats: xenophobia. From the outset of the Peninsular War, the British troops demonstrated a quasi-nationalistic self-belief in their superior skills as soldiers. This in itself is unsurprising, and forms part of a wider development of British national identity during the period. As Linda Colley has argued, the Napoleonic Wars marked the culmination of a century long trend of defining what it meant to be 'British' as simply being 'not French'.[40] As a result, popular culture sought to, quite literally, draw significant differences between British and French soldiers. The British, unsurprisingly, were depicted as a masculine figure, and it is noticeable that in caricatures British soldiers were always drawn with muscular physiques, in contrast to the French who were always portrayed as more 'feminine' and frail.[41] This was mirrored within the army itself, as British soldiers considered themselves to be vastly more capable than the soldiers of any other army (something which of course was not unique, and was equally apparent in the way that French soldiers perceived themselves).[42]

Honour also featured prominently in this self-perception, as George Bell's 1839 memoir summarised the character of the British soldier in the following terms:

> There was great hilarity, buoyant spirit and cheerfulness, a determined resolve to fight to the front, and never say die. When the British soldier is let loose in the field with all his steam up, the difficulty is to keep him in check, to stop his onward rapidity. When he sees the enemy in his front, he fights for his Queen, fights for Old England, fights for victory, and always wins. The British soldier is a queer sort of biped, fierce in battle, full of a child's simplicity and kindness when over. He will tear the shirt off his back to bind up the bleeding wounds of his fallen foe, carrying him away on his

---

38   Porter, *Letters from Portugal and Spain*, p.167. Porter to his unnamed friend, November 1808. Desertion rates represented 0.15% of British troops deployed that month.

39   Gavin Daly, *The British Soldier in the Peninsular War: Encounters with Spain and Portugal, 1808-1814* (Basingstoke: Palgrave Macmillan, 2013), pp.20-21.

40   Linda Colley, *Britons: Forging the Nation 1707-1837*, 3rd edn (London: Vintage, 1996), p.387.

41   See, for example, John Gillray, *Spanish Patriots attacking the French Banditti – Loyal Britons Lending a lift*, 15 August 1808, BM, Museum Number 185109011261; S.W. Forees, *Hogarth's Roast Beef Realised*, 28 November 1810, BM, Museum No.: 186808087962.

42   Hughes, *Forging Napoleon's Grande Armee*, p.117.

back to some quiet spot for medical care, lay him gently down, and divide with him the contents of his flask.[43]

This extract clearly mirrors Westbrook's theory, pointing to both camaraderie and fighting for the nation. However, it is noticeable that Bell was one of the few individuals to speak of the ordinary soldier fighting for his country, and, as the view of a single officer written in hindsight, it is important not to jump to conclusions that the motivation of British troops based on an isolated source.

Nonetheless, that eagerness to fight which Bell referenced emerged repeatedly in memoirs, letters and diaries. Indeed, it is not an exaggeration to say that there was a reckless, hubristic, self-belief amongst British troops that they would defeat the French regardless of the situation. Upon sailing for Corunna in 1808, an anonymous soldier of the 43rd Light Infantry expressed the sentiment particularly clearly:

> Eager for the fray, nothing was coveted save a clear stage and no favour; victory was reckoned on as a matter of course, and as to the hardships and disasters of a hostile or contested land, every inch of which was to be fought for, the idea had no existence, or was dismissed as a trifle.[44]

Exploring how the British soldier psychologically sought to reconcile this arrogant self-confidence with the strategic necessity of retreat is particularly revealing. Some expressed their frustration in terms that related to notions of honour and masculinity. Rifleman Harris recalled of the Corunna retreat: 'After this hasty meal we again pushed on, still cursing the enemy for not again showing themselves, that we might revenge some of our present miseries upon their heads. "Why don't they come on like men," they cried, "whilst we've strength left in us to fight them?"'[45]

A more common reaction, however, was to blame their Spanish and Portuguese allies. For much of the Peninsular War, the jury was out amongst British soldiers over the quality of their allies both in terms of their martial prowess and moral qualities. Frustration by British troops towards their allies should therefore be seen within the context of a wider disillusionment that they felt towards their supposed 'comrades in arms'. Letters and diaries from the period are full of unfavourable comments exemplifying this.[46] One officer was not unusual in expressing first his disgust of the Portuguese, for their lack of hygiene and poor sanitation, and subsequently for the Spanish for their idleness and apparent lack of zeal.[47]

---

43 Bell, *Soldier's Glory*, p.67.
44 Anon, *Memoirs of a Sergeant Late in the Forty-Third Light Infantry* (London: John Mason, 1835), p.39.
45 B. Harris (ed. H. Curling), *Recollections of Rifleman Harris* (London: Peter Davies Ltd, 1929), p.123.
46 Gavin Daly has written by far the best analysis of how the British perceived an interacted with the Spanish and Portuguese allies. Gavin Daly, *The British Soldier in the Peninsular War: Encounters with Spain and Portugal, 1808-1814* (Basingstoke: Palgrave Macmillan, 2013).
47 Porter, *Letters from Portugal and Spain*, pp.6-7, 162. Porter to his friend, 30 September 1808, November 1808.

Part of the issue lay in the negative reaction that many troops had to Lisbon upon arrival in the Peninsula.[48] As Private Wheeler put it: 'Without seeing them [the Portuguese] it is impossible to conceive there exists a people in Europe so debased'.[49] Equally, a number remained unconvinced about the qualities of the Portuguese as soldiers. Whilst some acknowledged that they could 'fight like tigers', others decried them as 'cowardly scoundrels', and 'the dirtiest and nosiest brutes, who have never been known to perform a gallant act'.[50] There is clear disillusionment here, partly due to the failure of reality to match up with the portrayal of the war back in Britain, touched upon above.

It is noticeable, however, that it was predominantly the Spanish who were the scapegoats whenever the British experienced privations or setbacks. Porter lamented the lack of Spanish zeal prior in November 1808 querying 'Where the promised patriots in arms? All we expected to meet *have made themselves air!*'[51] Similarly, John Mills opined in October 1811: 'I think Spain is already conquered and that the next campaign will show it us. They look upon us with a jealous eye and would rather submit to a French king than to be incorporated with England as Portugal is'.[52] These views were by no means restricted to the officers, as a soldier of the 71st summarised the general sentiment of the army during the Corunna retreat in the following terms: '"The British are here to fight for the liberty of Spain, and why is not every Spaniard under arms and fighting? The cause is not ours; and are we to be the only sufferers?" Such was the common language of the soldiers.'[53] It is therefore clear that nationalistic self-belief and xenophobia interacted in a complex way, with a disparaging attitude towards both their opponents and their allies being widespread amongst British troops throughout the conflict. Nonetheless, it is equally apparent that in times of hardship, these attitudes hardened, with frustration turning swiftly to anger which was directed at their allies, whilst leaving the men eager to 'prove' their superiority in battle with the French.

However, passing the blame to those of other nationalities was not the only way in which the troops dealt with the situation. The initial response of soldiers appears to have generally been one of irritation. The withdrawals in 1808-1809 and 1812 were both ordered without having fought the French, and it was the fact that they had not been beaten, but rather had a proven record of defeating their enemy, which particularly irked the troops and left them spoiling for a fight. In the words of one

---

48 Daly, *The British Soldier in the Peninsular War* pp.49-50.
49 Wheeler, *The Letters of Private William Wheeler*, pp.49-50. William Wheeler to his family, 13 March 1811.
50 George Simmons (ed. Lt-Col Willoughby Verner), *A British Rifleman* (London: Greenhill Books, 1986), p.126; Thomas Dyneley (ed. Col. F. A. Whinyates), *Letters Written by Lieut.-General Thomas Dyneley While of Active service Between the Years 1806 and 1815* (London: Ken Trotman, 1984), p.42; Edward Costello (ed. Anthony Brett-James), *The Peninsular and Waterloo Campaigns* (London: Longmans, 1967), p.28.
51 Porter, *Letters from Portugal and Spain*, p.162.
52 John Mills (ed. Ian Fletcher), *The Letters and Diaries John Mills, Coldstream Guards, 1811-1814* (Staplehurst: Spellmount, 1995), p.81.
53 Anon. (ed. Christopher Hibbert), *A Soldier of the Seventy-First: The Journal of a Soldier of the Highland Light Infantry 1806-1815* (London: Leo Cooper, 1975), p.24.

soldier 'the idea of running away from an enemy we had beat with so much ease at Vimeiro, without even firing a shot, was too galling to their feelings. Each spoke to his fellow even in common conversation, with bitterness, rage flashing from their eyes, even on the most trifling occasions of disagreement'.[54] This was not a sentiment that was limited solely to the NCOs and private men. William Webber observed the mood of the whole army as they prepared to face an overwhelmingly larger French force south of Salamanca in November 1812 on the same site which the Battle of Salamanca had been fought in July:

> The dismal appearance of the sky, the heavy rain, the immense body of troops drawn up on the very graves of their comrades and expecting the attack to commence (and so severe a contest as it would have been) rendered the scene truly awful: notwithstanding we all wished for it and hoped to decide the fate of Spain.[55]

Very rapidly, the British soldiers began to direct their anger towards their commanders for their unwillingness to commit to a battle, marking an important limitation to the confidence that men placed in their generals, and highlighting the complexity of the way in which these emotions interacted. It is here that the overweening extent of this self-confidence amongst British soldiers becomes most apparent, as the men were adamant that the circumstances in which they faced the French did not matter. Their raw skills as soldiers were, in their opinion, ample to compensate for any disadvantage in numbers or terrain. This quote from a soldier of the 71st Regiment summarises the sentiment with particular clarity:

> On the 24th of December [1808] our Headquarters were at Sahagun. Every heart beat with joy. We were all under arms and formed to attack the enemy. Every mouth breathed hope: "We will beat them to pieces and have our ease and enjoy ourselves", said my comrades. I even preferred any short struggle, however severe, to the dreadful way of life we were, at this time, pursuing. With heavy hearts, we received orders to retire to our quarters: "And won't we be allowed to fight? Sure we'd beat them", said an Irish lad near me. "By Saint Patrick, we'd beat them so easy, the General means to march us to death, and fight them after!"[56]

It was at these points that the differing layers of confidence conflicted, as the supremely self-confident British troops remained adamant that they could defeat the French, and resented the perceived lack of trust that their commander had in them. Self-confidence seemingly trumped everything, including reason.

---

54 Anon, *A Soldier of the Seventy-First*, p.23.
55 William Webber (ed. R. H. Wollcombe), *With the Guns in the Peninsula: The Peninsular War Journal of 2nd Captain William Weber, Royal Artillery* (London: Greenhill, 1991), p.113. 15 November 1812.
56 Anon, *A Soldier of the Seventy-First*, p.23.

Despite being a nationalistic form of self-confidence, these sentiments do not correlate with Westbrook's thesis, as the emphasis here is not on commitment to the nation and its goals. Instead the attitude appears to be one of, in Cruikshank's phrase 'tarnished valour', with the prospect of withdrawal reducing the honour and esteem with which the army, and therefore the individual soldier, could be held.

However, some soldier behaviour during withdrawals is more typical of the primary group concept. Both the 1808 and 1812 retreats were notable for the extent to which the troops suffered hugely from lack of supplies, a fact which the troops widely testified to.[57] The overall result was that troops straggled, and lost their cohesion and discipline, as they either fell behind due to fatigue caused by lack of food and constant marching, or deviated from the line of march in a desperate attempt to plunder food. As Edward Coss has so clearly demonstrated, in times such as these, it was a case of plunder, or starve.

There were repeated instances throughout the war, however, when discipline significantly improved at the prospect of fighting a battle. At such moments, the troops' irritation with their commander evaporated, and, surprisingly, straggling units re-formed. Porter and Hamilton observed a spike in morale following orders, in the last days of 1808, to prepare for an assault on French troops in Old Castille.[58] This positivity may be attributable to the basic British confidence in their combat ability, a notion which is further supported by a more careful examination of the Corunna retreat.

Contrary to popular belief, discipline did not collapse due to the appalling weather of the long retreat, as Moore complained about his troops' widespread misconduct from the first days of the withdrawal, when conditions were far less severe.[59] As Porter observed 'every countenance was changed; the proud glow on their cheeks was lost in a fearful paleness; [...] a few murmurs were heard, and the army of England was no more. Its spirit was fled [...] In my life I have never witnessed such an instantaneously withering effect upon any body of living creatures.'[60] A sudden and catastrophic change of mood overcame much of the army, which both Porter and Sergeant Hamilton suggest was due to the psychology of retreating without having been defeated, reinforcing the centrality of pride and tarnished valour to the soldiers' outlook.[61]

Primary groups, in these circumstances, seemed to largely collapse. Rifleman Harris recalled 'It was then pretty much "every one for himself"; those whose strength began to fail looked neither to the right nor the left, but with glassy eyes, they kept onward, [...] few were inclined to help their comrades when their own strength was

---

57 See, for example, Costello, *The Peninsular and Waterloo Campaigns*, p.114; Brown, *The Autobiography or Narrative of a Soldier*, p.113.
58 Porter, *Letters from Portugal and Spain*, p.222; Anthony Hamilton, *Hamilton's Campaign With Moore and Wellington during the Peninsular War* (Staplehurst: Spellmount, 1998), pp.26-27.
59 Quoted in John Fortescue, *A History of the British Army* (London: Macmillan, 1899-1930), Vol.VI, p.351.
60 Porter, *Letters from Portugal and Spain*, p.235. Porter to his friend, December 1808.
61 Porter, *Letters from Portugal and Spain*, pp.234-235. Porter to his friend, December 1808; Hamilton, *Campaign With Moore and Wellington*, p.43.

but small.'[62] Clearly the bonds of camaraderie had broken down the point where there was no primary group at all, as men left their friends and comrades to die.

After days of straggling and plunder however, the troops returned to their units, and inflicted a telling defeat on the French at the Battle of Corunna. 'Sir John Moore announced his intention to offer battle. Scarcely was the order issued, when the line of battle, hitherto so peeled and spread abroad, was filled with vigorous men, full of confidence and courage'.[63] The fact that soldiers regrouped so rapidly is a curious concept to reconcile with Westbrook's theory. In part, with their backs to the sea, it must have been apparent to the British that a battle was essential, but the rapid return of cohesion after such a widespread collapse in discipline and unity demonstrates that the British remained confident of victory despite the privations that they had experienced.

Admittedly, though, the improvement in morale must have been affected by availability of supplies from Corunna which had been a key operational bridgehead. Issues of supply were certainly one of a number of common factors between the Corunna retreat and the withdrawal from Burgos to Ciudad Rodrigo. Supplying the troops was a relentless struggle for Wellington and the commissariat department. First-hand accounts attest to the frequent and often prolonged issues of supply which plagued the army as they sought to maintain a supply network rather than live off the land. It is noticeable that at some moments of shortage, the confidence of the British troops did not collapse as it did in late 1808 and late 1812. In the opening stages of the Vittoria campaign, one Highlander recalled that 'we were only eight days on the march [at the start of the 1813 campaign] when the rations began to grow scarce; and for twelve days we had not, on any one day, a complete day's ration'.[64]

This makes a careful examination of the retreat from Burgos all the more revealing, as it demonstrates the significance of the multiple strands of confidence which existed amongst British troops, and the way in which they interacted. Wellington's mistakes in late 1812 were far from disastrous, and he displayed considerable skill in extracting his army during a difficult retreat. Nonetheless, by this point Wellington's presence was considered a guarantor for success. Even the war-weary Bragge remarked that he could not imagine Wellington being 'outdone at Burgos'.[65] That Wellington had seemingly lost his touch appeared to disconcert his men, and the loss of territory which had been liberated in the wake of their victory at the Battle of Salamanca in July unquestionably rankled.[66] A comment from Webber

---

62 Harris, *Recollections of Rifleman Harris*, p.42.
63 Anon, *Memoirs of a Sergeant Late in the Forty-Third*, pp.52-53.
64 Anon, *The Personal Narrative of a Private Soldier who served in the Forty-Second Highlanders* (London: Ken Trotman, 1996), p.184.
65 Bragge, *Peninsular Portrait*, p.75. William Bragge to his father, 25 September 1812. See also Jonathan Fremantle (ed. Gareth Glover), *Wellington's Voice: The Candid Letters of Lieutenant Colonel John Fremantle, Coldstream Guards, 1808-1837*, (London: Frontline Books, 2012), p.78, Jonathan Fremante to his uncle, 29 April 1811; Charles Boutflower, *The Journal of an Army Surgeon During the Peninsular War* (Staplehurst: Spellmount, 1997), p.85. Diary, 10 April 1811.
66 Bamford, *Sickness, Suffering and the Sword*, pp.56-57.

suggests that the troops clung to Wellington's reputation as a way of sustaining their morale, believing that his presence would somehow reverse the situation:

> Our spirits were a little cheered by the hope of our meeting Lord Wellington and his having some grand plan in contemplation to make some amends to the people of Madrid for their distress. I understand the generality of the men think so and are convinced of the necessity of sacrificing their present comforts for better prospects.[67]

This was a view echoed in remarkably similar terms by John Aitchison: 'While we remained encamped opposite Tordesillas, the most contradictory reports were circulated of our future operations; they generally breathed anything but despondency, and as they had credit for originating in a quarter which shall be nameless, we were far from expecting retreat. [...] we had unbroken spirits and former success in our favour'.[68]

Equally, the troops' high hopes of pushing the French beyond the River Ebro, which had been widespread after Salamanca, were dashed by the order to withdraw.[69] However, a lack of provisions turned these unfavourable circumstances into a collapse of discipline. It was the combination of all of these factors that had such a profound effect on the troops' morale. Insufficient rations were simply the last in a string of issues which contributed to the troops' low mood, and the shaking of the confidence in both Wellington's ability, and in the potential to win the war, were the unique issues which can account for such a rare widespread collapse in discipline. Furthermore, the perceived shame of failing to meet the public's expectations resurfaced during the retreat. Captain Bragge summarised the sentiment: 'I regret excessively having been obliged to have to recourse to this measure, which has disappointed the expectations of England'.[70] Boutflower described the prospect of retreat as 'mortifying in the extreme' for similar reasons.[71]

However, the prospect of battle on the same site as the Battle of Salamanca, had the same positive impact on the troops' morale that was witnessed at Corunna:

> He [Wellington] assumed his former position on the Arapiles, but here he had everything to hope – the ground was already consecrated by the blood of Heroes on 22 July, he still fought in the same righteous cause – the troops

---

67 Webber, *With the Guns in the Peninsula*, p.104. 31 October 1812.
68 John Aitchison (ed. W.F.K. Thompson), *An Ensign in the Peninsular War: The Letters of John Aitchison* (London: Michael Joseph, 1981), p.218. To his father, Mesquitello, 10 December 1812.
69 Mills, *The Letters and Diaries John Mills*, p.157. Jonathan Mills to his mother, 15 June 1812.; Boutflower, *The Journal of an Army Surgeon*, p.159. Diary, 15 September 1812, Wheeler, *The Letters of Private William Wheeler*, p.102. William Wheeler to his family, 10 December 1812.
70 Bragge, *Peninsular Portrait*, p.82. William Bragge to his father, 26 November 1812.
71 Boutflower, *The Journal of an Army Surgeon*, pp.167-168. Diary, 6 November 1812.

who that day had signalised themselves were still with him – *impatient* to repeat their former deeds [...] the army was confident of Victory.[72]

Similarly Wheeler commented that: 'Nothing now was thought of but a general engagement, and so eager were our men that I have no doubt but we should have given them a hearty drubbing'.[73] Clearly then, the prospects of fighting the French, on the assumption that victory would automatically follow, were an important motivator for British troops, providing an opportunity to reverse the strategic situation, regain honour that they perceived to have been lost by withdrawing without a fight, and in all likelihood, venting their frustration on their enemy.

There can therefore be no question that, whilst considerable elements of Westbrook's arguments on motivation, and particularly primary group theory, are indeed applicable to the context of British troops during the Napoleonic Wars, there are nonetheless facets of the behaviour of Wellington's men in times of failure that are difficult to reconcile with his otherwise compelling behavioural model. Whilst Westbrook's model is effectively able to explain how the British army managed to maintain its cohesion for much of the Peninsular War, it is clear that scholars must consider other elements of the psychological and behavioural traits of these men in order to appreciate how the individual sought to come to terms with the situation around him, and limit his despondency, in times of setback. The fact that such comparatively few men chose to desert is a clear indication of the extent to which British soldiers succeeded in overriding despair, suppressing that emotion by focusing outwards and blaming others. Most prominent in this 'blame game' were their allies, particularly the Spanish, although protracted withdrawals without committing to a battle could result in the troops' commanders becoming targets of their ire.

All of these emotions were underpinned by an intrinsic belief that the British soldier was vastly superior not only in comparison with his opponent, but also in comparison to his allies. This myth was perpetuated to a point of hubristic and reckless bravery, with the circumstances in which they faced the French being irrelevant, as the troops believed that they would prevail irrespective of whether they were at a tactical or numerical disadvantage. It was this fundamental self-belief that was capable of sustaining soldiers, and could cause them to regroup with astonishing speed, even when their other methods of sustaining motivation, and even the primary group, had failed.

There is, of course, scope for much more work on this topic. It is, for example, noticeable that this deeply rooted self-confidence was apparent from the outset of the Peninsular War. The existence of this confidence cannot therefore be attributed to the succession of victories that the army achieved under Wellington and must therefore have been sourced elsewhere. The inevitable question therefore arises of where this confidence originated from, especially given that the British Army's record of success during the Napoleonic Wars was not particularly illustrious until

---

[72] Aitchison, *An Ensign in the Peninsular War*, p.128. To his father, Mesquitello, 10 December 1812.
[73] Wheeler, *The Letters of Private William Wheeler*, p.102, Moimento, 10 December 1812.

the advent of the Peninsular War. It would also be interesting to determine how, if at all, this and the other types of confidence identified above differed in other British theatres during the period, and whether parallels can be identified in the armies of other nations which participated in the conflict. Most intriguingly, the question arises of whether this quasi-nationalistic sentiment was simply hubris, or is an indication that the process of formulating a 'British' identity was well advanced by this point in the nation's history, despite the fact that the union was still in its developmental stages. Whilst it may be anachronistic to talk of a 'British national identity' during this period, there is compelling evidence to suggest that the British soldier's self-perception was certainly construed in nationalistic terms. In times of setback, the question of whether the decision to retreat was prudent due to the strategic situation was, for them, irrelevant, as they presumed that British soldiers would automatically triumph irrespective of the circumstances. With national consciousness and pride being so central to the British soldiers' identity, retreat became tantamount to a national humiliation, which they considered to be unacceptable. Their allies might be to blame, their generals might be to blame, but they were not, and were adamant that they should be given the opportunity to prove it. The prospect of being responsible for 'Another Tarnish for British Valour' was ultimately too much for British soldiers to bear.

Select Bibliography

Bamford, A., *Sickness, Suffering and the Sword: The British Regiment on Campaign, 1808-1815* (Norman: University of Oklahoma Press, 2013).

Berkovich, I., *Motivation in War: The Experience of Common Soldiers in Old-Regime Europe* (Cambridge: Cambridge University Press, 2017).

Colley, L., *Britons: Forging the Nation 1707-1837*, 3rd edn (London: Vintage, 1996).

Coss, E., *All for the King's Shilling: The British Soldier Under Wellington, 1808-1814* (Norman: University of Oklahoma Press, 2010).

Daly, G., *The British Soldier in the Peninsular War: Encounters with Spain and Portugal, 1808-1814* (Basingstoke: Palgrave Macmillan, 2013).

Davies G., *Wellington and His Army* (Oxford: Blackwell & Mott, 1954).

Davies, H.J., *Wellington's Wars: The Making of a Military Genius* (London: Yale University Press, 2012).

Esdaile, C., *Napoleon's Wars* (London: Penguin, 2008).

Esdaile, C., *Peninsular Eyewitnesses: The Experience of War in Spain and Portugal 1808-1813* (Barnsley: Pen and Sword, 2008).

Esdaile, C., *The Peninsular War: A New History* (London: Penguin, 2003).

Hughes, M. J., *Forging Napoleon's Grande Armée: Motivation, Military Culture, and Masculinity in the French Army, 1800-1808* (New York: New York University Press, 2012).

Linch, K., *Britain and Wellington's Army: Recruitment, Society and Tradition, 1807-1815* (Basingstoke: Macmillan, 2011).

Lynn, J., *The Bayonets of the Republic: Motivation and Tactics in the Army of Revolutionary France, 1791-94* (Chicago: University of Illinois, 1984).

Muir, R., *Tactics and the Experience of Battle in the Age of Napoleon* (New Haven: Yale University Press, 1998).

Muir, R., *Wellington: The Path to Victory 1769-1814* (New Haven: Yale University Press, 2013).

Oman, C., *Wellington's Army* (London: Edward Arnold, 1912).

Sarkesian, S. (ed.) *Combat Effectiveness: Cohesion, Stress, and the Volunteer Military*, Sage Research Progress series on War, Revolution and Peacekeeping, Volume 9 (Beverly Hills: Sage Publications, 1980).

8

'Stand fast and defend yourself to the last!': the Experience of Battle in the French Revolutionary and Napoleonic Wars

Carole Divall

It is an obvious truism that the only people who know what it is like to experience a battle are the people who have experienced a battle. As John Keegan confessed: 'I have never been in a battle. And I grow increasingly convinced that I have very little idea of what a battle can be like'.[1] These simple statements emphasise that for us any battle fought in the convulsive period between 1792 and 1815 can never be more than a historical event from which we remain distanced spectators. Only for the combatants was it an action that placed them in a life-or-death situation and which would remain in their memory as a lived experience. Yet surely even those memories must have become distorted over time, as memories do? This then poses the pivotal question: how do we move from our understanding of the historical event in its time-context to our understanding of what the combatants actually experienced?

At this point, it is necessary to define what should be understood as a 'battle'. Keegan wrote that 'A battle must obey the dramatic unities of time, place and action'. He also maintained that there exists 'a fundamental difference between the sort of sporadic, small-scale fighting which is the small change of soldiering and the sort we characterize as a battle'. Furthermore, the action of a battle should be the means to a decisive end.[2] By this reckoning, the encounters between French soldiers and Spanish guerrillas in the Peninsula would not fit the definition of a battle since the latter's objective was to harass the former until their position in Spain became untenable. That is attrition rather than battle. For the purpose of this study, however, the term *battle* will not only be applied to encounters that were not properly battles in Keegan's sense but will also be extended in a further direction. Some of the fiercest and most costly encounters of the wars were sieges. Despite being the means to a decisive end, the experience was markedly different from the conventional set-piece battle of the time, and will be referenced as such.

---

1   John Keegan, *The Face of Battle* (London: The Bodley Head, 2014), p.1.
2   Keegan, *Face of Battle*, p.2.

Where do we look for our understanding of the human dimension of battle beyond the formal documentation of politicians and senior officers? A simple answer would be that we search through the accounts written by the participants. In theory, therefore, letters, journals, even memoirs, should give us a glimpse of those personal experiences, and to some extent they do. Yet we also need to be aware of their limitations. All written accounts have been edited. One has only to compare a spoken account with a written account to appreciate this. Furthermore, letters and memoirs have a reader in mind and the writing will be crafted for that reader. Journals may come closest to the actual moment. In a private journal the writer may even commit his fears to paper. Despite that, though, the journal cannot possibly recapture all the thoughts and feelings of the moment; what was understood and what remained unknown.

The difference between the letter and the reworked memoir is clearly demonstrated in the writing of Lieutenant James Hope of the 1/92nd. While he was in the Peninsula he wrote regularly to a friend. Then, in 1833, he produced *Campaigns with Hill and Wellington*. On 28 October 1811 Major General Rowland Hill, in command of the Second Division of the Anglo-Portuguese army and accompanied by Spanish troops under *Brigadeiro* Pablo Morillo, finally cornered *Général de Division* Jean-Baptiste Girard, whom he had been pursuing for some time, at Arroyo Molinos. The outcome was a decisive victory for Hill. Reporting this to his friend in a letter written on the 5 November, Hope described the part played by his own battalion as follows:

> The 71st and 92nd regiments moved forward to the village at a quick pace, and, in a few minutes, cleared it of the enemy, who were very far from being prepared for such an unceremonious visit. General Girard, driven from the village, formed his infantry in two squares; and, at the distance of two hundred yards from it, threw a very destructive fire towards the 71st and 92nd regiments. The first lined a wall outside the village, in column of sections. The 92nd regiment having orders to reserve their fire, beheld their companions fall around them, without being able to avenge their death. But they were not long in this situation. An order soon arrived for the regiment to form line, and prepare to charge. In a few minutes the line was formed, and the Highlanders only waited for the order to advance. All this time the enemy appeared extremely uncomfortable – something like hesitation was observed in their squares…[3]

At this point some Portuguese guns were brought up and wreaked havoc on the French squares. The Highlanders were ready 'to present the enemy with a little of their steel, when they, with the politeness for which Frenchmen are so remarkable, declined the honour we intended them', and precipitously withdrew. These last comments demonstrate a feature of Hope's letters: a certain satirical note that the

---

3   James Archibald Hope, *The Iberian Campaign* (Heathfield: Naval and Military Press, 2000), p.26.

writer obviously thought the recipient would appreciate. There is also an assumed familiarity with military terminology such as 'in sections of columns'.

The later account, however, adopts a very different tone.

> On arriving at the eastern extremity of the principal street, the 71st moved to their left – lined some of the village garden walls, and peppered their antagonists in very good style. The 92nd regiment following close on the heels of their companions, filed to the right, formed line, prepared to charge, but were not permitted to fire a single shot. This was extremely galling to the soldiers, who saw their officers and comrades falling around them without daring to retaliate upon the enemy. This was no doubt an unpleasant situation to be placed in but knowledge that the success of an enterprise frequently depends on the manner in which orders of this description are attended to, the Highlanders, with a praiseworthy forbearance, resisted every temptation to commit a breach of their orders, and with patience not very peculiar to their countrymen, waited the arrival of the decisive moment.[4]

These two accounts obviously describe the same event but there are marked differences in style, the second account being more carefully worked for effect than the first, evident in the details which the writer has chosen to include. It might be said that the second is more literary, whereas the first is more conscious of its very specific audience.

A more marked difference becomes apparent when a writer chooses to develop and elaborate on an account he wrote soon after the event. In a letter dated three weeks after the Battle of Waterloo, the very newly promoted Lieutenant Edward Nevil Macready of the 2/30th reported to his father some of his observations on the battle, with the proviso that he could only tell him 'how our Company and Regiment were employed'. He wrote, among other events, about the charges of the French cavalry:

> We then formed in square with the Reg. and the 73rd and advanced when a most murderous conflict took place. Their cuirassiers charged in every second, were every time repulsed and such numbers left dead, that latterly when we went out skirmishing we covered ourselves with dead men and horses.[5]

He added the proviso that 'I am endeavouring to do an impossibility to describe a battle, so little did we know of it the next morning..'. He also mentioned the extreme fatigue they suffered, so that after the battle was over he fell down and slept until the bugle sounded the advance the following morning.

---

4   James Archibald Hope, *Campaigns with Hill and Wellington* (Driffield: Leonaur, 2010), p.50.
5   Edward Nevil Macready, letter to his father written in Paris 7 July 1815, transcription kindly provided by Lieutenant Colonel John Downman.

Several months later he committed a much fuller account to his journal, including the French charges.

> Their first charge was magnificent. As soon as they quickened their trot into a gallop the Cuirassiers bent their heads, so that the peaks of their helmets looked like vizors [sic], and they seemed cased in armour from the plume to the saddle. Not a shot was fired until they were within thirty yards, when the word was given, and our boys peppered away at them. The effect was magical. Thro' the smoke we could see helmets falling, cavaliers starting and rearing in the agonies of fright and pain, and crowds of the soldiery dismounted; part of the squadrons in retreat, but the more daring remainder hacking their horses to force them on our bayonets. Our fire soon disposed of these gentlemen. The main body re-formed in our front, were reinforced, and rapidly and gallantly repeated their attacks. In fact, from this time (about four o'clock) till near six, we had a constant repetition of these brave but unavailing charges.[6]

This is just the start of an extended account of the great cavalry charges. We must assume, therefore, that between writing a letter to his father and deciding to compose a much fuller account of the battle Macready not only scoured his memory for recollections but also put them into some sort of order and then embellished them. Nevertheless, although his account of Waterloo is very detailed and often cited, Macready does not venture to describe what was happening elsewhere except when he was in a position to observe it, and such tends to be the approach adopted by anyone honestly trying to recall his own singular experience.

The problem of how far we can trust a written account was summed up by none other than the Duke of Wellington, in a comment he wrote a month after Macready penned his letter.

> The history of a battle is not unlike the history of a ball. Some individuals may recollect all the little events of which the great result is the battle won or lost, but no individual can recollect the order in which, or the exact moment at which they occurred, which makes all the difference to their value or importance...[7]

In other words, in the hurly-burly of action how much would a combatant understand of what was happening even in his immediate vicinity, let alone beyond it? At Waterloo, did the defenders of Hougoumont have any idea of the experiences of the defenders of La Haie Sainte? Did Major General Sir John Moore, defending the extreme right of the British position at Alexandria on 21 March 1801, realise what was happening on the extreme left? Furthermore, was there time to think as a battle raged? And if a combatant should have analysed his thoughts at the time, would he

---

6 NAM 6802-209, The Journal and Opinions of Edward Nevil Macready, Chapter 12.
7 Wellington to Croker, 8 July 1815, quoted in Elizabeth Longford, *Wellington: Pillar of State* (Frogmore: Panther Books, 1975), p.30.

remember them with any great clarity? Even the first letters or the hurried journal entries are already retrospective. An editorial process will have taken place to make sense of a jumble of sensory perceptions, because it is impossible to give a running commentary of what is happening, what the individual does and feels, while a battle is actually taking place.

Three examples make the point that the written account has to be treated with caution. Firstly, we have Sergeant Ewart's version of the taking of the eagle of the 45e Régiment de Ligne at Waterloo.

> The officer who carried it and I had a short contest for it; he thrust for my groin. I parried it off and cut him through the head; in a short time after whilst contriving how to carry the eagle (by folding the flag around my bridle arm and dragging the pole on the ground) and follow my regiment I heard a lancer coming behind me; I wheeled round to face him and in the act of doing so he threw his lance at me which I threw off to my right with my sword and cut him from the chin upwards through the teeth. His lance merely grazed the skin of my right side which bled a good deal but was well very soon. I was next attacked by a foot soldier who after firing a me, charged me with the bayonet; I parried it and cut him down through the head; this finished the contest for the eagle which I was ordered by General Ponsonby to carry to the rear.[8]

There is something almost analytical in this account, with its echo of the cavalryman's handbook. What is lacking is spontaneity, excitement, even the tone of a boastful hero. It tells us nothing of the human experience, although it is just possible, with some imagination, to glimpse the dilemma of how to carry an eagle out of the action. No doubt, when Ewart told his fellow soldiers how he had taken an eagle, it would have taken a very different form.

Ewart's account can be compared with others, like that of Lieutenant William Grattan of the 88th at Fuentes de Oñoro on 3 May 1810 or Ensign Edward Neville Macready's when going into battle for the first time at Quatre Bras.

Grattan was a spectator, but a spectator who knew he would soon be going into action as:

> The ninth corps, which formed the centre of the French army, advanced with the characteristic impetuosity of their nation, and forcing down the barriers which we had hastily constructed as a temporary defence, came rushing on, and torrent-like, threatened to overwhelm those that opposed them. Every street, and every angle of a street, were the different theatres of the combatants; inch-by-inch was gained and lost in turn. Whenever the enemy were forced back, fresh troops, and fresh energy on the part of their officers impelled them on again, and towards mid-day the town presented a shocking sight; our Highlanders lay dead in heaps, while the other

---

8   Harold F.B. Wheeler, *The Story of Wellington* (London: George G, Harrap & Co., N.D.), p.227.

regiments, while less remarkable in dress, were scarcely so in the numbers of their slain; the French grenadiers, with their immense caps and gaudy plumes, in piles of twenty and thirty together...[9]

This is lively writing that enables readers to create the scene in their imagination, thus putting them in the position of spectators at a public event caught up in the atmosphere of that event, but it tells us little about the writer's feelings as he watched the scene of slaughter (the accurate identification of the French corps is also a feature of retrospective accounts, when details not known at the time can be added). Macready takes this descriptive process a step further. The light company of the 2/30th, to which Macready was attached, had been posted at Nivelles, and reached the battlefield when the action was already raging:

We soon reached Quatre Bras, where the Brunswickers and some of Picton's people were in square; and on turning the end of the wood, found ourselves in the hurly-burly of battle. The roaring of great guns and musquetry [sic], the bursting of shells, and shouts of the combatants raised an infernal and indescribable din: while the galloping horses, the mingled crowds of wounded and fugitives, the volumes of smoke, the flashing of fire, struck a scene which accorded admirably with the music.[10]

It probably comes as no surprise that Macready was the son and brother of notable actors. There is drama, but it is fashioned drama. It gets us closer to the reality of battle, just as a film can recreate the noise and confusion of historical events. Yet the writer is a spectator. He is, in effect, in the audience of his own drama; an audience that the reader is invited to join. It is worth emphasising, perhaps, that although both Macready and Grattan were on the verge of joining the action, they were granted a moment to look and think. Such thoughts and impressions would be more coherent than those that followed, and easier to recollect.

One way to get closer to the personal experience is to consider how men coped with the inherent dangers of battle once they went into action. It needs to be remembered, however, that the response of an eighteenth- or nineteenth-century soldier would be very different from a modern soldier's response, simply because life then was very different from life now. There is nothing to suggest that human emotions have changed over the centuries, but what provoked those emotions and how they were managed certainly have. A different state of mind may well militate against the blood, thunder and agony of high drama. For example, was there less fear of the risk of death in battle because life itself was so uncertain? Rich and poor alike were liable to the diseases or accidents that might carry them off prematurely. For the poor, the harsh social conditions, shortage of food, and accommodation that was damp, overcrowded, probably rat-infested, made the risk of death in battle something that could be contemplated with resignation, if not with equanimity. It is worth noting

---

9   William Grattan, *Adventures of the Connaught Rangers* (London: Henry Colburn, 1847), Vol.I, p.95.
10 NAM 6802-209, The Journal and Opinions of Edward Nevil Macready, Chapter 9.

that the average life expectancy for males as late as 1841 was 40.[11] Such factors could easily breed fatalism, instanced by the soldier's acceptance that if your name was on a bullet nothing could save you.

Furthermore, and perhaps easy to forget, is the significance of how battles were fought and how troops were trained and conditioned to fight them. The means of battle were more limited, so that the course a battle might take was more predictable. The man standing in the ranks knew what was expected of him and he could anticipate to a fair degree how the enemy would behave. He was familiar with the commands that he would be given and he knew how to respond. He also knew himself to be one of a body of like-minded men. During the action fought on 13 March 1801 at Mandorah in Egypt the men of the 92nd found themselves in 'a situation of great danger' as they awaited the onslaught of the advancing French line, supported by cavalry.

> [W]e were not above 500 strong and every minute were getting fewer. The enemy had some fieldpieces in front which were making sad havoc amongst us, every shot sweeping down some of our men. Our commanding officer ordered us not to fire but to stand firm until we could see their feet as they advanced from the hollow in front of us. When the order to fire was given, like magic it dispelled the gloom from our countenances and everyone did his duty manfully. We encouraged one another and at the same time, praying, for soldiers do pray and that very fervently on occasions of this kind and, I believe, serious thoughts were with most of us, even the most profligate.[12]

This extract from the journal of Private Daniel Nichol illustrates not only the benefits of thorough training and obedience to command, but also the ability to stand fast in a critical situation when the instinct may have been to flee, both because one was obedient to command and because of a sense of loyalty to one's comrades.

Similarly, the rifleman acted in accordance with learnt procedures, although his was a looser set of orders. Benjamin Harris of the 95th later recalled his impressions of the Battle of Roliça, the first battle of the Peninsular War that involved the British Army, fought on 17 August 1809. He prefaced it with a significant reminder of the limitations of recall:

> I do not pretend to give a description of this or any other battle I have been present at. All I can do is to tell the things which happened immediately around me, and that, I think, is as much as a private soldier can be expected to do.

---

11 'Mortality in England and Wales: Average life span, 2010', *Office of National Statistics*, at <https://www.ons.gov.uk/peoplepopulationandcommunity/birthsdeathsandmarriages/deaths/articles/mortalityinenglandandwales/2012-12-17>, viewed 22 September 2020.
12 Journal of Daniel Nichol, quoted in Edward Bruce Low (ed.), *With Napoleon at Waterloo* (London: G. Bell and Sons Ltd., 1911), pp.30-31.

> Soon afterwards the firing commenced and we advanced pretty close upon the enemy. I took advantage of whatever cover I could find, throwing myself down behind a small bank where I lay so secure that, although the Frenchmen's bullets fell pretty thickly around, I was able to knock several over without being dislodged. Whilst lying in this spot, I fired away every round I had in my pouch.[13]

This is obviously a very different experience of battle from that of Daniel Nichol; the difference between the men standing in line in close order and those skirmishing in loose order.

Gunners followed a procedure so familiar that it needed little conscious thought; so familiar, in fact, that it is well nigh impossible to find a journal, letter or memoir that describes it. Captain Cavalié Mercer made what might seem like a slight concession to the reader's presumed ignorance in his account of the sharp action at Genappe on 17 June 1815 when he wrote:

> "Reverse by unlimbering" was the order. To do this the gun was to be unlimbered, then turned round, the one wheel run at the bank, which just left space for the limber to pass it. The gun is then limbered up again and ready to move to the rear. The execution, however, was not easy, for the reversing of the limber itself in so narrow a lane, with a team of eight horses, was sufficiently difficult, and required first-rate driving. Nothing could exceed the coolness and activity of our men; the thing was done quickly and well, and we returned to the chaussée without hindrance. How we were permitted to do so, I am at a loss to imagine; for although I gave the order to reverse, I certainly never expected to see it occupied.[14]

The final sentence makes clear that the technicalities are introduced not so much to inform as to emphasise the unlikely success of the manoeuvre.

The cavalryman did what his textbook training had conditioned him to do. This last has already been illustrated in Ewart's account, which implies that, even during the excitement of taking an eagle, training was not forgotten. The heavy cavalry, of course, were shock troops. The light cavalry was used very differently, the men spending much of their time on outpost duty and tending to skirmish rather than charge *en masse*. They were more likely to engage with the enemy cavalry than with ranks of infantry, although they might play a significant part in dispersing a defeated foe, infantry or cavalry. A historian of the 13th Light Dragoons describes an encounter at St Gaudens on 22 March 1814 which came about because the regiment was performing 'the advance duties of the army', which brought them repeatedly into collision with the enemy:

---

13   Benjamin Harris (Ed. Eileen Hathaway), *The Recollections of Benjamin Harris* (Swanage: Shinglepicker, 1995), p.41.
14   Cavalié Mercer, *Journal of the Waterloo Campaign* (London: Greenhill Books 1985), p.149.

> [F]our squadrons of French cavalry were discovered drawn up in front of the town. Undismayed by the superior numbers, the THIRTEENTH advanced to the charge, and such was the ardour and determined bravery with which they rushed upon their numerous opponents, that the French horsemen were overthrown at the first shock, and they galloped in disorder through the streets; but they rallied at the other side of the town, and prepared to resist the few British troopers whose audacity they were desirous to punish. The THIRTEENTH being supported by the 3rd Dragoon Guards, dashed through the town, and rushing sword in hand upon the French squadrons, broke them in an instant, and pursued them for two miles, cutting many down and taking above a hundred prisoners and sixty horses.[15]

This last account describes men going into action, which leads on to a point made by John Douglas of the Royal Scots, that the worst time for the soldier preceded the onset of a battle.

> I am fully persuaded that the man possessed of a belief that there is a God... will have a kind of terror over him for which he cannot account, owing to the reflection that the next moment he may be numbered with the dead... to bear me out in this, let 20, 30, nay as many thousands as ever mixed in battle, be advancing to the deadly strife and not one word can be heard in all that number, but move on silent as the grave... I now ask the reason for that awful silence. The answer is that each man is employed as he ought to be with his maker. But when the fire is opened all is forgotten save king and country.[16]

That was but one man's opinion. Ensign George Gleig of the 85th, young and with very limited experience, remembered how he felt before the onset of action at the Nivelle:

> I perfectly recollect, that any feeling of seriousness pervaded my own mind, nor, if I am to judge from appearances, the minds of those around me. Much conversation, on the contrary, passed among us in whispers, but it was all of as light a character, as if the business in which we were about to engage was mere amusement, and not that kind of play in which men stake their lives.[17]

Experience of the reality of battle against inexperience? Or do we conclude that John Douglas and George Gleig were men of very different temperaments? If such be the case, then it enables us to appreciate that each man's response will be peculiarly his

---

15 Richard Cannon, *Historical Records of the Thirteenth Regiment of Light Dragoons* (London: John W. Parker, 1842), pp.63-64.
16 John Douglas (ed. Stanley Monick), *Tale of the Peninsula and Waterloo 1808-1815* (Barnsley: Leo Cooper, 1997), p.44.
17 George Robert Gleig (ed. Ian C. Robertson), *The Subaltern: a Chronicle of the Peninsular War* (Barnsley: Leo Cooper, 2001), p.63.

own. On the other hand, even allowing for inexperience, Gleig demonstrates that one way of dealing with tension is to distract oneself with trivialities.

To take up Douglas's final 'that when fire is opened all is forgotten', Gleig presented a similar idea in his thoughts on siege work: 'There is no species of duty in which a soldier is liable to be employed so galling, or so disagreeable as a siege… it ties him so completely down to one spot, and breaks in so repeatedly upon his hours of rest, and exposes him so completely to danger, and that too at times and places where no honour is to be gained'.[18] Gleig was obviously thinking of the work that preceded a final assault, since the assault itself would be a very different matter. The men waiting in the shadow of Ciudad Rodrigo, Badajoz, or San Sebastian for the commencement of the assault would certainly have been aware of the even greater risk of death, an awareness that must have sharpened over time as each siege produced its bloody butcher's bill. It is difficult to imagine that there was no excitement, however. What can certainly be suggested is that when involved in an assault the infantryman lost the familiarity of learnt orders and procedures, and that must have created its own disturbance.

Captain Edward McCarthy of the 50th Foot, serving as assistant engineer to the 3rd Division, watched the division attempting to escalade the castle of Badajoz during the third, and successful, siege. What he saw might best be described as chaos. Even as the ladders were being raised, the French guns were sweeping the walls.

> [T]heir discharges of round-shot, broken shells, bundles of cartridges, and other missiles, and also from the top of the wall, ignited shells, etc, [meant] that it was almost impossible to twinkle the eye of any man before he was knocked down. In such an extremity, four of my ladders with troops on them, and an officer on the top of each, were broken, successively, near the upper ends, and slided [sic] into the angle of the abutment; - dreadful their fall, and appalling their appearance at daylight…On the remaining ladder was no officer; but, a private soldier at the top, in attempting to go over the wall, was shot in the head, as soon as he appeared above the parapet, and tumbled backwards to the ground.[19]

In such circumstances, men had to rely on instinct rather than orders.

Another element of those pre-battle moments that Gleig recognised was the conditions under which a man went into battle. Douglas had been thinking of the slow, measured advance. Macready, at Quatre Bras, described the experienced of rushing into an action already in full flow. Gleig noted the distinction:

> [T]he feelings of a man hurried into battle, as we were today [Arcangues], are totally different form those of the same man who goes gradually, and as it were preparedly into battle… Everything was accordingly done, every word

---

18 Gleig, *The Subaltern*, p.21.
19 Edward John Connor McCarthy, *Recollections of the Storming of the Castle of Badajoz* (London: W. Clowes & Sons, 1836), pp.44-45.

spoken, and every movement made, under the influence of that species of excitement, which absolutely shuts out all ideas, except those which spring from the circumstances around you.[20]

Significantly, Gleig does not try to recall those ideas. Instead, he remembers the rush of blood and the flow of adrenaline caused by excitement in its literal sense. Then came the stirring of the senses and the emotions which carried a man towards '*Tod*'.

There is also an obvious difference between attacking the enemy and waiting to be attacked. On 27 September 1810 Lieutenant Grattan, posted on the ridge of Bussaco, observed, as the fog cleared, that 'a bright sun enabled us to see what was passing before us. A vast crowd of *tirailleurs* were pressing onward with great valour…' The 88th and the other regiments under Major General Picton's command had no choice but to stand and face the imminent attack. The initial skirmishing took casualties but behind the tirailleurs was a larger force which threatened to sweep the defenders off the ridge. Lieutenant Colonel Wallace, in command of the 88th, sent his captain of grenadiers to ascertain the situation. Captain Dunne returned with the information that 'a heavy column was coming up the hill':

> Wallace, with a steady but cheerful countenance, turned to his men, and looking them full in the face, said, "Now, Connaught Rangers, mind what you are going to do; pay attention to what I have so often told you, and when I bring you face to face with those French rascals, drive them down the hill – don't give the false touch, but push home to the muzzle! I have nothing more to say, and if I had it would be of no use, for in a *minit* or two there'll be such an infernal noise about your ears, that you won't be able to hear yourselves."
>
> This address went home to the hearts of us all, but there was no cheering; a steady but determined calm had taken the place of any lighter feeling, and it seemed as if the men had made up their minds to go to their work unruffled or too much excited…[21]

And that is precisely what they did. Joined by the 45th and led by Wallace, who had dismounted from his horse, they awaited the moment and then overwhelmed the French and drove them down the hill. Just as the 92nd at Mandorah had been held on a tight rein until the time came to fire, the 45th and 88th at Bussaco took their cue from their commander to devastate the enemy assault.

Very different was the advance of the 5th Division at Salamanca on 22 July 1812, the advance that Douglas was describing when he considered the state of mind of a man going into battle. Captain Andrew Leith Hay, aide-de-camp to the divisional commander, Lieutenant General James Leith, recorded his impression of the long advance, from its beginning to its successful conclusion:

---

20 Gleig, *The Subaltern*, pp.89-90.
21 Grattan, *Connaught Rangers*, Vol.I, pp.49-51.

Lord Wellington arrived from the right and communicated to General Leith his intention of immediately attacking the enemy.

It is impossible to describe the energetic exultation with which the soldiers sprung to their feet; if ever primary impulse gained a battle, that of Salamanca was won before the troops moved forward...

The general [Leith] desired me to ride forward, make the light infantry press up the heights to clear his line of march, and if practicable make a rush at the enemy's cannon. In the execution of this service, I had to traverse the whole extent of surface directly in front of the 5th division: the light troops soon drove back those opposed; the cannon were removed to the rear, every obstruction to the regular advance of the line had vanished. In front of the centre of that beautiful line rode General Leith, directing its movements, and regulating its advance. Occasionally, every soldier was visible, the sun shining brightly upon their arms, while at intervals all were enveloped in a dense cloud of dust, from whence, at times, issued the animating cheer of British infantry.[22]

Grattan's account of the Anglo-Portuguese attack at Bussaco, which was actually a defensive tactic – a counter-attack, to nullify the French attack – materialised into the tumult of battle so that 'All was now confusion and uproar, smoke, fire, and bullets, officers and soldiers, French drummers and French drums knocked down in every direction; British, French, Portuguese mixed together'.[23] At Salamanca, the advance, as an offensive move, produced a markedly different result. Already having seen some of their fellows rolled up by the 3rd Division, and then suffering the collapse of their own squares under the threat of cavalry, the French did not stand. Instead:

[T]he victorious [Fifth] division pressed forward, not against troops opposed, but a mass of disorganized men, flying in all directions. General le Marchant's brigade of heavy cavalry dashed forward on the right flank of the 5th division, while General Packenham, having overthrown everything before him, added an immense number to the mass of fugitives escaping from this brilliant attack.[24]

What, though, if one had to stand and wait, as the 92nd did at Mandorah? What thoughts might fill a man's mind? Young Ensign Macready might have been a tyro but he had certainly heard of the Imperial Guard. To stand and wait for an attack by the Middle Guard was enough to make any man quail.

It was near seven o'clock, and our front had sustained three attacks from fresh troops, when the Imperial Guard was seen ascending our position,

---

22 Andrew Leith Hay, *Narrative of the Peninsular War* (Edinburgh: Henry Washbourne, 1834), Vol.I, pp.55-57.
23 Grattan, *Connaught Rangers*, Vol.I p.53.
24 Leith Hay, *Narrative*, Vol.I p.57.

in as correct order as at a review. As they rose step by step before us, and crossed the ridge, their red epaulettes and cross belts, put on over their blue greatcoats, gave them a gigantic appearance, which was increased by their high hairy caps and long red feathers, which waved with the nod of their heads as they kept time to a drum in the centre of their column. "Now for a clawing", I muttered; and I confess, when I saw the imposing advance of these men, and thought of the character they had gained, I looked for nothing but a bayonet in my body, and I half breathed a confident sort of wish that it might not touch my vitals…

The enemy halted, carried arms about forty paces from us, and fired a volley. We returned it, and giving our "hurra!" brought down the bayonets. Our surprise was inexpressible when, pushing thro' the clearing smoke, we saw the backs of the Imperial Grenadiers.[25]

It is worth noting that between his confession of fear and the unexpected departure of the French, Macready references the words of the commander of the brigade, Major General Sir Colin Halkett. This raises a significant point. The relationship between the men and their commanders could prove crucial, as with Wallace at Bussaco, Halkett at Waterloo, and Leith at Salamanca, where, according to Douglas, he urged the 3/1st Royal Scots into action: 'This shall be a glorious day for Old England, if these bragadocian rascals dare but stand their ground, we will display the point of the British bayonet, and where it is properly displayed no power is able to withstand it'.[26]

John Keegan draws attention to another of the issues that contribute to the experience of battle, the condition of the men as they prepared for action. Had they marched far with heavy kit? Were they cold, wet, hungry? Keegan suggests these factors might have produced a state of *semi-anaesthesia*, which raises the question, how many of the allied combatants at Waterloo were in such a condition. The previous day they had retreated from Quatre Bras in pouring rain, which continued throughout the night. Furthermore, the men of Halkett's British brigade had been without food. James Goodall Elkington, the surgeon of the 2/30th, noted in his journal: 'Early in the morning [the rain] began to clear, the men and officers were actually benumbed, being so saturated with the wet. After a little running about, wringing their blankets, and the issue of some spirits, the circulation returned…'.[27] It is possible to posit, however, that not everyone was fully recovered by the time the French launched their first attacks.

Whatever the feelings of men going into action and experiencing action, a very different mood may be detected in those accounts that consider the aftermath. Elkington, for example, having been sent 'to report on the number of French wounded still to be removed' and witnessed the suffering of those who were still

---

25 NAM 6802-209, The Journal and Opinions of Edward Nevil Macready, Chapter 12.
26 Douglas, *Tale of the Peninsula and Waterloo*, p.45.
27 Wellcome Institute (WI), RAMC/336, 'The Diary of James Goodall Elkington', p.13.

awaiting succour, commented that 'a day or two after a general action is the period to gain a fine idea of the miseries of war'.[28]

Sergeant Benjamin Miller of the Royal Artillery certainly found himself reflecting on the reality of battle and the miseries of war, two days after the Battle of Alexandria:

> I took a solitary walk amongst the scattered graves [French and British having been buried indiscriminately] to ruminate upon the implacable lot of men until I would come to some of my companion's graves. And, thinks I, here lie the mangled remains of a comrade, who but the other day, he and I were very jovial, drinking wine together, and perhaps the next destructive day of carnage it may be my lot at no great distance from this awful spot to be laid where no relation or friend will ever have the melancholy satisfaction to drop a sympathetic tear. Then I would reflect how dreadful it was to be cut off so suddenly...[29]

If nothing else, the aftermath of a battle would impress upon the survivors the mutability of human existence, which explains the urgent and understandable need for company. Time and again we are presented with an image of men huddled round a fire, talking over what they had experienced, perhaps, or deliberately choosing not to think about it. Gleig, again, tells us how he and his fellow officers reacted after the third day of the Battle of the Nive.

> A supply of beef, biscuit, and rum had… been issued out… Then the grog being passed round, and pipes and cigars lighted, we lay not down to sleep, till many a rude joke had been bandied around, and many a merry catch chanted. Not that we were altogether insensible to more melancholy feelings. Our ranks were a good deal thinned; of our beloved companions many had fallen; and I speak truly when I say, that we lamented their fall, even in the midst of our mirth. But a state of warfare is productive, and necessarily productive, of more consummate selfishness than any other situation into which man is liable to be thrown… it must be confessed that soldiers think less of the dead than of the living.[30]

For Sergeant James Hale of the 1/9th, the most crucial element after a battle was food. He and his comrades were particularly fortunate after the Battle of Salamanca when they came across a good supply of French provisions: biscuit, flour, mutton and goat.

> So when our camp was formed, and our picquets posted, the remaining part were soon busily ployed [sic] providing for the belly, some making hard dumplings with the flour we had found, some getting wood, and others

---

28   WI, RAMC/336, 'The Diary of James Goodall Elkington', p.13.
29   Benjamin Miller, *The Adventures of Sergeant Benjamin Miller* (Uckfield: The Naval and Military Press, N.D.), pp.18-19.
30   Gleig, *The Subaltern*, p.99.

searching for water for our cooking, which by chance was found at about one mile distant from our camp. Therefore towards the middle of the night we enjoyed ourselves over a most able supper, and after a little conversation over what had passed during the day, we wrapped ourselves in our blankets, with accoutrements on, and lay down in the hopes of getting a few hours' good rest, for we were getting very much fatigued for want of sleep.[31]

From this survey of the experience of battle as it has come to us from the testimony of the men who went into action and recorded not only what happened but also their thoughts and feelings, certain assumptions may be drawn. Firstly, it is inevitable that sensual responses will become distorted. Against the roaring of the guns, the bursting of shells, the shouts, yells, screams of combatants, it might become increasingly difficult, if not impossible, to maintain coherent and rational thought. The result might well be that men would abandon thought and act like automatons. Or, if they tried to think, they would battle against disorientation, taking refuge in the here and now, and even that might be limited by smoke from guns and muskets, and by opponents pressing in from all sides. And those opponents might be on horseback. *Lieutenant* Martin, in D'Erlon's corps at Waterloo, describes the experience as the Union Brigade descended on them:

When infantry is in disorder and the cavalry has broken into its ranks, resistance is useless and it can massacre them almost without danger. That is what happened. In vain did our soldiers try to get to their feet and raise their muskets; they were unable to strike this cavalry, and the few shots that were fired in this confused crowd were as likely to hit our own men as the English. We were thus defenceless against a fierce enemy, who, in the excitement of battle, sabred without pity even the drummers and fifers. It was then that our eagle was taken, and it was there that I looked death in the face, for my best friends fell around me and I awaited a similar fate, whilst swinging my sword mechanically.[32]

Beyond sight and sound there would be the smell; the smell of powder, of course, but also something worse than that:

The odour, even of an ordinary field of battle, is extremely disagreeable. I can compare it to nothing more aptly than the interior of a butcher's slaughter-house, soon after he may have killed his sheep or oxen for the market.[33]

This leaves little to the imagination.

---

31 James Hale, *The Journal of James Hale* (Windsor: IX Regiment, 1998), pp.91-92.
32 Martin, *Souvenirs d'un ex-officier 1812-1815* (Paris: Cherbulier, Paris 1867), pp.288-289; quoted in Andrew Field, *Waterloo, the French Perspective* (Barnsley: Pen & Sword, 2012), p.110.
33 Gleig, *The Subaltern*, p.105.

Then, as *Lieutenant* Martin remembered, there was the moment when a man could envisage his own death. Edward Costello of the 95th Rifles was part of the ladder party on the 6 April 1812, the night of the assault of Badajoz. The ladders were not for an escalade but to climb out of the ditch in front of the breach. Having been knocked over as he rushed forward, he suddenly found himself up to his neck in water. He was able to swim to the other side, but then received a blow to the breast.

> [D]own I rolled senseless, drenched with water and human gore.
>
> I could not have lain long in this plight, and when my senses started to return, I saw our gallant fellows still rushing forward, each seeming to meet a fate more deadly than my own. The fire continued in one horrible and incessant peal, as if the mouth of the infernal regions had opened to vomit forth destruction upon all around us. Even more appalling were the fearful shouts of the combatants, and cries of the wounded that mingled in the uproar.
>
> Strange to say, I now began to feel my arms and legs were entire. At such moments a man is not always aware of his wounds. I had lost all the frenzy of courage that had first possessed me and felt weak, my spirits prostrate. Among the dead and wounded bodies around me, I endeavoured to screen myself from the enemy's shot. While I lay in this position, the fire continued to blaze over me in all its horrors, accompanied by screams, groans, and shouts, the smashing of stones and the falling of timbers. For the first time for many years, I uttered something like a prayer.[34]

To fully understand the experience of battle we need to move beyond the machinations of politicians which bring about war and the decisions of senior officers who, in theory, determine the course of a campaign, including its battles. Even what might be called the paraphernalia of battle, strategy, tactics, weaponry, all of which have their place in the study of military history and the form that war takes, leave us at one remove from what it was like to take part in a battle, in the Revolutionary and Napoleonic period or at any other time. Instead, we need to acknowledge the personal dimension, and accept that the combatants are not mere pawns on a chessboard but thinking and feeling human beings with their own hopes and fears. What they tell us, even if only in part, allows us at least the glimpse the reality of their experience.

There is no better ending for this survey that the words of John Keegan, whose seminal work did so much to make the pawns the heroes of their own story.

> The soldier is vouchsafed no such well-ordered and clear-cut vision [as the commander]. Battle, for him, takes place in a wildly unstable physical and emotional environment; he may spend much of his time in combat as a mildly apprehensive spectator, granted, by some freak of events, a comparatively danger-free grandstand view of others fighting; then he may suddenly

---

34   Eileen Hathaway, *Costello: the True Story of a Peninsular Rifleman* (Swanage: Shinglepicker, 1997), pp.170-171.

be able to see nothing but the clods on which he has flung himself for safety, there to crouch – he cannot anticipate – for minutes or for hours; he may feel in turn boredom, exultation, panic, anger, sorrow bewilderment, even the sublime emotion we call courage.[35]

With these comments in mind, supported by the wealth of letters, journals and memoirs through which we are able to trawl, we should be able to appreciate a battle as both a historical event and a personal experience.

Bibliography

Archival Sources

Edward Nevil Macready, letter to his father written in Paris 7 July 1815, transcription kindly provided by Lieutenant Colonel John Downman.

National Army Museum, NAM 6802-209, 'The Journal and Opinions of Edward Nevil Macready'.

Wellcome Institute, RAMC/336, 'The Diary of James Goodall Elkington'.

Published Sources

Cannon, Richard, *Historical Records of the Thirteenth Regiment of Light Dragoons* (London: John W. Parker, 1842).

Douglas, John (ed. Stanley Monick), *Tale of the Peninsula and Waterloo 1808-1815* (Barnsley: Leo Cooper, 1997).

Field, Andrew, *Waterloo, the French Perspective* (Barnsley: Pen & Sword, 2012).

Gleig, George Robert (ed. Ian C. Robertson), *The Subaltern: a Chronicle of the Peninsular War* (Barnsley: Leo Cooper, 2001).

Grattan, William, *Adventures of the Connaught Rangers* (London: Henry Colburn, 1847).

Hale, James, *The Journal of James Hale* (Windsor: IX Regiment, 1998).

Harris, Benjamin (Ed. Eileen Hathaway), *The Recollections of Benjamin Harris* (Swanage: Shinglepicker, 1995).

Hathaway, Eileen, *Costello: the True Story of a Peninsular Rifleman* (Swanage: Shinglepicker, 1997).

Hay, Andrew Leith, *Narrative of the Peninsular War* (Edinburgh: Henry Washbourne, 1834).

Hope, James Archibald, *Campaigns with Hill and Wellington* (Driffield: Leonaur, 2010).

Hope, James Archibald, *The Iberian Campaign* (Heathfield: Naval and Military Press, 2000).

Keegan, John, *The Face of Battle* (London: The Bodley Head, 2014).

Longford, Elizabeth, *Wellington: Pillar of State* (Frogmore: Panther Books, 1975).

---

35 Keegan, *Face of Battle*, pp.31-32.

Low, Edward Bruce (ed.), *With Napoleon at Waterloo* (London: G. Bell and Sons Ltd., 1911).
McCarthy, Edward John Connor, *Recollections of the Storming of the Castle of Badajoz* (London: W. Clowes & Sons, 1836).
Mercer, Cavalié, *Journal of the Waterloo Campaign* (London: Greenhill Books 1985).
Miller, Benjamin, *The Adventures of Sergeant Benjamin Miller* (Uckfield: The Naval and Military Press, N.D.).
Wheeler, Harold F.B., *The Story of Wellington* (London: George G, Harrap & Co., N.D.).

General Index

Albuera, Battle of 77, 157-158
Alexandria, Battle of 175, 185
American War of Independence 51, 55, 84, 96-97, 108, 116
Amherst, Gen. Jeffery, Baron 110-114, 118, 122
Amherst, Lt Gen. William 110-111
Arroyo Molinos, Battle of 173-174 173
Articles of War 160
Atrocities, alleged after Culloden 48-50

Bank of England 103, 113, 116-117, 119, 121, 123, 126-127, 130
Barrington, William Barrington, Viscount 109, 116, 118, 130
Bathurst, Henry Bathurst, Earl 56, 61
Belford, Gen. William 34, 122
Beresford, Lt Gen. William Carr 157
Bexhill 56, 65
'Black Wednesday' 103, 115, 117, 121
Blakeney, Lt Gen. Sir William 131, 136-138, 143-149, 151
Burgos, Retreat from 67-68, 78, 154, 159, 167
Byng, Adm. George 132, 134-137, 143, 145, 149, 152

Cadiz 54, 66, 68, 78
Calvert, Lt Gen. Sir Harry 60, 97-98
Cambridge, Gen. HRH Prince Adolphus, Duke of 60-61
Cape Mola 139-140
Chaplains 34, 48, 87-89, 97-89
Cintra, Convention of 153-154, 157
Ciudad Rodrigo 71, 154, 159-161, 167, 181
Ciutadella 139-140, 142-143, 145, 147
Clinton, Col William Henry 97
Clinton, Lt Gen. Henry 97
Commissary General, post of 133, 138, 152
Common Law 104-107

Cooper, Pte John 157-158, 160-161, 188
Corunna 59, 163; Battle of 167-168; Retreat to 73-74, 154, 157, 161-164, 166-168
Culloden, Battle of 31-33, 35, 37-38, 40-41, 44, 48, 50-53; casualties at 43-47
Cumberland, Capt. Gen. HRH Prince William, Duke of 31, 33, 35, 39-42, 47, 49-51, 53, 89, 99, 117
Cunninghame, Maj. William 131-132, 135, 137-140, 142-146, 148-149

D'arvey, Capt. 138, 145, 148
Dalrymple, Lt Gen. Sir Hew 62, 153
Desertion 54-55, 59, 61, 63, 67-70, 72-73, 79, 81, 94, 155, 160-161
Dettingen, Battle of 92
Discharge, from the Army 23-27, 90-91, 97
Drummond's Bank 111

Émigrés, Recruitment of 55; see also under Foreign Corps in Index of Regiments
Employment, conditions of in eighteenth century 20-21
Ewart, Sgt Charles 176, 179

Falkirk, Battle of 24, 33, 39, 41, 48-49
'Fear God and Honour the King', Methodist doctrine of 85-86, 95
Foot Guards 22-23, 25, 28, 38, 103, 108, 110-113, 115-117, 119-121, 124, 127, 130; see also under individual units in Index of Regiments
Foreign Depot 56, 58-59, 67
Foreigners, Recruitment of, 35, 54-80; see also under Foreign Corps in Index of Regiments
Fornelles 139, 142-143
Fort Marlborough 142
Fuentes de Oñoro, Battle of 78, 176

GENERAL INDEX

Gibraltar 21, 28, 35, 59, 78, 85, 97, 99, 130, 148-149, 151-152
Gleig, Lt George Robert 180-182, 185
Gordon Riots 102-129
Grattan, Lt William 176-177, 182-183

Haime, Pte John 87-89, 93-94
Harris, Pte Benjamin ('Rifleman Harris') 45, 163, 166, 178, 188
Heligoland 58
Hill, Major General Rowland 173
Hillsborough, Wills Hill, Viscount 110-111, 122
Honour 42, 73, 79, 85-86, 95, 149, 162-163, 166, 169, 173, 181
Horse Guards (War Office) 58-59, 127
Hospitals 56, 121; see also Royal Hospital, Chelsea
Household Cavalry 108, 116; see also under individual units in Index of Regiments

Iberian Peninsula 56, 58-61, 63-64, 69, 71-77, 80-81, 153-154, 157, 162, 164, 172-173, 188
Identity 82-83, 85, 99, 162, 170
Inverness 47-48
Isle of Wight 56, 65

Jenkinson, Charles 109-111, 113, 116

Keith, Action at 39 39

Lamb, Sgt Roger 96-97, 99
Lambeth 110, 112, 122, 125, 127
Lauffeld, Battle of 92, 94
Literacy 29, 32, 39, 154
Liverpool, Robert Jenkinson, Earl of 54, 67, 78
Lothian, Maj. Gen William Kerr, Marquis of 110
Lymington 56, 59

Macready, Lt Edward Neville 174-177, 181, 183-184, 188
Magistrates 103-107, 109-112, 115-116, 120, 134, 151
Mahon 131, 139-144, 146
Mansfield, William Murray, Earl of 105, 112-113, 119-120, 122
Militia 33-35, 44, 55-56, 64, 74, 79, 102, 111-113, 116-117, 119, 122, 124-125; see also under individual units in Index of Regiments

Minorca 21, 64, 131-140, 142-143, 145-146, 149-152
Minorcans 134, 147, 150
Moore, Lt Gen. Sir John 70, 73-74, 96, 161, 166-167, 175
Moorfields 103, 119
Mosheim, Col. Lewis von 59, 62-63, 67
Munro, Col Sir Robert 49, 92

New Orleans, Battle of 160
Newcastle, Thomas Pelham-Holles, Duke of 39, 133
Newgate 103, 112, 114, 116, 119, 128
Nive, Battle of the 185
Nivelle, Battle of the 180
North America 55-56, 61, 72, 101, 108, 111, 117

Oporto, 2nd Battle of 62, 72
Ordnance Office 133, 138, 144, 147, 152

Pakenham, Maj. Gen Sir Edward 158, 161, 183
Pell, Sgt William 115; account of Gordon Riots by 127-129
Peninsular War 61, 64, 79-81, 153-154, 159, 161-163, 169-170, 178, 188
Pensions: Dealers in 26-27; Qualifications for 20; Rates of 19, 26-27
'Peterloo' 102, 104, 123
Phillipet 142
Picton, Lt Gen Sir Thomas 177, 182
Poor Law 20, 28-29, 47
Pringle, Dr John 47, 52
Pyrenees, Battles of the 68, 77

Quatre Bras, Battle of 176-177, 181, 184
Queen Anne's Fort 139-140, 150

Rainsford, Lt Gen. Charles 121-122
Recruits, ages of 22-24, 29
Richelieu, *Maréchal* Louis François Armand du Plessis, duc de 134, 136, 143, 147
Riot Act 105, 112, 118-120
Rolica, Battle of 154, 157
Royal Hospital, Chelsea 17-20, 24, 26-27, 29-30, 33, 51, 97; Commissioners of 17-18, 20, 26; In-pensioners; 19, 24; Out-pensioners 17, 19, 24-25, 27, 29, 97; see also Pensions

Salamanca 70, 73-74, 165; Battle of 165, 167-168, 182-185
Savile, Sir George 112, 119, 126
Savoy 110-111, 117, 119, 126
Secretary-at-War, post of 26, 130
Seven Years War 23, 51, 61, 84, 88, 95-96, 111, 132, 135, 143, 151
Southwark 110, 121
St George's Fields 103, 127-128; Riots at (1768), see Wilkes Riots
St Philip's 131, 134, 137, 139-144, 146-151
St Philip's Town 141, 149
Stair, Field Marshal John Dalyrmple, Earl of 90, 92
Staniforth, Pte Sampson 91-94, 98-99
Stormont, David Murray, Viscount 110-111, 126
Straslund 58

Tents 70, 75, 159
Tiltyard, The 110, 117
Toulon 131-132, 143
Treasury 108, 133, 139, 144

Vimeiro, Battle of 61, 64, 154, 157, 165

Vittoria, Battle of 67, 78, 159-160, 167

War of Jenkin's Ear 23
War of the Austrian Succession 23, 83-84, 87, 90-92, 98-100, 111, 142
War of the Spanish Succession 19, 22, 26, 39, 84
Waterloo, Battle of 159, 174-176, 184, 186, 188-189
Wellington, Field Marshal Arthur Wellesley, Duke of 54-55, 58-64, 67-81, 98, 153-160, 167-171, 173, 175, 183, 188-189
Wesley, John 82-101
Wesley, Charles 83, 86, 88, 90, 94
West Indies 21, 57, 59, 62, 70, 77
Wheeler, Pte William 156-159, 164, 169
Wilkes Riots 108, 118

Xenophobia, in character of British soldier 155, 162, 164

York, Field Marshal HRH Prince Frederick, Duke of 56, 58-61, 70, 80, 90, 100-101, 130, 170

Index of Regiments and Corps

Household Troops
Horse Guards 19, 110, 117, 121, 124
Horse Grenadier Guards 112, 117, 120, 124
1st Foot Guards 111-112, 115, 119, 124
Coldstream Guards 119, 121, 124
3rd Foot Guards 28, 110, 116, 120, 124

Ordnance Troops
Royal Artillery 19, 34, 41, 122, 185
Royal Horse Artillery 71

Cavalry
1st (Irish) Horse 97
4th Horse 29
10th Light Horse 34, 38-39, 42, 44
3rd Dragoon Guards 112, 117, 124-125, 180
3rd Dragoons 112, 124-125
4th Dragoons 112, 124-125
8th Dragoons 28
10th Dragoons 34, 42, 44, 46
11th Dragoons 34, 44, 117, 124-125
13th Light Dragoons 179
16th Light Dragoons 76, 103, 110, 112, 117, 124
23rd Light Dragoons 71
Cobham's Dragoons; see 10th Dragoons
Kerr's Dragoons; see 11th Dragoons
Kingston's Light Horse; see 10th Light Horse
St. George's Dragoons; see 8th Dragoons
Wade's Horse; see 4th Horse

Infantry
1st Foot 35, 117, 125, 180, 184
2nd Foot 117, 124
3rd Foot 34, 43
4th Foot 34-35, 39-40, 42-44, 48
5th Foot 22, 57
7th Fusiliers 22-23, 71
8th Foot 28, 34, 42-43
9th Foot 185
10th Foot 88, 96
13th Foot 34, 43, 72-73, 179
14th Foot 34, 43, 49
18th Foot 29, 117, 121, 124-125, 127, 130
20th Foot 33-34, 42-43
21st Fusiliers 34-35, 40, 43
23rd Fusiliers 23, 57, 71
25th Foot 34-35, 38, 42-44
26th Foot 28
27th Foot 34, 43, 72
28th Foot 24
29th Foot 158
30th Foot 174, 177, 184
32nd Foot 76
34th Foot 22, 34, 41, 43, 57
36th Foot 24, 34, 43
37th Foot 34, 38, 40-44, 48-49, 72
39th Foot 97
42nd Highlanders 71, 75, 92, 97, 163
43rd Highlanders (pre-1748 numbering); see 42nd Highlanders
43rd Light Infantry 34, 92
45th Foot 182
50th Foot 76, 181
52nd Foot (Light Infantry post-1803) 71, 117, 124-125
55th Foot (pre-1748 numbering) 28
58th Foot 95
59th Foot (pre-1748 numbering) 34, 43
60th Foot 54, 59-64, 67, 70-80, 161; see also Battalion of Foreign Recruits
62nd Foot (disbanded 1748) 34, 43
71st Highland Light Infantry 73, 164-165, 173-174
85th Light Infantry 79, 180
87th Foot 57
88th Foot 71, 176, 182
92nd Highlanders 173-174, 178, 182-183
95th Rifles 71, 178, 187
97th Foot 64

Anstruther's Foot; see 26th Foot
Barrell's Foot; see 4th Foot
Battereau's Foot; see 62nd Foot
Blakeney's Foot; see 27th Foot
Bligh's Foot; see 20th Foot
Bragg's Foot; see 28th Foot
Campbell's Foot; see 21st Fusiliers
Cholmondeley's Foot; see 34th Foot
Conway's Foot; see 59th Foot
Dejean's Foot; see 37th Foot
Fleming's Foot; see 36th Foot
Howard's Foot; see 3rd Foot
Lee's Foot; see 55th Foot
Murray's Highlanders; see 42nd Highlanders
Pearce's Foot; see 5th Foot
Price's Foot; see 14th Foot
Pulteney's Foot; see 13th Foot
Royal Fusiliers; see 7th Fusiliers
Royal Highland Regiment; see 42nd Highlanders
Royal Irish Regiment; see 18th Foot
Royal Scots; see 1st Foot
Royal Welch Fusiliers; see 23rd Fusiliers
Sempill's Foot; see 25th Foot
Wolfe's Foot; see 8th Foot

Foreign Corps
Battalion of Foreign Recruits (later 8/60th) 54, 78
Brunswickers 54, 58, 63, 65, 68, 72, 74, 76, 78-79, 177
Chasseurs Britanniques 54, 63, 67-69, 74, 78-79, 161
De Meuron's Regiment 72
De Watteville's Regiment 72, 78
King's German Legion (KGL) 54, 56, 58-61, 64-66, 70-72, 74-78, 80-81
Minorca Regiment; see 97th Foot
York Light Infantry Volunteers 59, 70

Militia
2nd West Yorkshire Militia 117, 124
Buckinghamshire Militia 117, 124-125
Cambridgeshire Militia 117, 124
Hertfordshire Militia 117, 124-125
Middlesex Militia 113, 124-125
North Hampshire Militia 117, 124
Northamptonshire Militia 117, 124-125
Northumberland Militia 112-113, 117, 124-125
South Hampshire Militia 117, 122, 124-125
Staffordshire Militia 117

From Reason to Revolution series – Warfare 1721-1815

http://www.helion.co.uk/published-by-helion/reason-to-revolution-1721-1815.html

The 'From Reason to Revolution' series covers the period of military history 1721–1815, an era in which fortress-based strategy and linear battles gave way to the nation-in-arms and the beginnings of total war.

This era saw the evolution and growth of light troops of all arms, and of increasingly flexible command systems to cope with the growing armies fielded by nations able to mobilise far greater proportions of their manpower than ever before. Many of these developments were fired by the great political upheavals of the era, with revolutions in America and France bringing about social change which in turn fed back into the military sphere as whole nations readied themselves for war. Only in the closing years of the period, as the reactionary powers began to regain the upper hand, did a military synthesis of the best of the old and the new become possible.

The series will examine the military and naval history of the period in a greater degree of detail than has hitherto been attempted, and has a very wide brief, with the intention of covering all aspects from the battles, campaigns, logistics, and tactics, to the personalities, armies, uniforms, and equipment.

Submissions

The publishers would be pleased to receive submissions for this series. Please contact series editor Andrew Bamford via email (andrewbamford18@gmail.com), or in writing to Helion & Company Limited, Unit 8 Amherst Business Centre, Budbrooke Road, Warwick, CV34 5WE

Titles

No 1   *Lobositz to Leuthen. Horace St Paul and the Campaigns of the Austrian Army in the Seven Years War 1756-57* Translated with additional materials by Neil Cogswell (ISBN 978-1-911096-67-2)

No 2   *Glories to Useless Heroism. The Seven Years War in North America from the French journals of Comte Maurés de Malartic, 1755-1760* William Raffle (ISBN 978-1-1911512-19-6)

No 3   *Reminiscences 1808-1815 Under Wellington. The Peninsular and Waterloo Memoirs of William Hay* William Hay, with notes and commentary by Andrew Bamford (ISBN 978-1-1911512-32-5)

No 4   *Far Distant Ships. The Royal Navy and the Blockade of Brest 1793-1815* Quintin Barry (ISBN 978-1-1911512-14-1)

No 5   *Godoy's Army. Spanish Regiments and Uniforms from the Estado Militar of 1800* Charles Esdaile and Alan Perry (ISBN 978-1-911512-65-3) (large-format paperback)

No 6   *On Gladsmuir Shall the Battle Be! The Battle of Prestonpans 1745* Arran Johnston (ISBN 978-1-911512-83-7)

No 7   *The French Army of the Orient 1798-1801. Napoleon's Beloved 'Egyptians'* Yves Martin (ISBN 978-1-911512-71-4)*

No 8   *The Autobiography, or Narrative of a Soldier. The Peninsular War Memoirs of William Brown of the 45th Foot* William Brown, with notes and commentary by Steve Brown (ISBN 978-1-911512-94-3)

No 9   *Recollections from the Ranks. Three Russian Soldiers' Autobiographies from the Napoleonic Wars* Translated and annotated by Darrin Boland (ISBN 978-1-912174-18-8)

No 10 *By Fire and Bayonet. Grey's West Indies Campaign of 1794* Steve Brown (ISBN 978-1-911512-60-8)

No 11 *Olmütz to Torgau. Horace St Paul and the Campaigns of the Austrian Army in the Seven Years War 1758-60* Translated with additional materials by Neil Cogswell (ISBN 978-1-911512-72-1)

No 12 *Murat's Army. The Army of the Kingdom of Naples 1806-1815* Digby Smith (ISBN 978-1-912390-09-0)

No 13 *The Veteran or 40 Years' Service in the British Army. The Scurrilous Recollections of Paymaster John Harley 47th Foot – 1798-1838* John Harley, with notes and commentary by Gareth Glover (ISBN 978-1-912390-25-0)

No 14 *Narrative of the Eventful Life of Thomas Jackson. Militiaman and Coldstream Sergeant, 1803-15* Thomas Jackson, with notes and commentary by Eamonn O'Keeffe (ISBN 978-1-912390-12-0)

No 15 *For Orange and the States! The Army of the Dutch Republic 1713-1772. Part I: Infantry* Marc Geerdinck-Schaftenaar (ISBN 978-1-911512-15-8)*

No.16 *'Men who are Determined to be Free': The American Assault on Stony Point 15 July 1779* David Bonk (ISBN 978-1-912174-84-3)*

No 17 *Next to Wellington. General Sir George Murray. The Story of a Scottish Soldier and Statesman, Wellington's Quartermaster General* John Harding-Edgar (ISBN 978-1-912390-13-7)

No 18 *Between Scylla and Charybdis: The Army of Friedrich August II of Saxony, 1733-1763. Part I: Staff and Cavalry* Marco Pagan (ISBN 978-1-912174-89-8)*

No 19 *The Secret Expedition: The Anglo-Russian Invasion of Holland 1799* Geert van Uythoven (ISBN 978-1-912390-20-5)

No 20 *'We Are Accustomed to do our Duty' German Auxiliaries with the British Army 1793-95* Paul Demet (ISBN 978-1-912174-96-6)

No 21 *With the Guards in Flanders. The Diary of Captain Roger Morris 1793-95* Peter Harington (ISBN 978-1-911628-15-6)

No 22 *The British Army in Egypt 1801. An Underrated Army Comes of Age* Carole Divall (ISBN 978-1-911628-17-0)*

No 23 *Better is the Proud Plaid. The Clothing, Weapons, and Accoutrements of the Jacobites in 1745* Jenn Scott (ISBN 978-1-911628-16-3)*

No 24 *The Lilies and the Thistle. French Troops in the Jacobite '45* Andrew Bamford (ISBN 978-1-911628-17-0)*

No 25 *A Light Infantryman With Wellington* Gareth Glover (ed.) (ISBN 978-1-911628-10-1)

No 26 *Swiss Regiments in the Service of France 1798-1815. Uniforms, Organisation, Campaigns* Stephen Ede-Borrett (ISBN 978-1-911628-12-5)*

No 27 *For Orange and the States! The Army of the Dutch Republic 1713-1772. Part II: Cavalry and Specialist Troops* Marc Geerdinck-Schaftenaar (ISBN 978-1-911628-13-2)*

No 28 *Fashioning Regulation, Regulating Fashion. Uniforms and Dress of the British Army 1800-1815 Volume I* Ben Townsend (ISBN 978-1-911628-09-5)

No 29 *Riflemen. The History of the 5th Battalion 60th (Royal American) Regiment, 1797-1818* Robert Griffith (ISBN 978-1-911628-46-0)

No 30 *The Key to Lisbon. The Third French Invasion of Portugal, 1810-11* Kenton White (ISBN 978-1-911628-52-1)

No 31 *Command and Leadership. Proceedings of the 2018 Helion & Company 'From Reason to Revolution' Conference* Andrew Bamford (ed.) (ISBN 978-1-911628-53-8)

No 32 *Waterloo After the Glory. Hospital Sketches and Reports on the Wounded After the Battle* Michael Crumplin and Gareth Glover (ISBN 978-1-911628-48-4)

No 33 *Fluxes, Fevers, and Fighting Men. War and Disease in Ancien Regime Europe 1648-1789* Pádraig Lenihan (ISBN 978-1-911628-51-4)

No 34 *'They Were Good Soldiers'. African-Americans Serving in the Continental Army, 1775-1783* John U. Rees (ISBN 978-1-911628-54-5)*

No 35 *A Redcoat in America. The Diaries of Lieutenant William Bamford, 1757-1765 and 1776* Edited and Annotated by John B. Hattendorf (ISBN 978-1-911628-47-7)

No 36 *Between Scylla and Charybdis: The Army of Friedrich August II of Saxony, 1733-1763. Part II: Infantry and Artillery* Marco Pagan (ISBN 978-1-911628-08-8)*

No 37 *Québec Under Siege: French Eye-Witness Accounts from the Campaign of 1759* Translated and Annotated by Charles A. Mayhood (ISBN 978-1-912866-73-1)

No 38 *King George's Hangman: Henry Hawley and the Battle of Falkirk 1746* Jonathan D. Oates (ISBN 978-1-912866-64-9)

No 39 *Zweybruken in Command: The Reichsarmee in the Campaign of 1758* Translated with additional materials by Neil Cogswell (ISBN 978-1-911628-55-2)*

No 40 *So Bloody a Day: The 16th Light Dragoons in the Waterloo Campaign* David J. Blackmore (ISBN 978-1-912866-66-3)

No 41 *Northern Tars in Southern Waters: The Russian Fleet in the Mediterranean 1806-1810* Vladimir Bogdanovich Bronevskiy, translated and annotated by Darrin Boland (ISBN 978-1-912866-71-7)

No 42 *Royal Navy Officers of the Seven Years War: A Biographical Dictionary of Commissioned Officers 1748-1763* Cy Harrison (ISBN 978-1-912866-68-7)

No 43 *All at Sea. Naval Support for the British Army During the American Revolutionary War* John Dillon (ISBN 978-1-912866-67-0)

No 44 *Glory is Fleeting. New Scholarship on the Napoleonic Wars* Andrew Bamford (ed.) (ISBN 978-1-912866-69-4)

No 45 *Fashioning Regulation, Regulating Fashion. Uniforms and Dress of the British Army 1800-1815 Volume II* Ben Townsend (ISBN 978-1-911628-45-3)

No 46 *Revenge in the Name of Honour. The Royal Navy's Quest for Vengeance in the Single Ship Actions of the War of 1812* Nicholas James Kaizer (ISBN 978-1-912866-72-4)*

No 47 *They Fought With Extraordinary Bravery. The III German (Saxon) Army Corps in the Southern Netherlands 1814* Geert van Uythoven (ISBN 978-1-912866-65-6)*

No 48 *The Danish Army of the Napoleonic Wars 1807-1814, Organisation, Uniforms & Equipment: Volume 1: High Command, Line and Light Infantry* David Wilson (ISBN 978-1-913118-91-4) (large-format paperback)

No 49 *Neither Up Nor Down: The British Army and the Flanders Campaign 1793-1895* Phillip Ball (ISBN 978-1-913118-90-7)

No 50 *Guerra Fantastica: The Portuguese Army and the Seven Years War* António Barrento (ISBN 978-1-911628-11-8)*

No 51 *From Across the Sea: North Americans in Nelson's Navy* Sean M. Heuvel and John A. Rodgaard (eds) (ISBN 978-1-913118-92-1)

No 52 *Rebellious Scots to Crush: The Military Response to the Jacobite '45* Andrew Bamford (ed.) (ISBN 978-1-912866-74-8)

No 53 *The Army of George II 1727-1760: The Soldiers who Forged an Empire* Peter Brown (ISBN 978-1-913118-96-9)*

No 54 *Wellington at Bay: The Battle of Villamuriel, 25 October 1812* Garry David Wills (ISBN 978-1-913118-95-2)*

No 55 *Life in the Red Coat: The British Soldier 1721-1815. Proceedings of the 2019 Helion & Company 'From Reason to Revolution' Conference* Andrew Bamford (ed.) (ISBN 978-1-913118-94-5)

No 56 *Wellington's Favourite Engineer. John Burgoyne: Operations, Engineering, and the Making of a Field Marshal* Mark S. Thompson (ISBN 978-1-913118-93-8)

* indicates 'Falconet' format paperbacks, page size 248mm x 180 mm, with high visual content including colour plates; other titles are monographs unless otherwise noted.